IMAGES
of America

TROUTDALE

On the Cover: Commercial smelt dippers lift nets laden with "eulachon"—the scientific name for smelt—above their barges on the Sandy River near Troutdale. (Courtesy of the Troutdale Historical Society.)

IMAGES
of America

TROUTDALE

Julie Stewart

ARCADIA
PUBLISHING

ISBN 978-0-7385-9334-0

Published by Arcadia Publishing
Charleston, South Carolina

Printed in the United States of America

Library of Congress Control Number: 2012932295

For all general information, please contact Arcadia Publishing:
Telephone 843-853-2070
Fax 843-853-0044
E-mail sales@arcadiapublishing.com
For customer service and orders:
Toll-Free 1-888-313-2665

Visit us on the Internet at www.arcadiapublishing.com

Contents

ACKNOWLEDGMENTS

For a small community, Troutdale has produced a prolific number of dedicated writers who have meticulously documented the town's history. Mention the names Sharon Nesbit and Clarence Mershon in Troutdale and you will receive nods of recognition. They are the "heavy hitters" of local lore.

Sharon has been a columnist for the *Gresham Outlook* for decades and has had firsthand access to history as it happened. Her book, *It Could Have Been Carpdale*, written for Troutdale's 2007 centennial anniversary, is the magnum opus of Troutdale's past. Clarence, a retired math teacher, possesses more knowledge about the area around Troutdale than Wikipedia has in all its files . . . and he is a whole lot more accurate.

It is to these two that I owe the most thanks. Without their records of the "who, what, when, where, and why" about things that happened in Troutdale, this book would have been impossible to write. Sharon was indispensable to me, editing all of my work through cyberspace from Hawaii, and Clarence was my "go-to man" when I needed nitty-gritty pieces of trivia.

Len Otto deserves a pat on his back for his gracious sharing of photographs and information about his father, Glenn Otto, and smelt dipping. Terry Huston, director of the Troutdale Historical Society, good-naturedly helped me wade through books, articles, and albums to retrieve information I needed.

And to all the friends, former colleagues, neighbors, and people affiliated with Troutdale, I give my thanks for their support and encouragement. Unless otherwise noted, all photographs in this book came from the archives of the Troutdale Historical Society.

INTRODUCTION

Attempting to reconstruct any town's history is a bit like trying to untangle a skein of ensnarled yarn. You know there is a logical beginning, but finding your way back through it requires sorting through the knots and tangles. Meriwether Lewis and William Clark first noted the Sandy River, near the present site of Troutdale, on their Corps of Discovery exploration in 1805. Although a small landing spot called Sandy, nearer the Columbia River, preceded it, Troutdale itself dates back to 1907 as an incorporated community.

From its rough beginnings as a settlement at the western end of the Columbia River Gorge, Troutdale has been an amalgamation of immigrants from back east, hardened loggers in the forests around it, and farmers who learned to work with the fickle weather and grow fine produce and flowering bulbs. Its first industry—a slaughterhouse and meatpacking factory—employed hard-drinking, unpolished workers who caroused in the town's saloons at night. Their boisterous behavior led to the establishment of a city government to deal with the problems they created. Interestingly, women played some key roles as mayors in that government at a time when they had barely gained the right to vote.

Until the arrival of the railroad, the Sandy River, which runs along the east side of Troutdale, was vital to commerce. Its confluence with the Columbia River allowed early settlers arriving by boats from The Dalles, on the eastern side of the Cascades, to camp, reassemble their wagons, and graze their stock before moving on into the Willamette Valley or finding work locally felling trees in the woods or sending logs to the government sawmill in Vancouver. Many new arrivals settled on the low lands bordering the Columbia and began farming and grazing cattle on some of the only ground available without dense trees.

A ferry service across the Sandy provided a dry crossing until a road bridge was built. Once Troutdale was granted a railroad depot, its growth as a railroad boomtown began. Linked to other communities along the Columbia, as well as to destinations back east, the trains that stopped in Troutdale carried passengers, and, eventually, logs, meat and fish, crossties for railroad building, and local produce across the nation. The completion of the Historic Columbia River Highway through the downtown in 1916 brought traffic from the newly developed automobile to the town. Those visitors, as well as tourists and outdoor enthusiasts, engendered more jobs in service stations, restaurants, inns, and roadhouses, serving those traveling on the first highway along the gorge.

Through pluck and ingenuity, the town of Troutdale kept its pioneer spirit, fending off the typical small-town withering that dried up other communities. Conveniently located on the banks of the nearby Sandy River, the town hosted an impromptu fishing spree for the annual smelt runs during its heyday. Yielding to the inevitable loss of traffic when Interstate 84, which runs parallel to Highway 30, was constructed in the 1950s, Troutdale struggled to reinvent itself in 1991 by building an entirely new business district on the north side of the Historic Columbia River Highway. Today, it is still a feisty little town that retains the can-do attitude of its ancestors, typified in an arch over the entrance to downtown, proclaiming itself the "Gateway to the Gorge."

One

A Boomtown Appears on the Map

No one sat down in front of a map in the 1850s and said, "I want to go to this spot on the Columbia River in the Oregon Territory and establish a town called Troutdale." Pioneers on the Oregon Trail had other sites in mind at the end of their journey. A group fresh off the treacherous 70-mile boat trip from The Dalles in the mid-1800s found that a small community called Sandy had been established to serve new Oregon residents right where they disembarked, but these hardy souls chose a spot farther uphill for a new town.

Until the establishment of a railroad depot, Troutdale remained part of a series of far-flung communities from Portland eastward to the Sandy River. The original village, four blocks square, grew primarily as a result of a meatpacking/slaughterhouse, which used "everything but the squeal" from the cattle, sheep, and hogs fattened at nearby farms. By 1880, the town had a post office, followed by a rail depot two years later. In 1891, the editor of the local newspaper wrote that Troutdale was only about a year old and had a population of 300. "It has mostly been built in the past three months," he reported.

When the Oregon-Washington Railway and Navigation Company built a railroad line through Troutdale in 1882, the village became a boomtown. The editor of the *Troutdale Champion* described Troutdale in 1891 as having "two hotels, three general stores, one hardware store, one restaurant, one opera hall, two meat markets, one shoemaker, one barber, one blacksmith, one saloon, one lumberyard, one laundry, one livery stable, two doctors, two real estate firms, two painters, nineteen carpenters, and one newspaper." By October 1907, Troutdale officially incorporated itself with a population of 450 and set up its initial government.

The first general merchandise store in Troutdale was owned and operated by Aaron Fox, who would also become the first postmaster and mayor. The general store remained in the family for 50 years before passing into new ownership in 1944.

By 1929, there were other mercantile establishments, a hotel, several automobile dealerships and garages, a lumberyard, a sauerkraut factory, and a large number of nurseries and a bulb-growing organization. The burgeoning tourist business enabled some locals to open roadhouses and restaurants, automobile repair shops, and other enterprises that catered to the travelers.

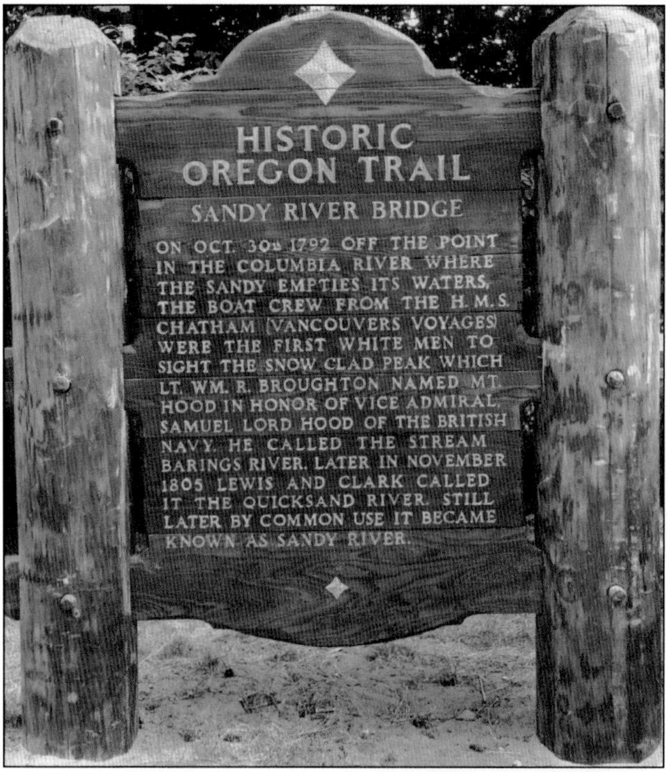

This wooden sign marks the area where Lt. William Broughton and his crew on the HMS *Chatham* first sighted and named Mount Hood in 1792. They named the river where they stood the Baring River, which Lewis and Clark renamed the Quicksand River in 1805.

This historical information signpost details the early years of Troutdale, including its role in the settlement of the end of the Oregon Trail. The sign also mentions that unemployed demonstrators, part of Coxey's Army, tried to commandeer a train in an attempt to reach Washington, DC, in 1894.

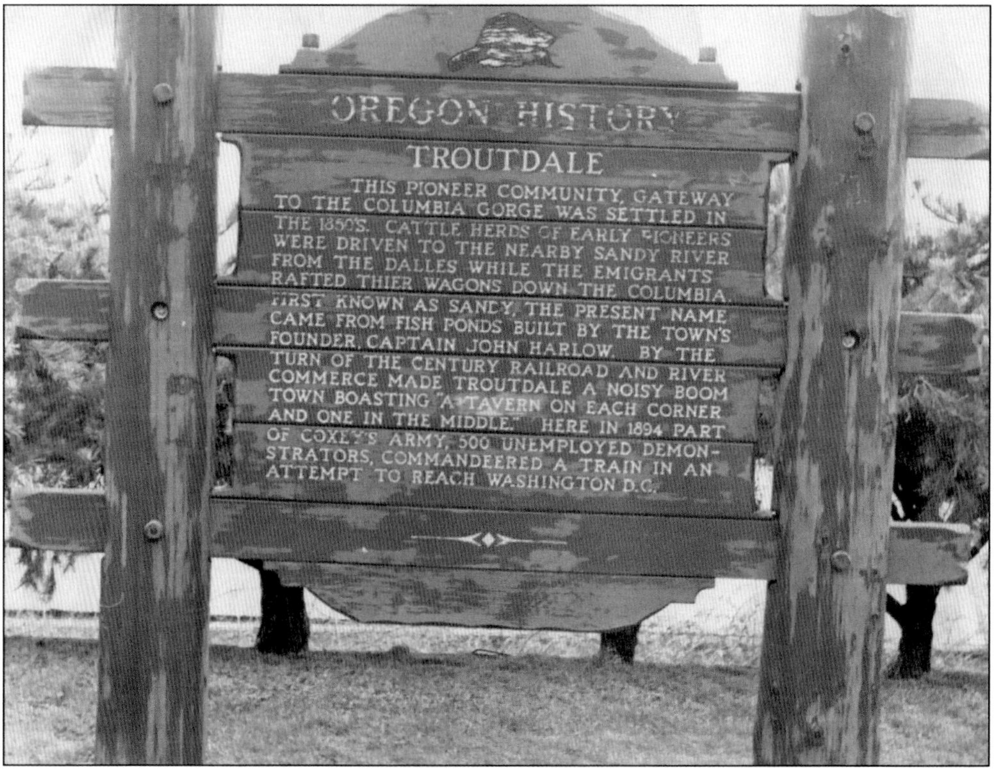

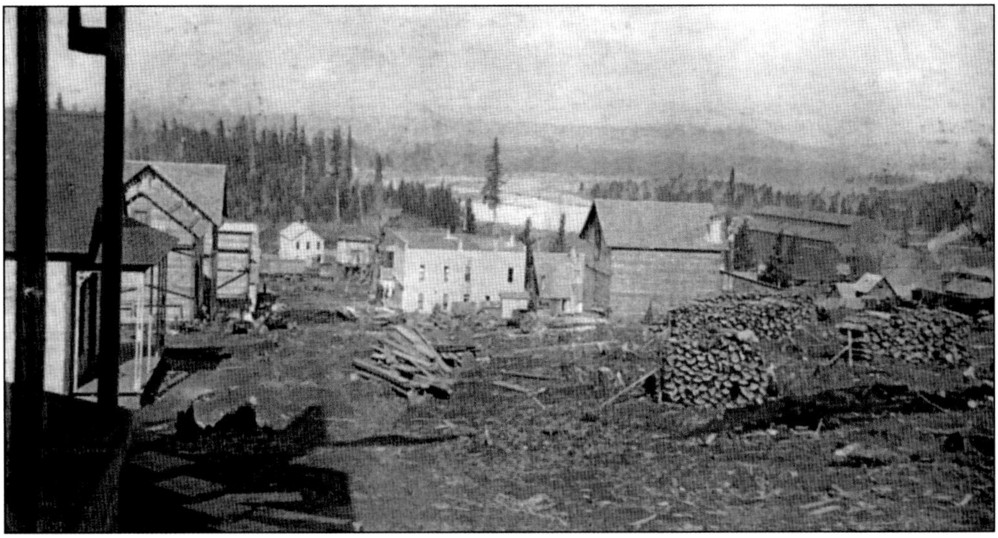

An 1890s photograph shows a raw new town with stacks of lumber and firewood piled beside unpaved streets. The white buildings in the background are beyond the railroad tracks.

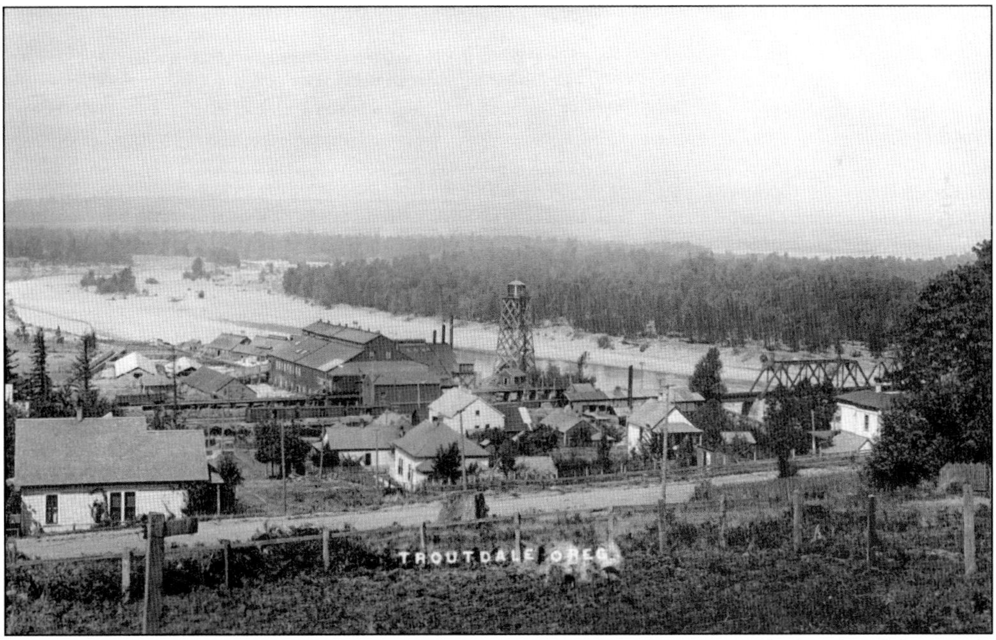

The Union Meat Company's operation sat north of the railroad tracks on the banks of the Sandy River around 1905. Much of the town was built on the hill overlooking the Sandy River to escape its frequent floods.

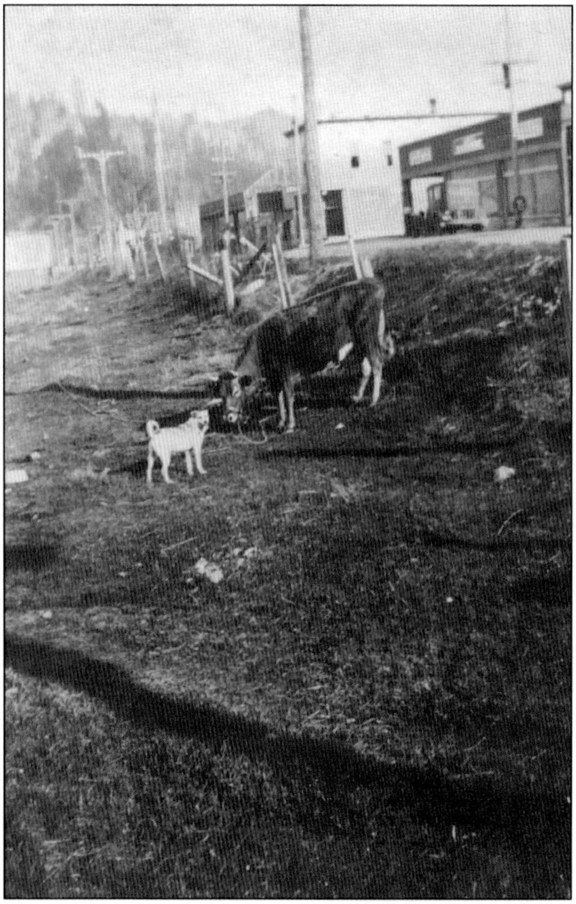

A local dog watches over the family cow grazing on what is now part of the business district on the north side of the Historic Columbia River Highway. The photograph depicts the bucolic nature of small Oregon towns around 1900.

A comment at the top of this postcard asks, "Don't you think this is a lovely little town?" Though still sparsely populated, Troutdale had incorporated by the time this photograph was taken in 1908.

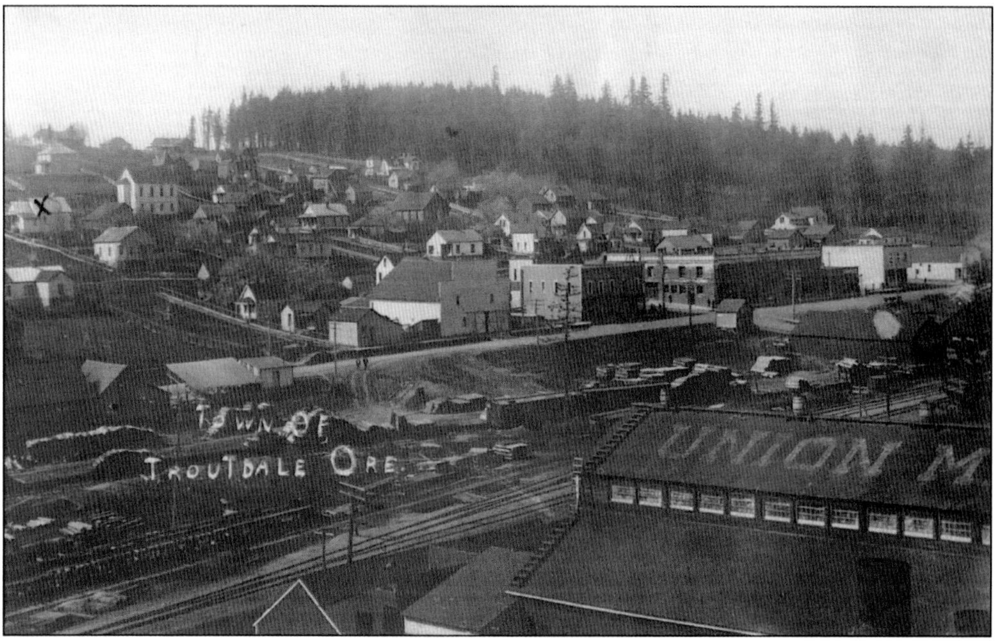

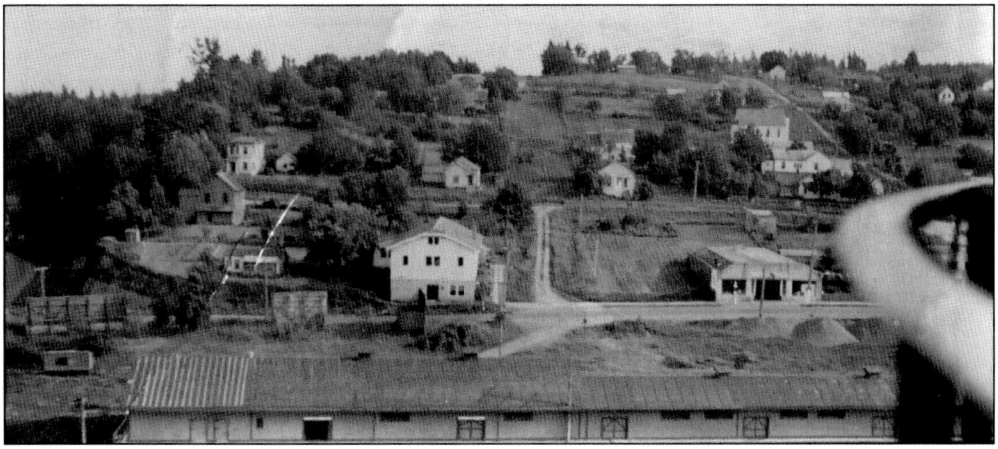

This photograph, taken from the water tower of Bissinger & Company around 1930, shows the houses dotting the hill above the main street. The white building in the foreground housed city hall until 2012.

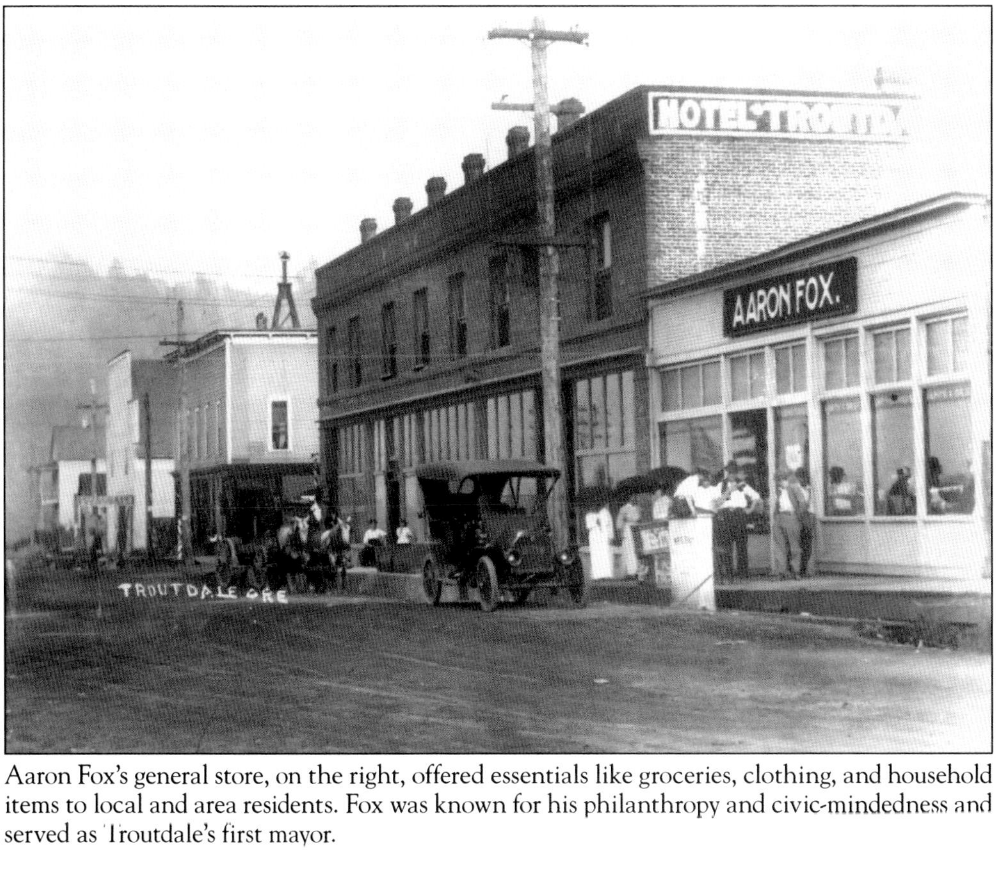

Aaron Fox's general store, on the right, offered essentials like groceries, clothing, and household items to local and area residents. Fox was known for his philanthropy and civic-mindedness and served as Troutdale's first mayor.

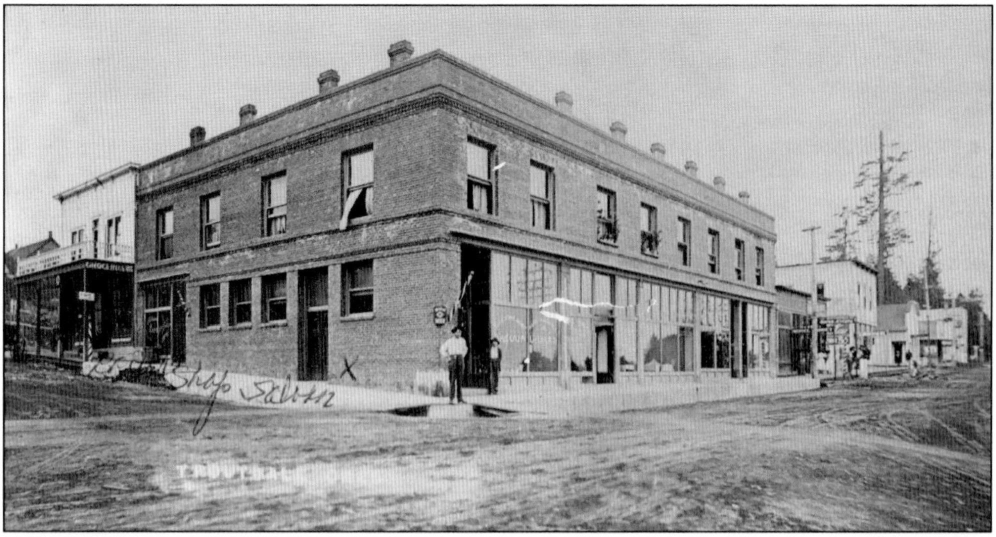

A fire that destroyed much of downtown Troutdale in 1907 was started by a boarder at a town hotel and boardinghouse who tipped over a kerosene lamp in his room after a night of drinking at a saloon. It was the first of two fires to burn the town.

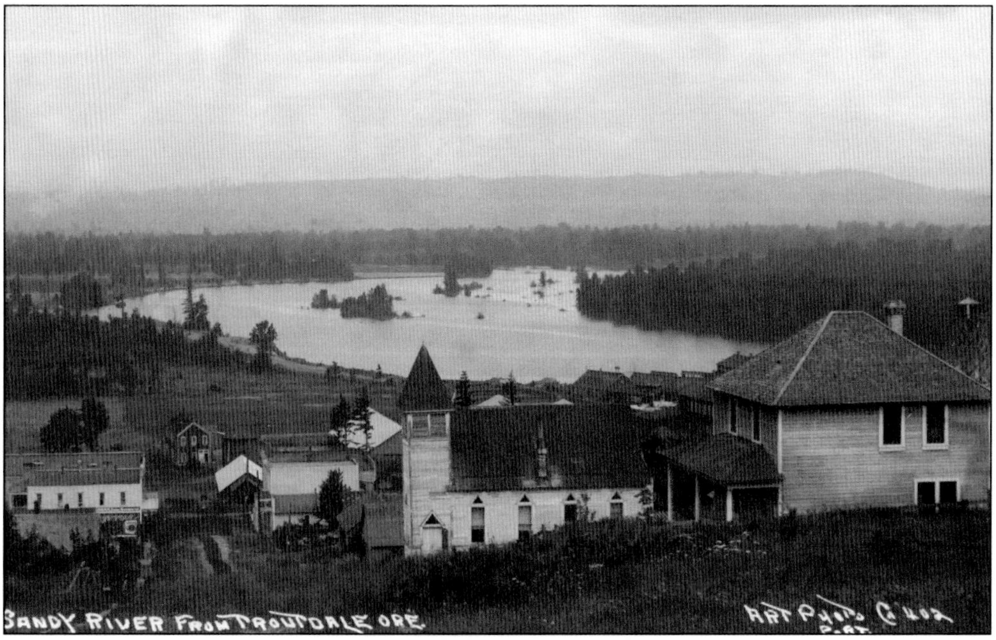

An overview of Troutdale from the top of "Hungry Hill" (what is now Third and Harlow Streets) in 1900 shows the Methodist-Episcopal church and the beginnings of a business district. The two-story building at the bottom of the street was a boardinghouse.

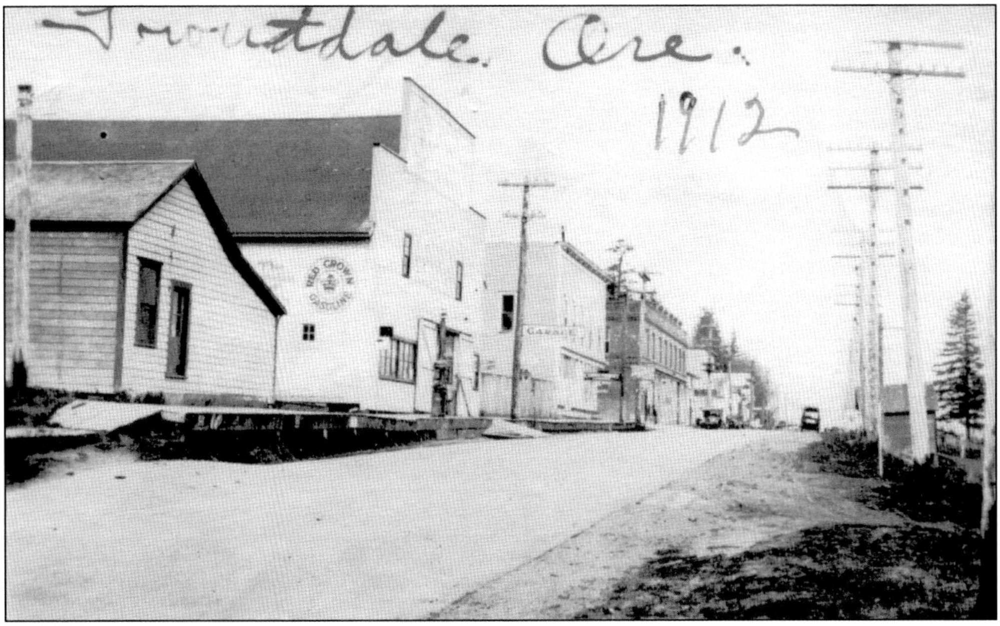

This 1912 view of downtown Troutdale shows a family home and a livery stable with a gas pump and a Red Crown gas sign. Next door is a confectionary/restaurant/hotel, and the Troutdale Hotel is the last brick building on the left.

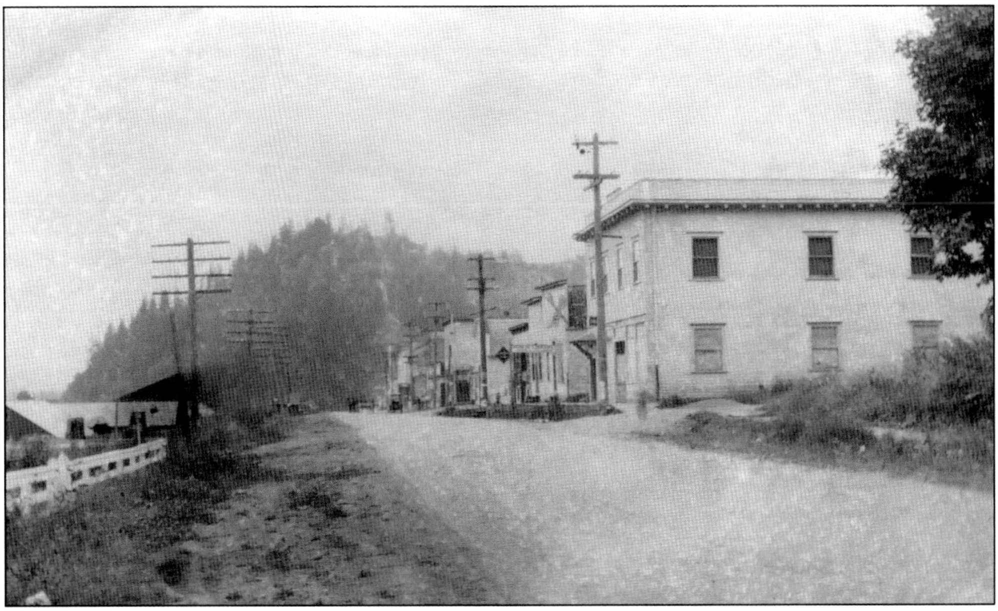

A 1912 photograph, looking east toward Broughton Bluff, shows the still undeveloped highway through Troutdale. A note on the backside of the photograph identifies the buildings on the immediate right as the Masonic Hall and the Davis Red and White store. A bicycle path paralleled the roadway.

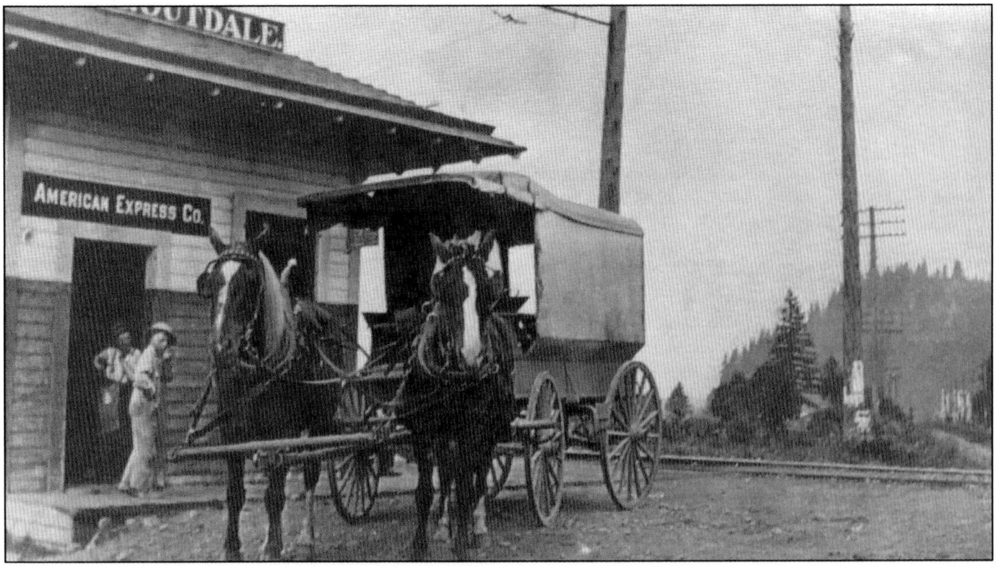

This undated photograph of the American Express office at the Troutdale interurban railway depot shows a horse-drawn livery truck waiting for its load, suggesting that it predates the general use of automobiles. The power line brought electricity to town when the urban rail line was built in 1908.

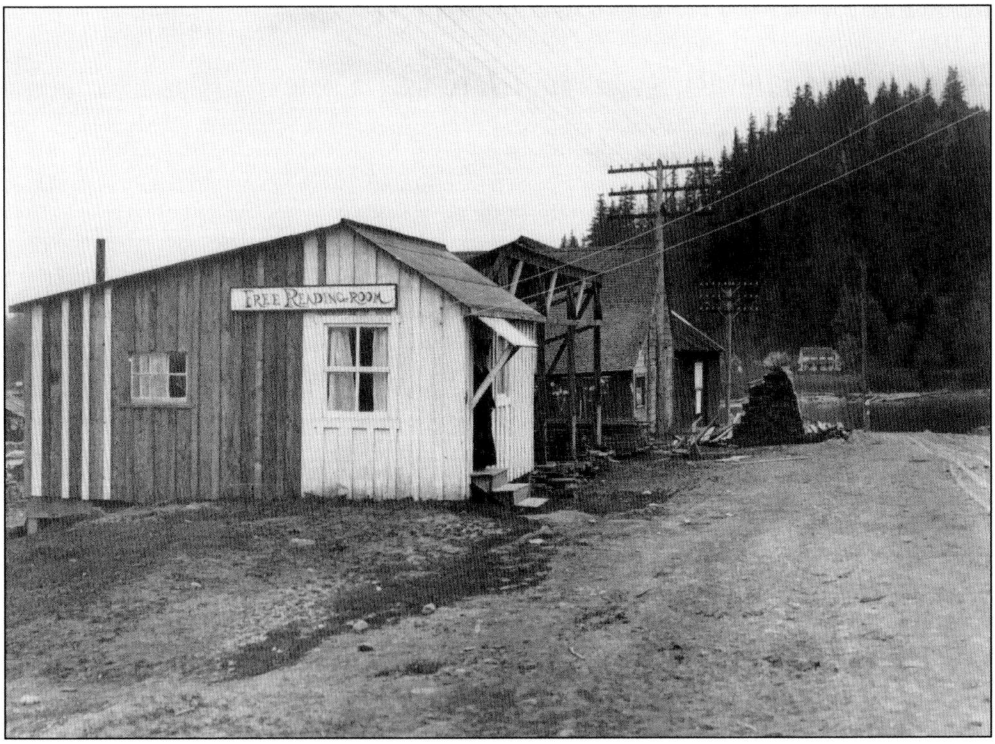

Troutdale's first "library" was called the "Free Reading Room" and occupied a one-room building on the dirt road, now the historic highway, leading out of town. Most likely, the collection would have been made up of books from local residents' own collections. This photograph was taken in 1900.

Longtime resident Walter Nasmyth published a book of his memories of Troutdale. The book, filled with personal anecdotes of his observations and experiences, provides a unique insight on a young town. His list of the early businesses in Troutdale gives a vivid portrait of small-town USA.

MAIN STREET TROUTDALE BEGINNING AT :

AS REMEMBERED BY HERB & WALT NASMYTH

1- THE HARLOW HOUSE.
2- EVANS BUILT HOUSE
3- BRINKS HOUSE
4- BLACKIE'S HOUSE COVERED BY SLIDE-JUST EAST OF CITY HALL
5- CITY HALL
6- THE NASMYTH HOUSE- BURNED IN 1925
7- JOHN LARSON'S GARAGE.
8- BRINKS MEAT MARKET.
9- MACK'S HOTEL
10- SOUTH OF MACKS- STATE SURVEYORS & POST OFFICE-HUDSON P.M.
11- RED AND WHITE STORE- DOOLITTLES
12- MALCOMS-KENDALL-PARSONS—BULB HOUSE.
13- PHARMACEY-SHELLEYS
14- GENERAL STORE— MILT FOX
15- POOL HALL— JESS WIGGINS
16- BARBER SHOP— FELIX STRAUSSER
17- HOTEL—TILLERS
18- GARAGE—JOHN MCGINNIS
19- SALOON— LOUIE HELMING
20- SHOE SHOP
21- STOREFRONT APARTMENT
22- RED AND WHITE STORE—HARRY AND LOUISE DAVIS
23- BANK— H.E. BLOYD
24- BEAUTY SALON
25- DOCTOR MANGLES
26- GROCERY STORE— R.D. HEWITT
27- HANDY GARAGE— ENTIRE BUILDING CONSTRUCTED BY BILL WEISER
28- RESTAURANT— CURLEY THARP— FLORIST SHOP— IG WAND
29- A.D. KENDALL HOUSE
30- SPENCE'S FIELD
31- DRIVEWAY TO SPENCE HOUSE
32- JIM SPENCE HOUSE
33- PELTON HOUSE
34- ERICKSON'S HOUSE
35- GARAGE— ART MATCHES
36- REST ROOMS— OLD TROLLEY STOP— JEAN BUCK LIVED IN OLD TROLLEY STOP
37- LUMBER YARD— MURPHEY'S
38- STOREFRONTS
39- MURPHEY'S HOUSE— OFF THE HIGHWAY
40- LORENZO HOUSE

41- RUSS WILSON HOUSE
42- GARAGE— BILL WEISER
43- COUNTY DOCTORS HOUSE— BEFORE THAT A HOUSE OF ILL REPUTE

NORTH OF THE HIGHWAY

44- FRANK CRAWFORD HOUSE
45- JIM SIMONE HOUSE
46- DOMINIC GIANCONI HOUSE
47- SAUERKRAUT FACTORY
48- OWRRN OVERPASS TO FARMS
49- CHASES GARAGE
50- PASTURE
51- GARBAGE DUMP
52- PASTURE— BARN ON LOWER SECTION
53- RAILROAD OUTHOUSE
54- RAILROAD HOUSE
55- PASTURE
56- SIGNBOARD— FOSTER & KLEISER
57- ROAD TO DEPOT
58- GRAVEL STORAGE AREA
59- UNDEVELOPED TO BEAVER CREEK
60- FOUNDATION OF OLD MEAT PLANT NEAR TRACKS
61- SMALL SHACK AT CORNER OF HIGHWAY— MAYBE READING ROOM

ALONG TRACKS

62- FRANK CRAWFORD'S HOUSE
63- RAILROAD TURNTABLE
64- JIM SIMONE FARM
65- DOMINIC GIANCONI FARM
66- TRUELOVE— DELPHINIUM FARM
67- R.R.BUNKHOUSE
68- RAILROAD HOUSE
69- PARSON'S & MCGINNIS TRUCK GARDENS
70- WOOL PULLERY— BISSINGER
71- MAGGOT PILE
72- RAILROAD BRIDGE

SOUTH OF TRACKS

73-ACROSS FROM DEPOT— AARON FOXES— WAREHOUS
74-BLAZER'S— BOX FACTORY— RUN BY MILO COONS
75-EAST OF DEPOT ROAD— R.R. PACKING SHEDS

Walter Nasmyth had a nearly photographic memory of his childhood in Troutdale. In his self-published book, he detailed his childhood memories, as well as the people and businesses that inhabited that early town. Most of the businesses in this list are long gone. A close look at the list details the intermix of private homes, farms, and businesses (including the garbage dump and a "maggot pile") along the highway.

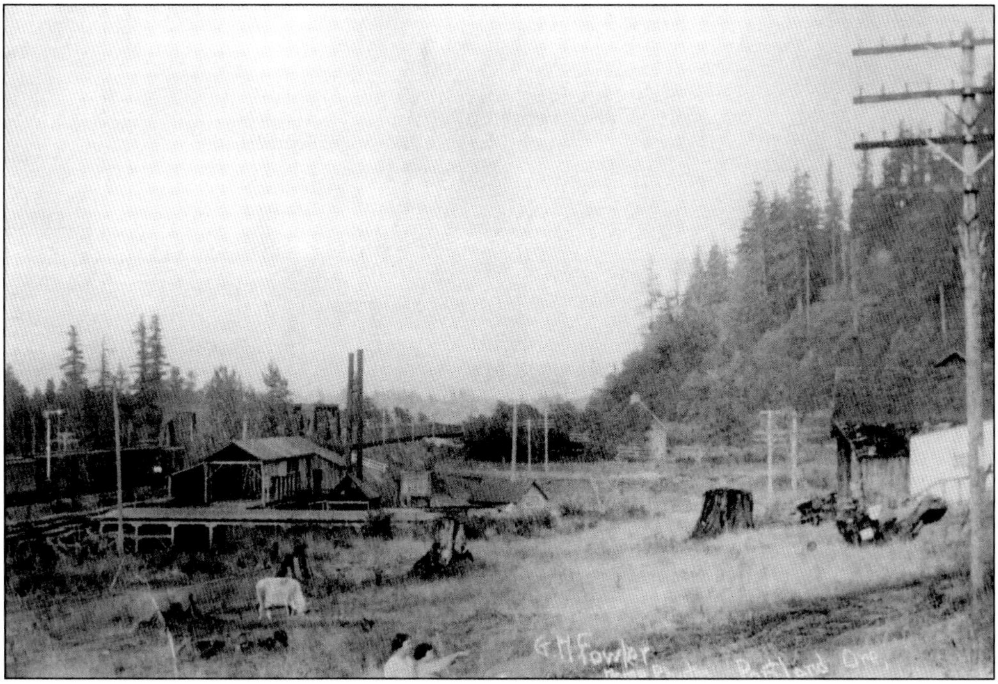

The Davenport Lumber Mill was located by the railroad tracks, where railroad ties and lumber could be loaded onto trains. The tie drive of 1913 ended that practice as the Davenport Mill decided that ties could more easily be hauled out by truck.

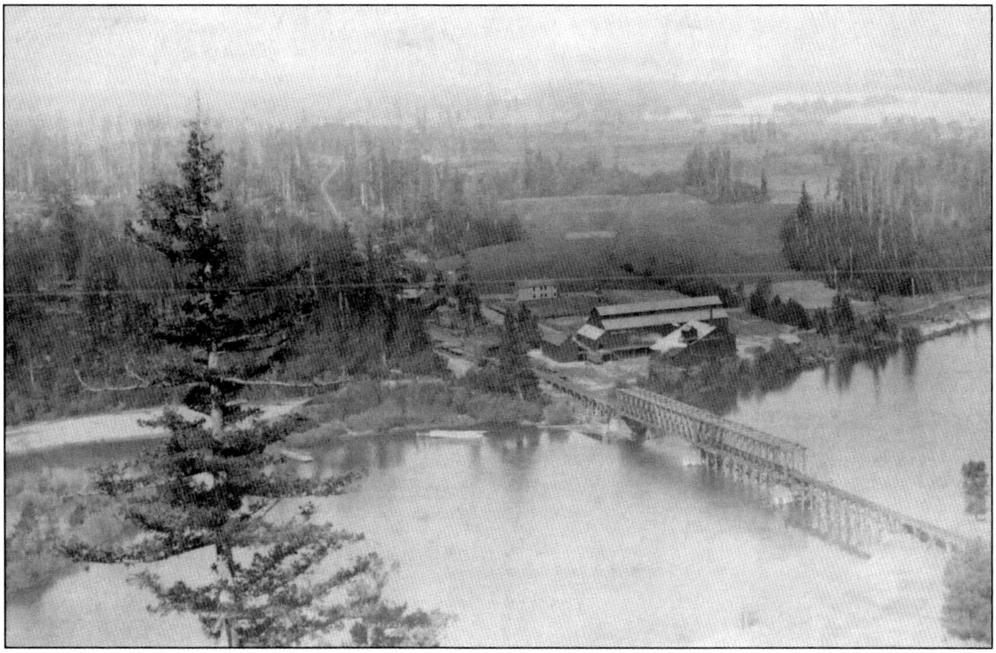

The American Dressed Meat Company, the first industry in Troutdale, was located next to the railroad track in 1890, and employed about 100 men. The Sun Dial Ranch, which stretched from the Sandy River to Fairview along the south shore of the Columbia River, provided grazing and feed lots for the plant.

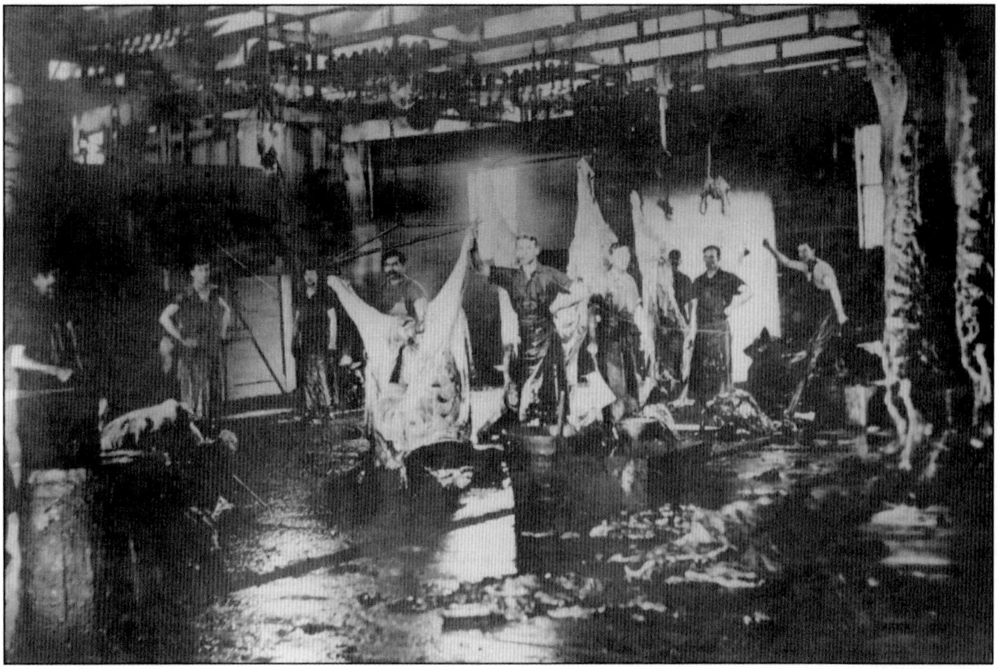

Workers stand among hanging beef carcasses at the American Dressed Meat Company, also known as the Union Meat Company. The slaughterhouse and packinghouse handled 1,500 beef cattle a month, as well as hogs and sheep. A cattle feed company with a five-story-high distillery was nearby.

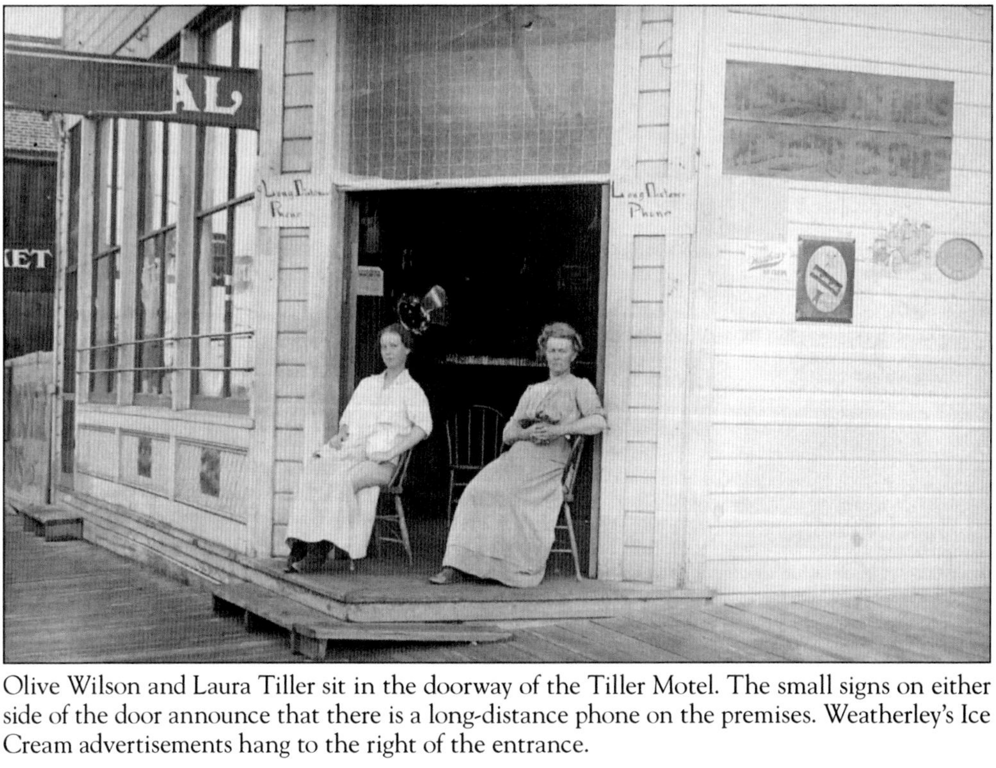

Olive Wilson and Laura Tiller sit in the doorway of the Tiller Motel. The small signs on either side of the door announce that there is a long-distance phone on the premises. Weatherley's Ice Cream advertisements hang to the right of the entrance.

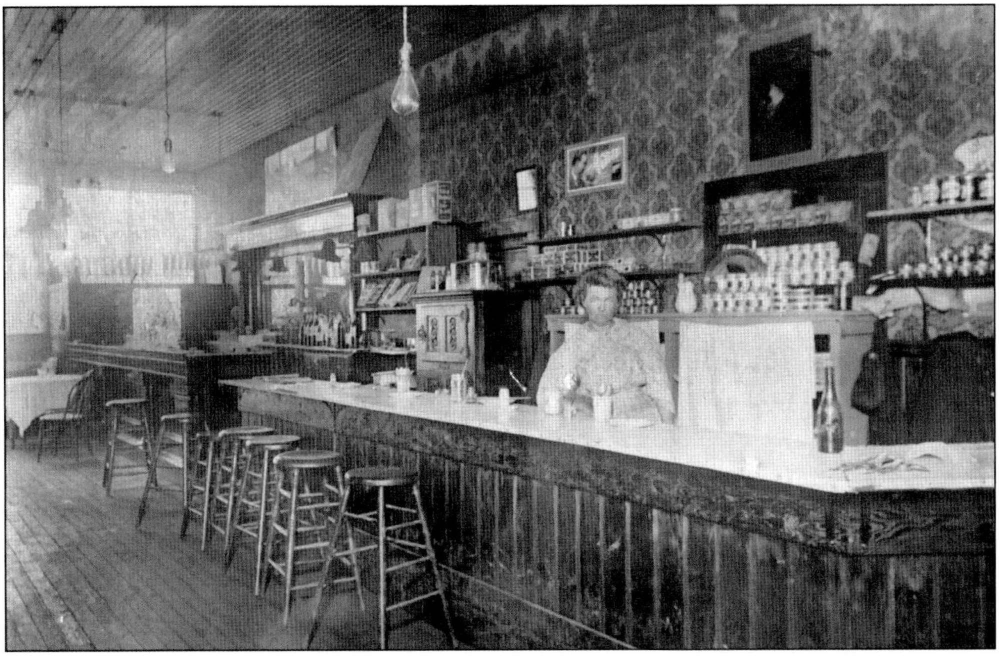

The Tiller family operated a hotel and an adjacent pool hall, the Tiller & Loser Pool Hall. Laura Tiller is seen here at her lunch counter. Contrary to many communities at the time, Troutdale boasted several female-owned businesses including this pool hall.

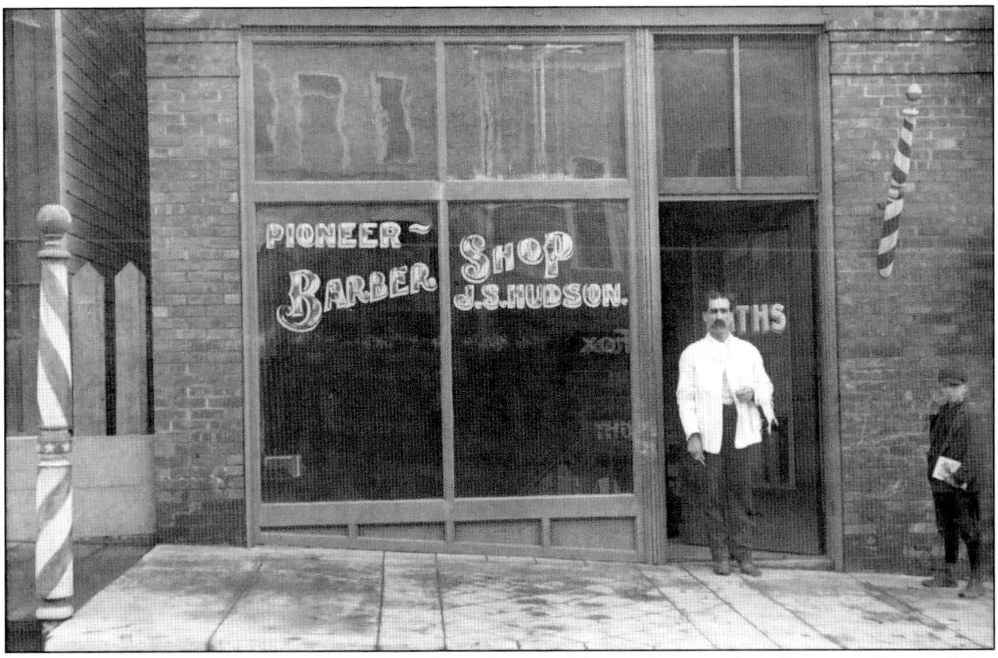

Customers at John Hudson's Pioneer Barber Shop could use the raised walkway in front of the establishment to keep their shoes from getting soiled by dust and mud. Barbershops at the time offered baths as part of their services. Hudson also served as the city recorder in Troutdale in 1920.

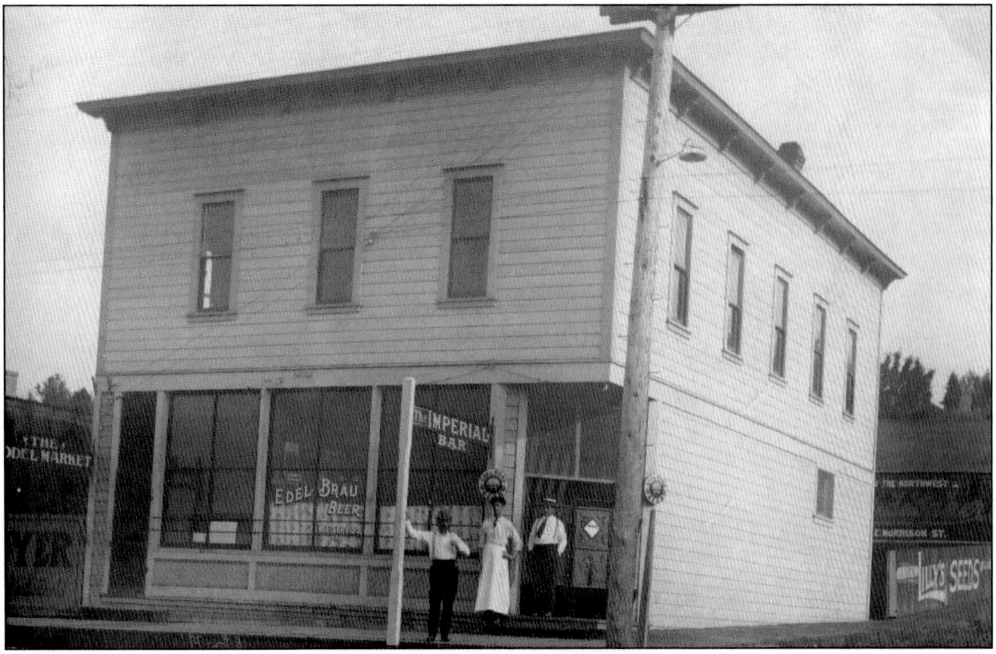

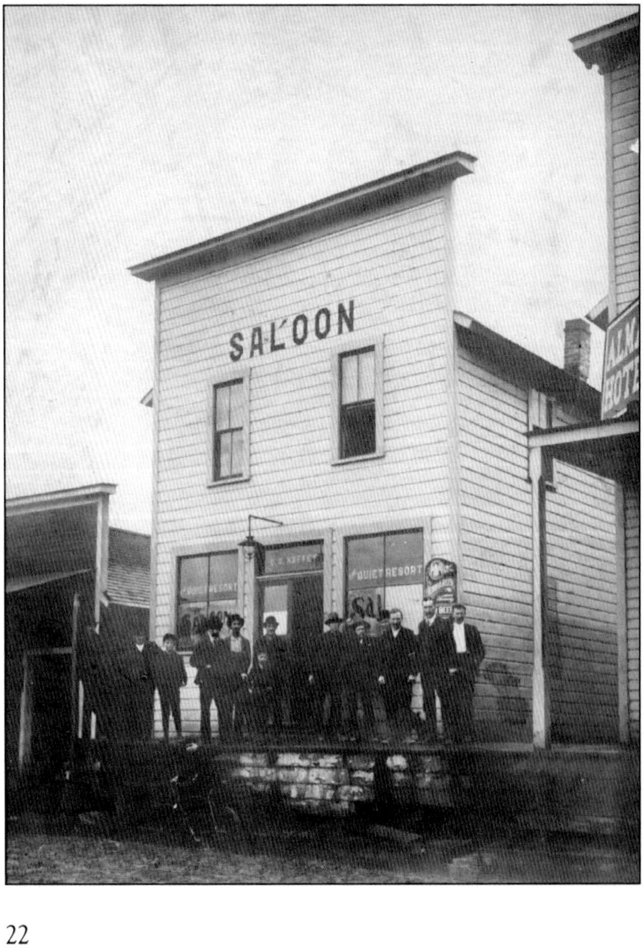

The Imperial Bar was on the corner of the Historic Columbia River Highway and Dora Street. The building was constructed by A.M. Tiller after the 1907 fire that destroyed most of downtown. The window advertises Edelbrau Beer and names W.T. Serviss as the proprietor.

In the early 1900s, Troutdale had a well-deserved reputation as a saloon town, with six, and possibly seven, bars lining the main street through the village. The problems associated with them caused local wives to demand city ordinances to control their husbands' drinking and to curtail their rowdy behavior.

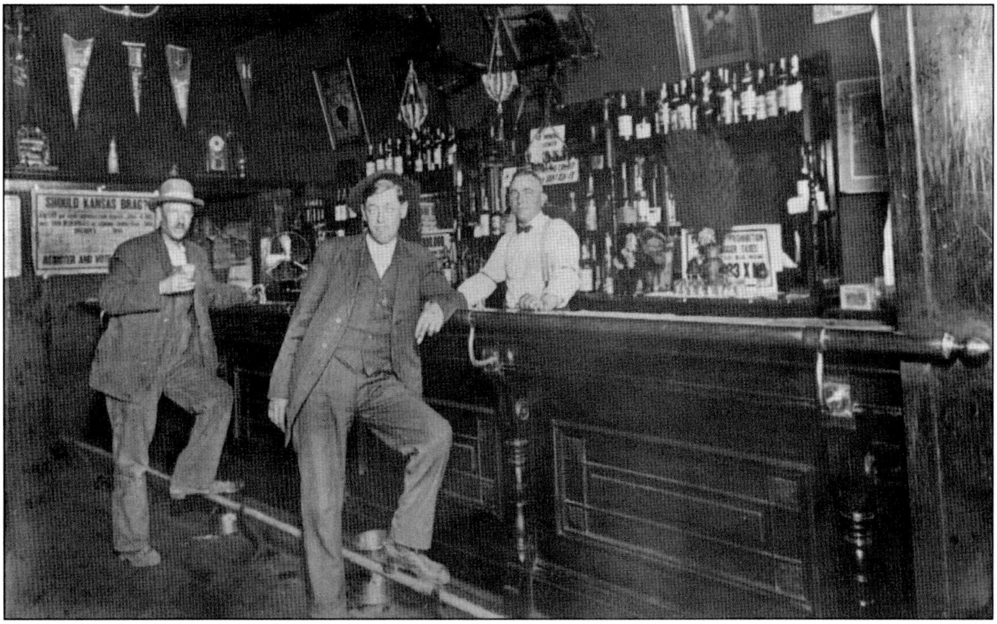

Louis Helming made a written request for the first drinking establishment license in the newly incorporated city of Troutdale. The cost for the license was a hefty $400. Taverns were Troutdale's main industry in 1913 because neighboring towns either limited or outlawed bars, enabling Troutdale to draw thirsty patrons.

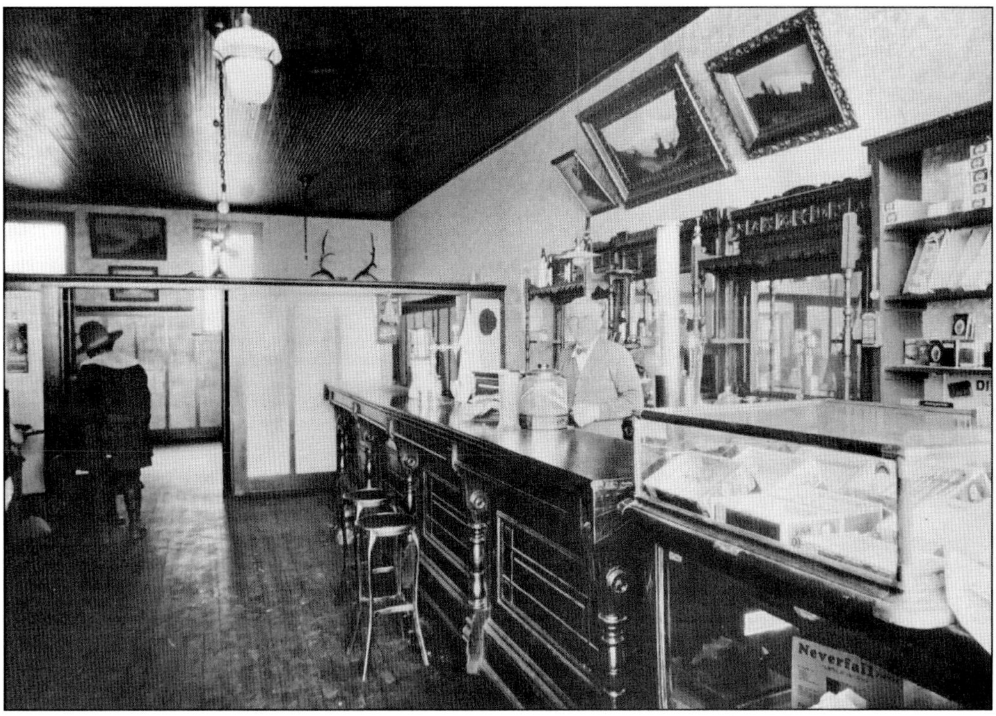

Seen here behind the counter at his confectionary shop, Helming sold sodas and ice cream to customers after the closure of Troutdale's saloons. However, even after the closure, people knew where to get the spirits they desired from local "vendors."

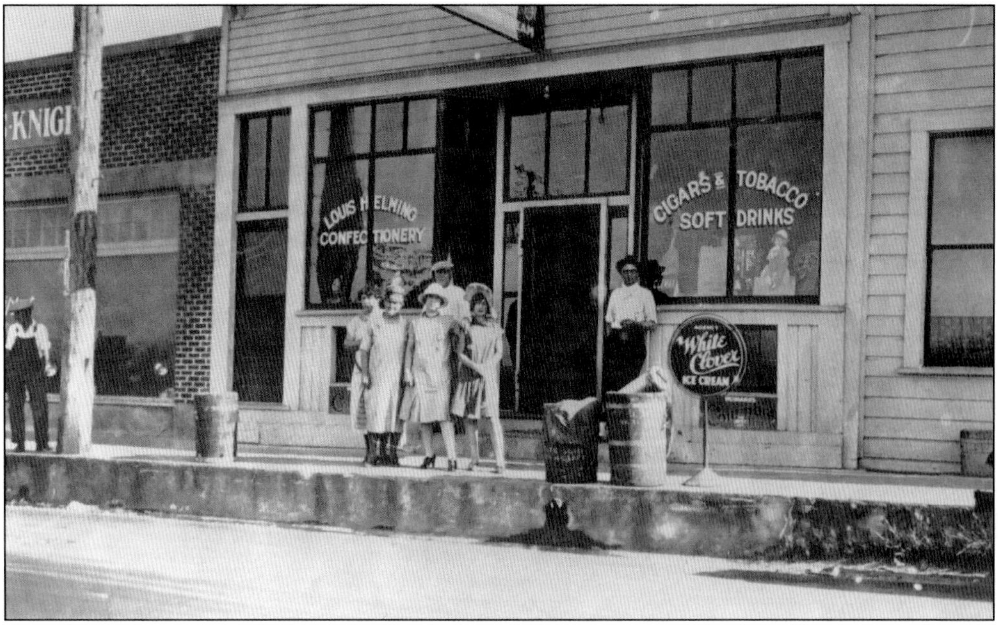

Clara Larsson, the wife of a saloonkeeper, was mayor of Troutdale in 1915, when female voters in town, spearheaded by Louise Surber, approved a local option law, closing all the town's saloons. Barkeepers, to save their businesses, converted their saloons into confectionary shops, selling nonalcoholic beverages.

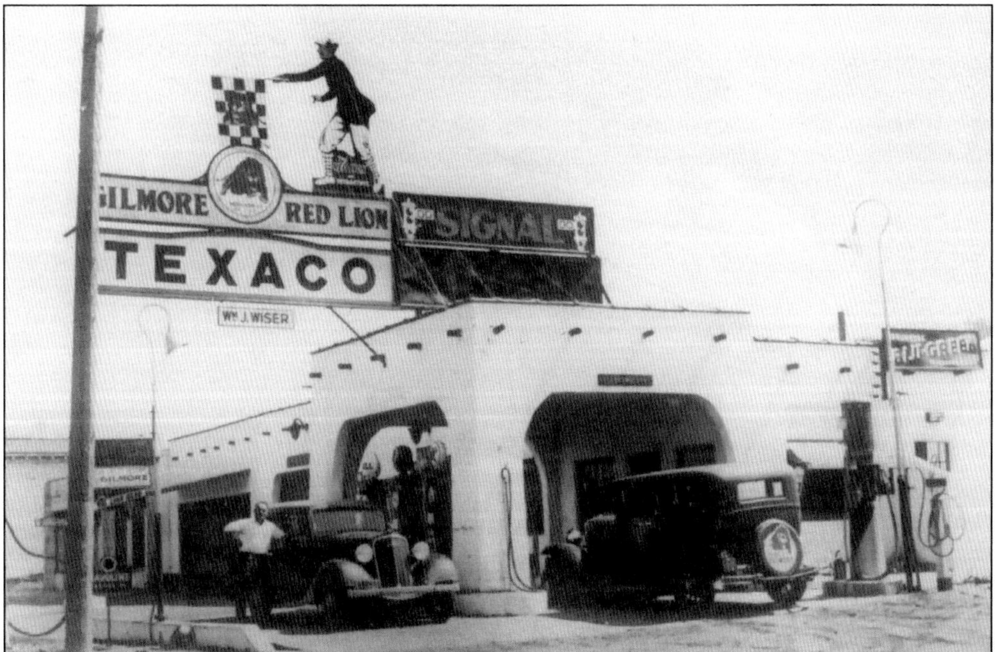

This service station, built by Bud Wiser, featured the sign "Gilmore Red Lion, Signal, Texaco and Gilmore Blu-Green." Ike and June Handy owned and operated the station from 1940 on and actually lived in the office of the service station, using the same outside restrooms as the customers.

M.C. Federspeil's Blue Ribbon Sauer Kraut Manufacturing Company, built in 1925, powered the kraut cutter with a 1914 Model T Ford that had its rear end elevated and connected to a belt used to run the blades. The cabbage was soaked in a salt brine and vinegar mixture in large wooden vats.

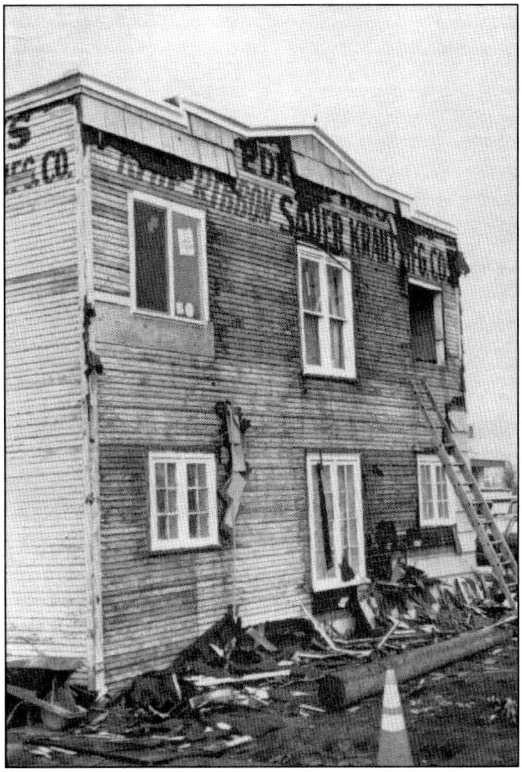

Harlan Cone owned the sawmill on the Sandy River near the confluence of Beaver Creek around 1895. The location allowed easy access to the logs sent downriver from the logging operations farther up the mountain, where the towering fir trees were cut for railroad ties and lumber.

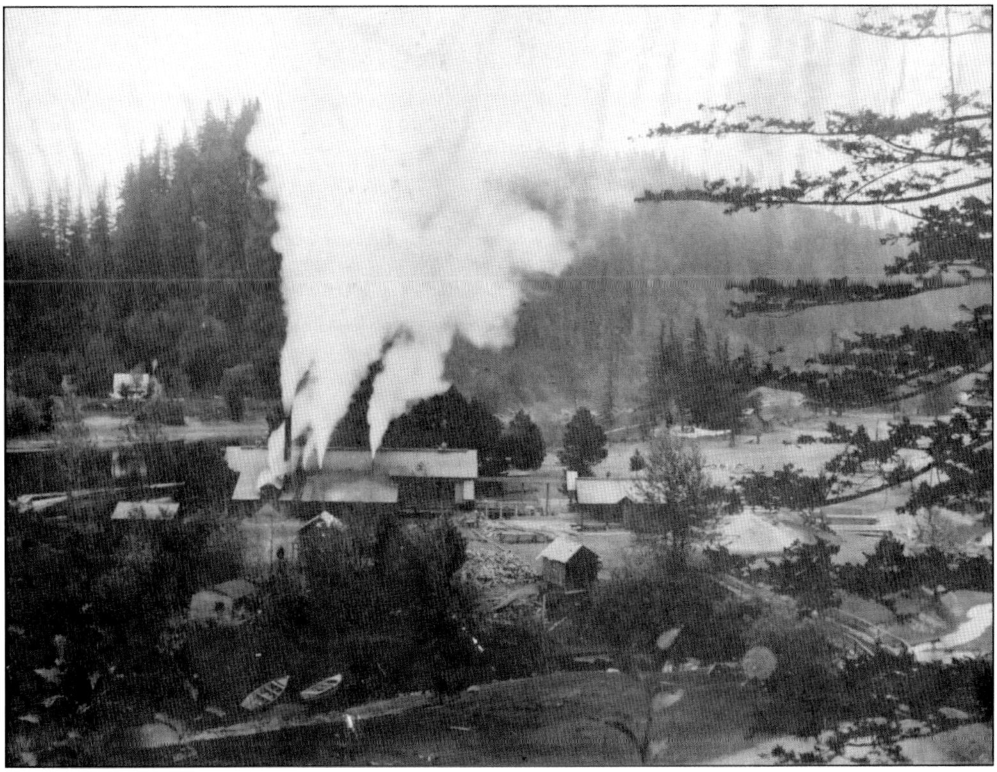

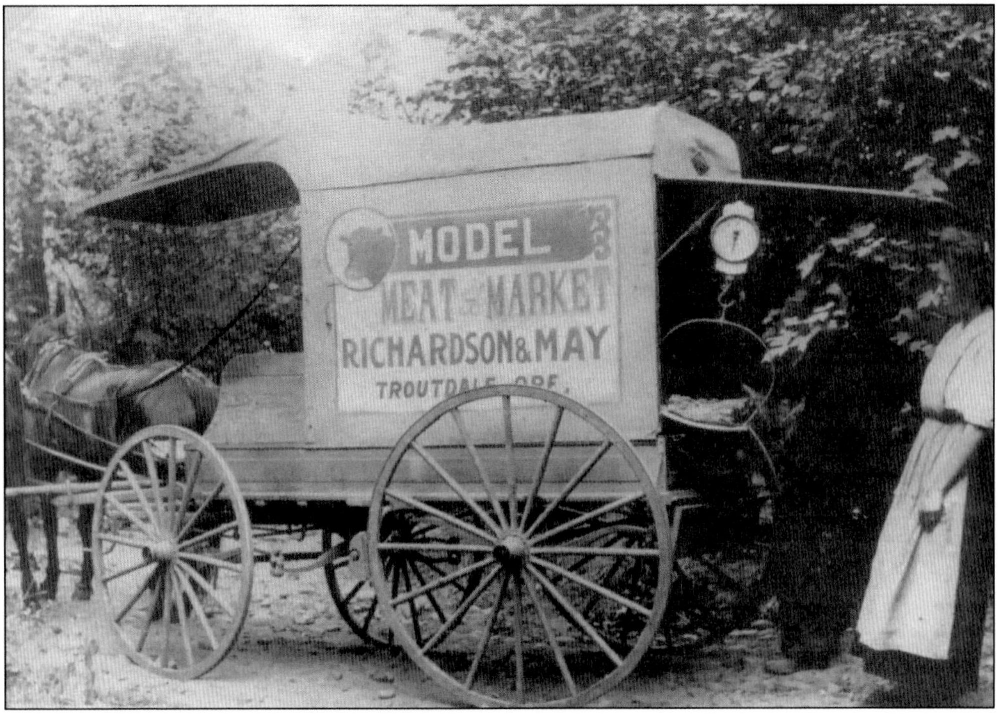

The Richardson and May Model Meat Market of Troutdale ran a small business out of a wagon in about 1910, serving residents in the Columbia River Gorge area as well as summer campers along the river. A scale on the back of the wagon weighed the meat for purchase.

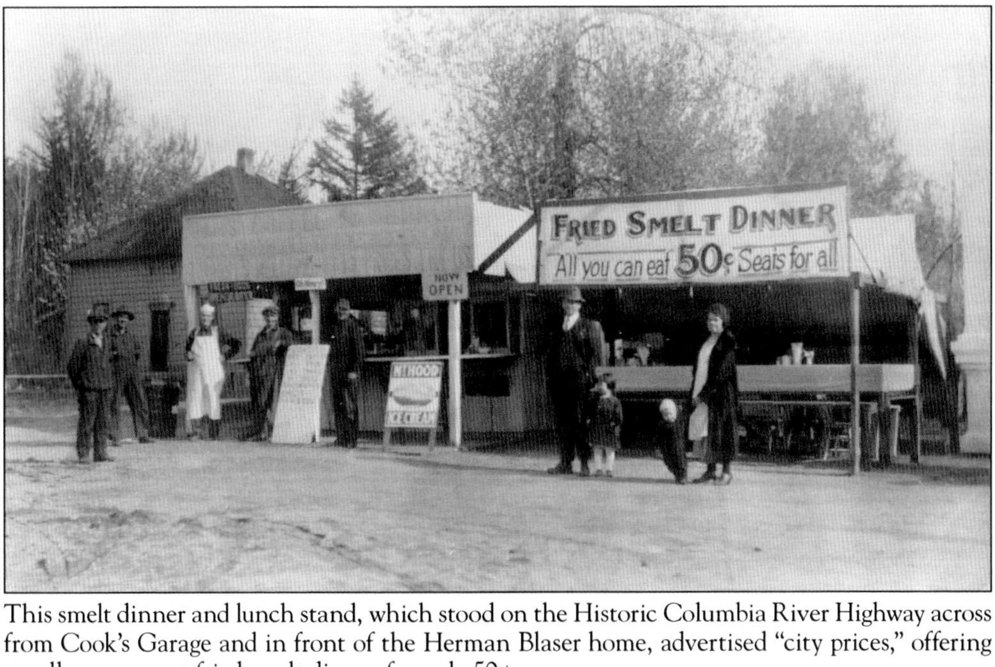

This smelt dinner and lunch stand, which stood on the Historic Columbia River Highway across from Cook's Garage and in front of the Herman Blaser home, advertised "city prices," offering an all-you-can-eat fried smelt dinner for only 50¢.

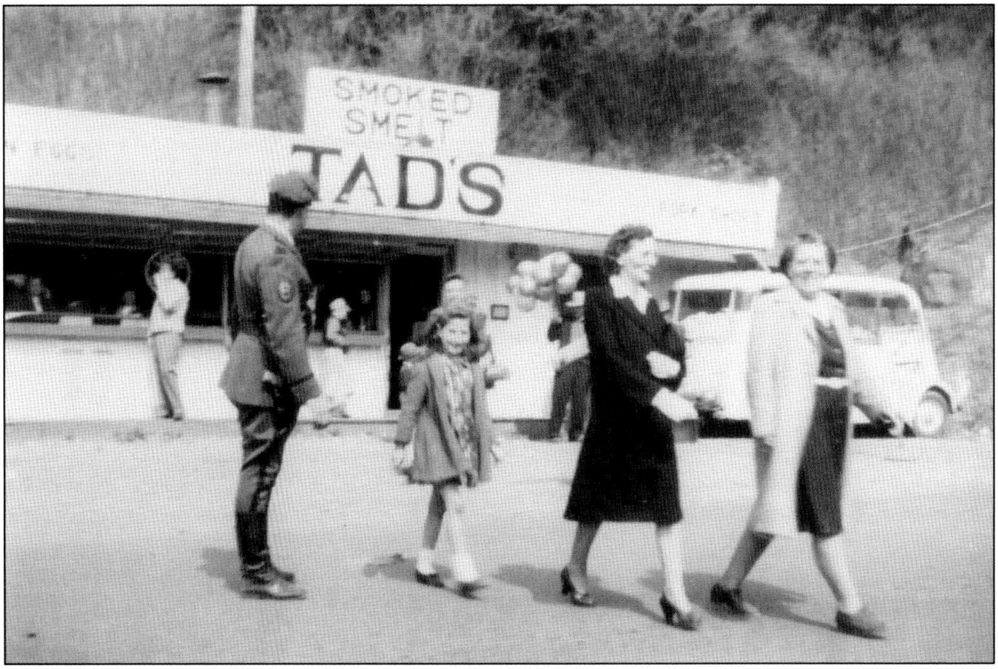

Tad Johnson was one of a series of owners of a food stand/restaurant on the Sandy River. During smelt season, he served up smoked smelt dinners. In 1946, Paul and Echo Mumpower bought the restaurant, moved it upriver, and added the still existing "Tad's Chicken 'n Dumplins'" sign.

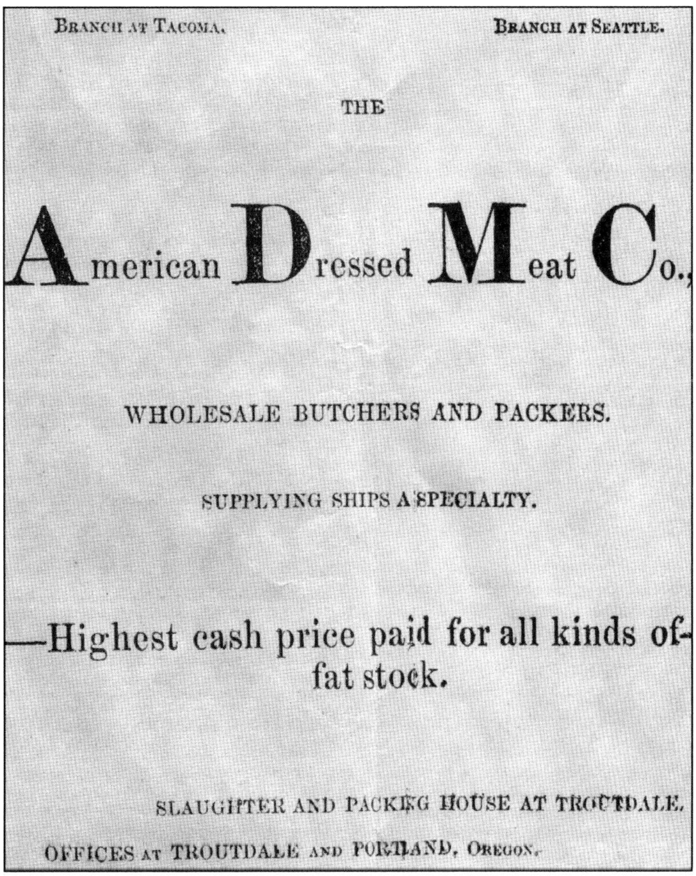

BRANCH AT TACOMA. BRANCH AT SEATTLE.

THE

American Dressed Meat Co.,

WHOLESALE BUTCHERS AND PACKERS.

SUPPLYING SHIPS A SPECIALTY.

—Highest cash price paid for all kinds of fat stock.

SLAUGHTER AND PACKING HOUSE AT TROUTDALE.

OFFICES AT TROUTDALE AND PORTLAND, OREGON.

This 1891 advertisement for the American Dressed Meat Company, the predecessor to the Union Meat Company, shows that supplying ships was a specialty. The business was obviously successful, with branches in Tacoma and Seattle and offices in Troutdale and Portland.

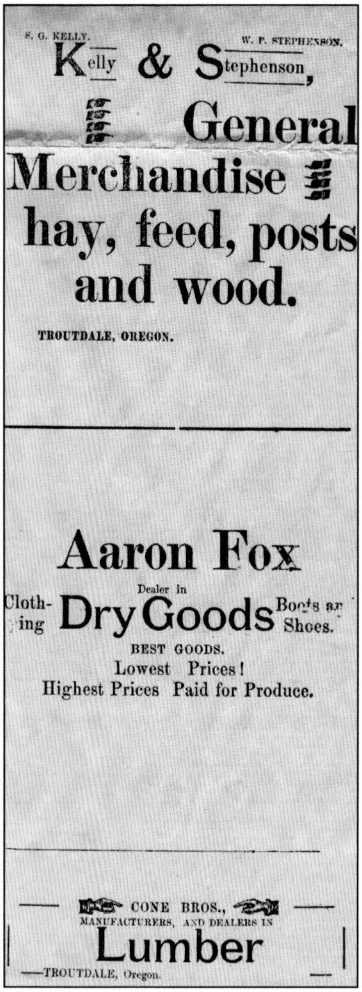

An advertisement from the January 7, 1892, *Troutdale Champion* was for Aaron Fox's general store, which served Troutdale area residents and sold shirts and socks to cowboys riding trains from eastern Oregon loaded with cattle for the slaughterhouse.

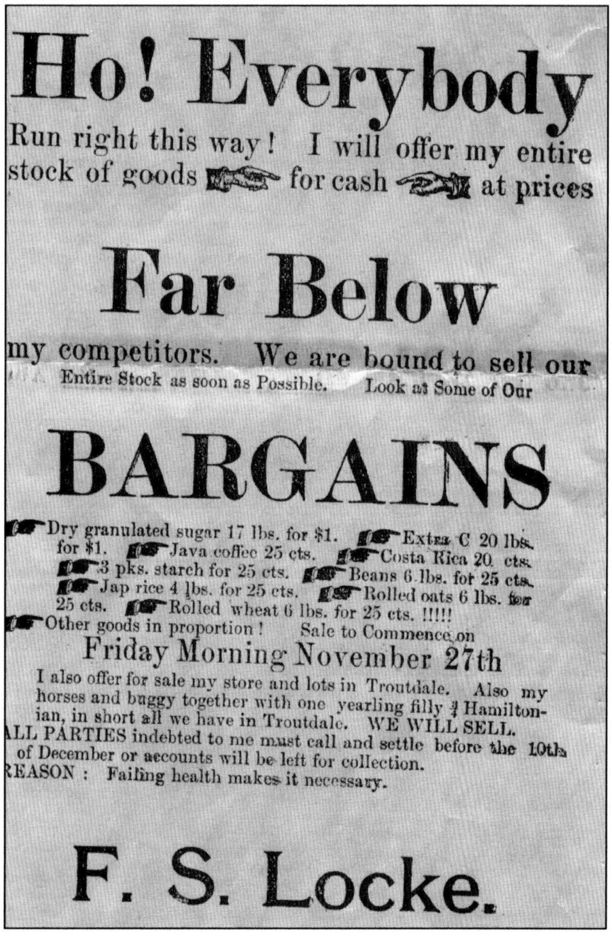

F.S. Locke's advertisement in the *Troutdale Champion* in 1891 announced that he was selling his business, store stock, horses and buggy, as well as his lots in Troutdale due to his failing health. Ladies paddled across the Columbia River from the state of Washington to shop at his store.

Two

Getting From Here to There

From wagon-wheel ruts to the first paved highway in the northwest, Troutdale has seen transportation carve its way through the town. Ferries crisscrossed the Sandy River as early as 1855, transporting passengers, their wagons, and stock to and from the community.

Early gorge travelers on foot or horseback could choose to go east from Troutdale by an old Native American trail running from the Sandy River along the south bank of the Columbia. This route was locally referred to as the "Wire Trail" because a telegraph line had been laid along it to points farther east in the Gorge. In the 1890s, a wooden bridge was built to span the Sandy River at Troutdale. Until that time, people either used the aforementioned ferry to cross the river to the east or rode west through the still-developing areas to reach Portland.

Riverboats also plied the Columbia River, carrying passengers between Cascade Locks and Portland for less than $1. Travelers stood on the southern bank of the Columbia and put up a flag on what is now Sun Dial Beach, indicating that they wanted the boat to stop. Area ranchers used the steamboats and flatboats to transport their livestock to market into the 1900s.

By 1882, Troutdale secured a rail depot when the Oregon Railway and Navigation Company opened a line between Portland and Bonneville, making it a railroad town. Once local farmers realized that they could use the railroad cars to ship their produce, the market for their goods increased. When refrigerated cars were introduced, they began shipping perishable goods to eastern US cities.

The Columbia River Gorge is the only passage through the Cascade Mountains that is near sea level, making it a logical place for a highway linking Portland with the rest of the gorge. With the road's completion, Troutdale began to enjoy its new status as the "Gateway to the Columbia Gorge," and the new stretch of pavement became a part of the burgeoning US highway network.

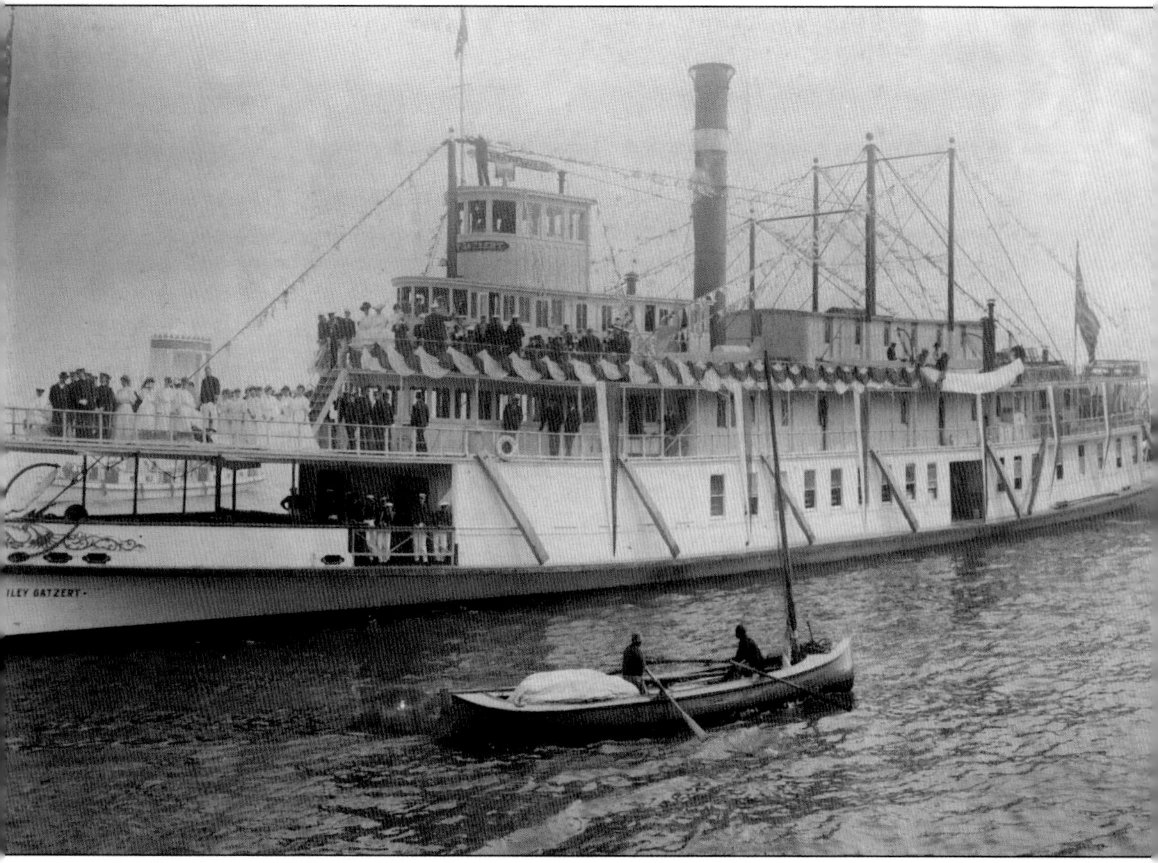

Early sightseers and tourists on the Columbia River took one of several sternwheelers such as the *Bailey Gatzert* to ply the waters between Portland and Cascade Locks, east of Troutdale. It was especially popular during the 1905 Lewis and Clark expedition in Portland. It made two daily runs from Portland to Cascade Locks and was one of the fastest on the river at a time when captains raced to pass each other on daily routes. Captains of other ships on the river at the time called it "the Daily Bastard" because of the large wakes it made.

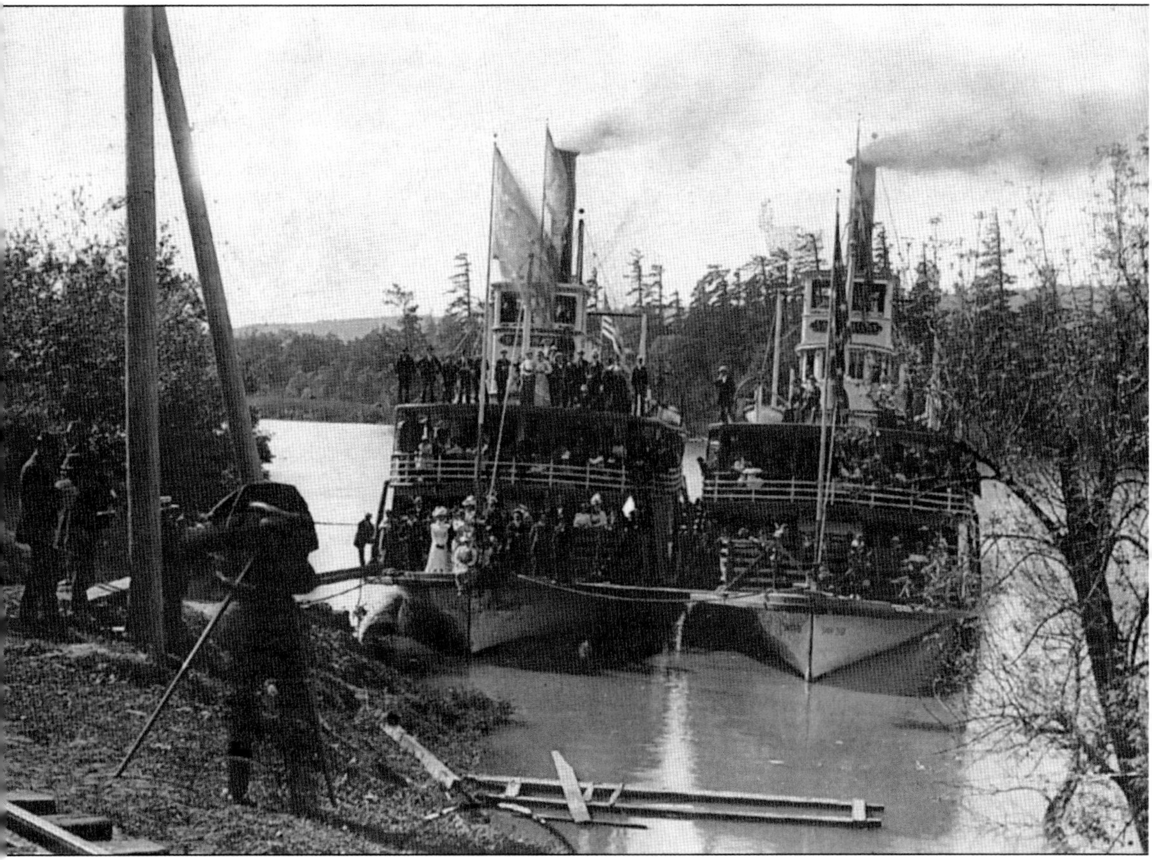

Excursion steamers took passengers from spot to spot on the river, often from impromptu landings. The cost for a ride from Cascade Locks to Portland was only 50¢, with a meal thrown in. The menu depended on what was in season. In the early 1900s, steamers could travel from The Dalles to Portland in five hours.

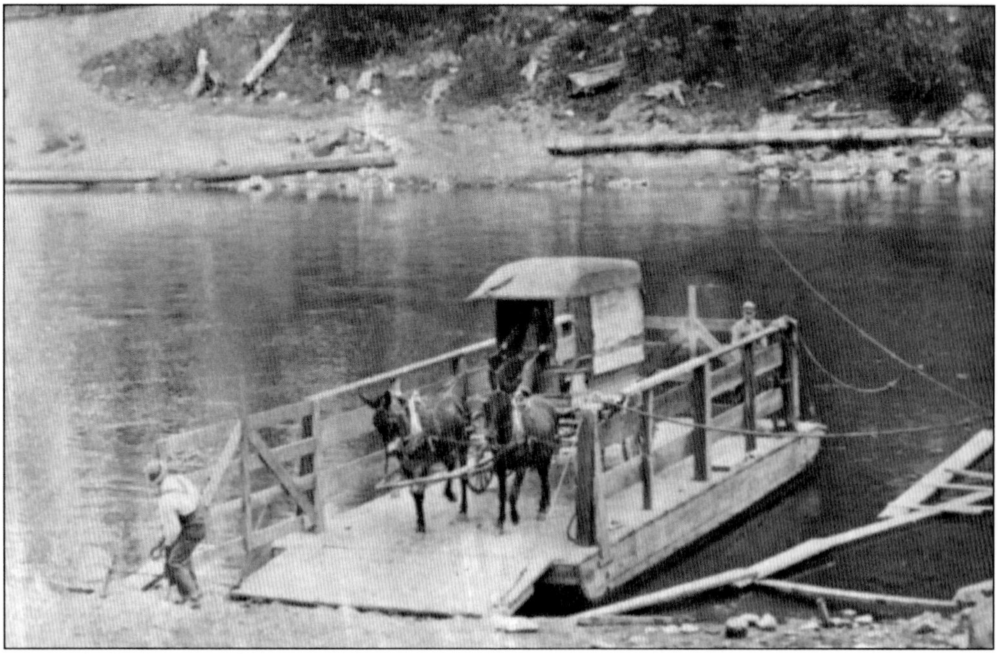

Before the highway bridge was built across the Sandy River, early settlers in the Troutdale-Corbett area took the ferry across the river from what was then called the Hicklin Ranch. The ferry landing was near the present boat ramp at Lewis and Clark State Park.

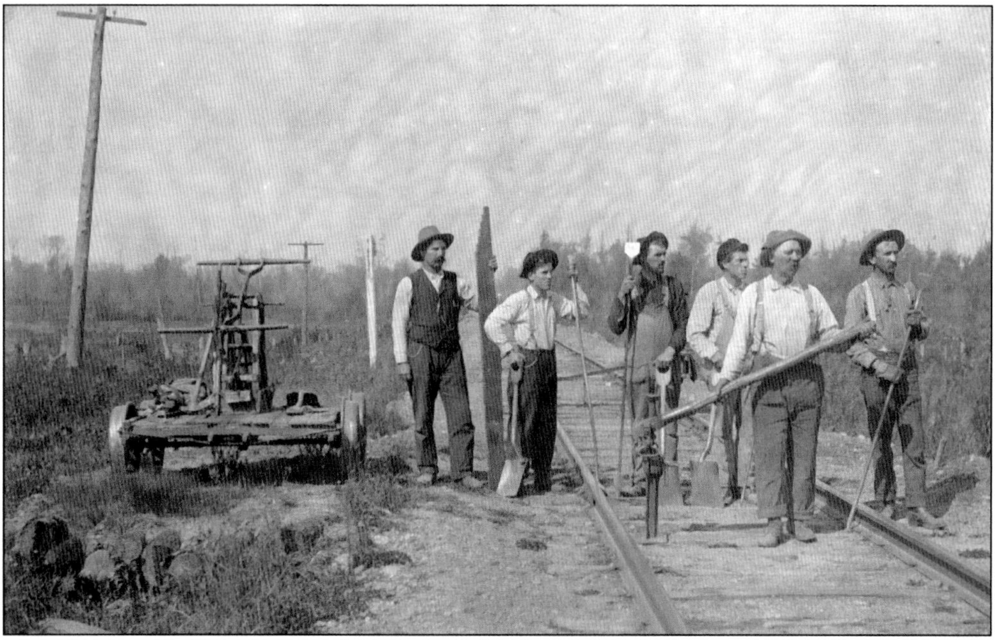

The Oregon Railway and Navigation Company's rail line opening from Portland to Bonneville with a stop at Troutdale allowed passengers and local products to be moved by rail. Here, railroad workers repair the railroad crossties and rails using tampers and pry bars.

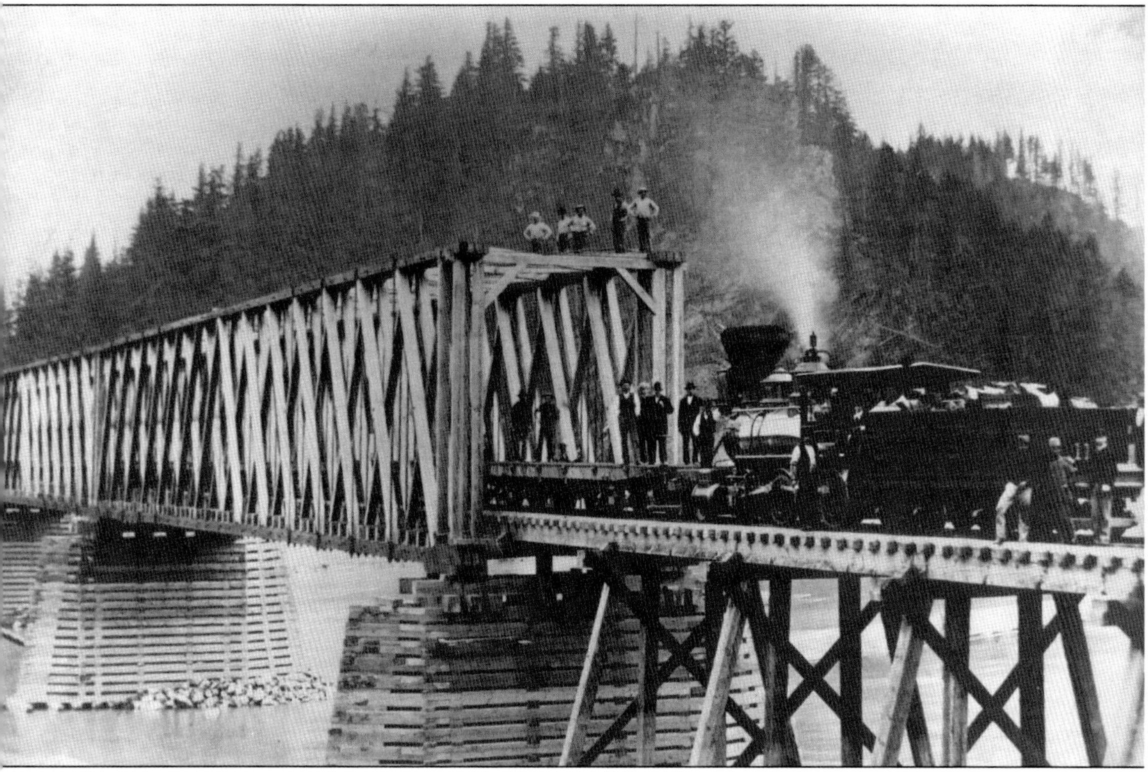

The first wooden railroad bridge was constructed over the Sandy River at Troutdale in 1882. Capt. John Harlow waged a one-man battle with the railroad by using his own ship to sail up the Sandy River from its juncture with the Columbia to prove that if the railroad did not build a railroad bridge over the river, Captain Harlow would have to use a ship to move his farm products by water routes. This would have necessitated a more costly drawbridge to be built to accommodate boats; thus, the railroad agreed to build the depot at Troutdale, securing the bridge as part of the deal.

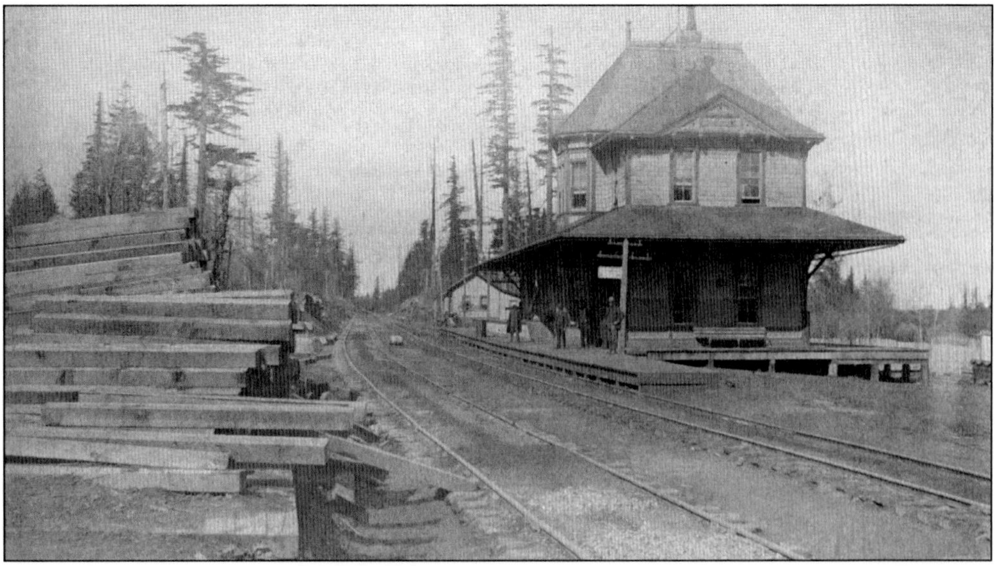

The first passenger train rolled through Troutdale in November 1882. The railroad depot was then a two-story structure with living quarters for the station agent and his family on the second floor. The depot burned in 1907 and was replaced with a new building.

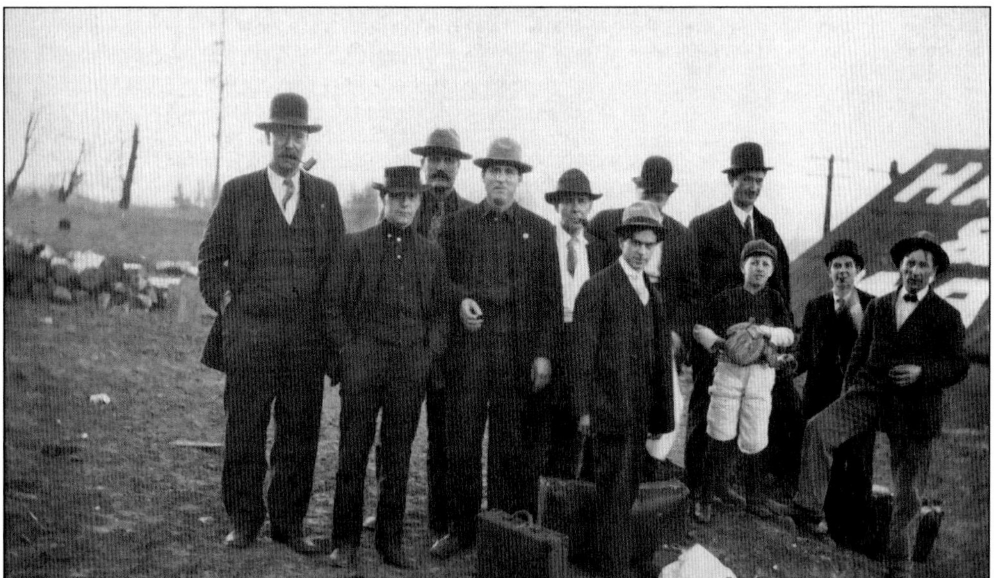

A group of businessmen and a boy wearing a baseball uniform and his catcher's mitt wait beside the tracks for the train's arrival in 1905. Some people used the train to travel to nearby Latourell to attend all-night dances or to go into Portland to shop.

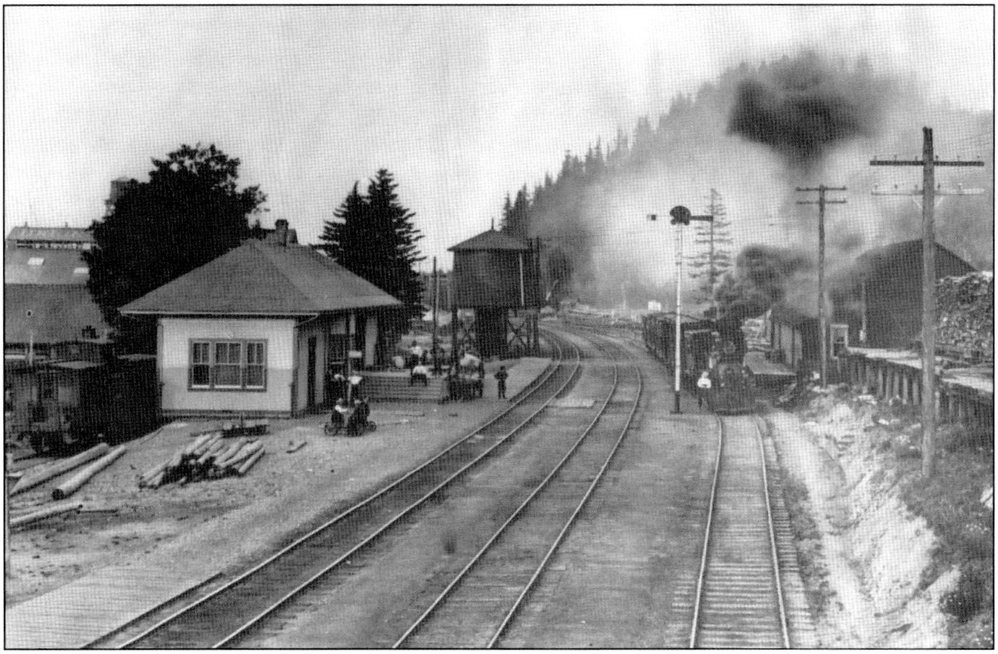

The transcontinental rail link at Troutdale allowed local farmers to ship produce all over the nation, but it also connected the tiny communities eastward along the Columbia River Gorge. One local resident surmised that shipping lettuce on refrigerated cars helped many families in Troutdale to survive the Depression.

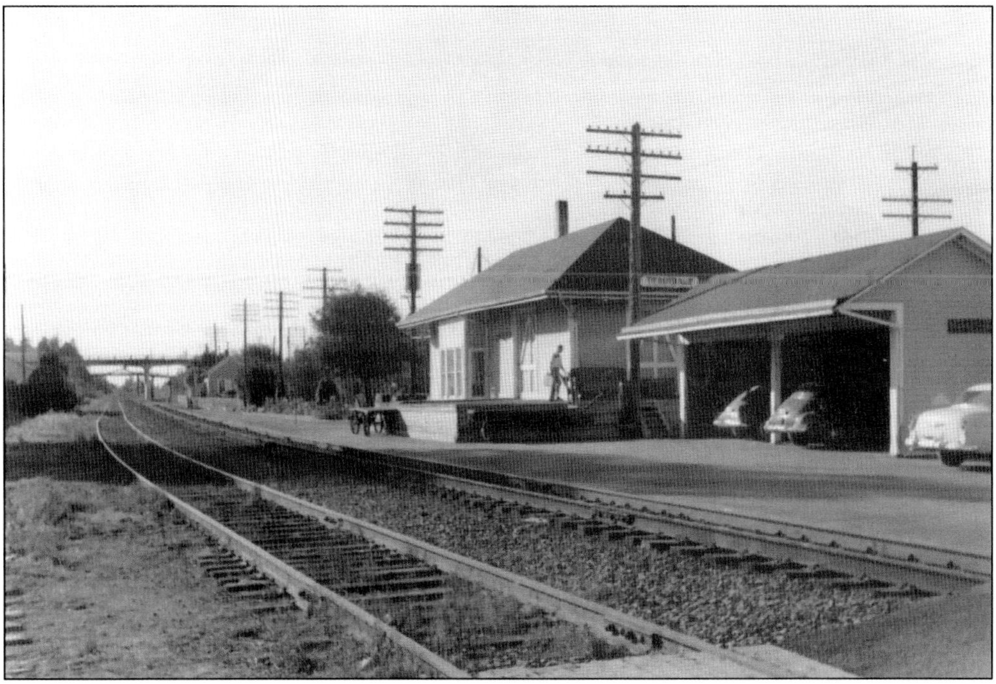

A view to the west shows the second railroad depot, built in 1907 after the first depot burned. The depot has since been moved to the south side of the tracks and is being used as the Rail Depot Museum for the Troutdale Historical Society.

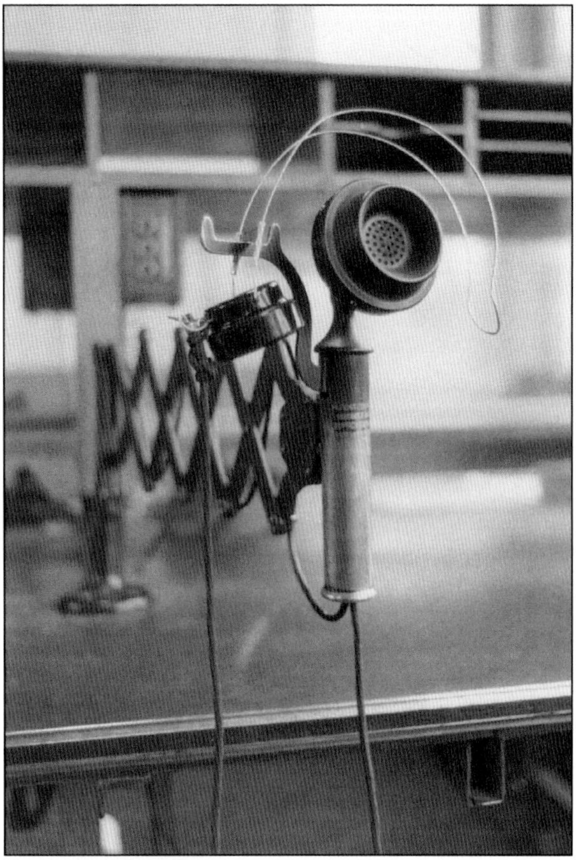

Pictured is the telephone dispatcher's phone from the 1907 rail depot. It remains in the Rail Depot Museum, which has a full room set up as the depot would have looked around 1900.

Passenger service at Troutdale ended in 1965 when people began using cars instead of trains to travel. The Union Pacific sold the building to Troutdale for $1. The Troutdale Historical Society used a $2,500 US Bicentennial grant to move it to the opposite side of the tracks in 1976.

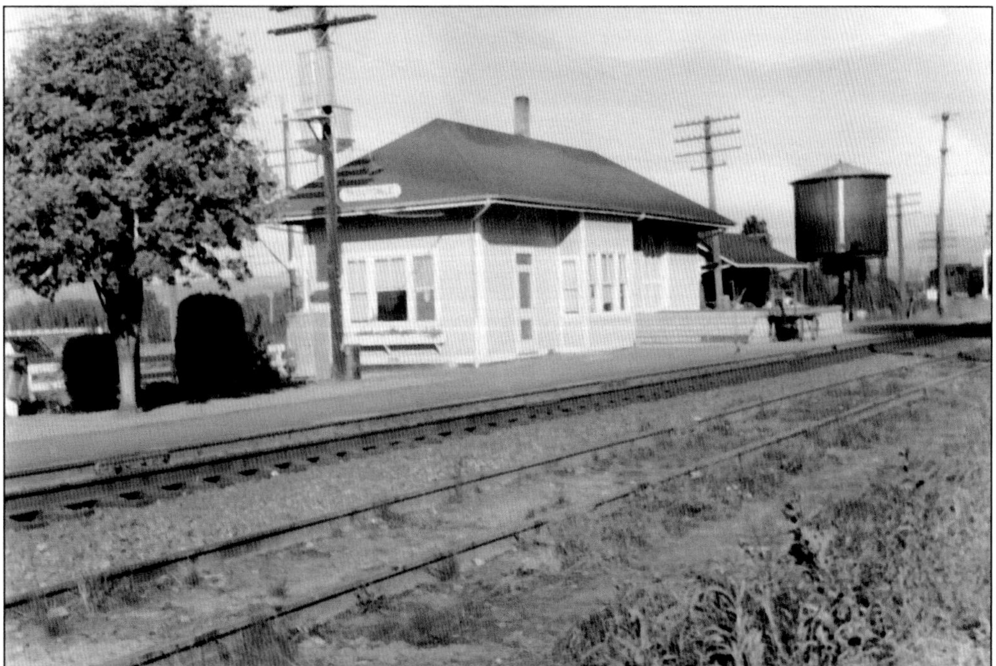

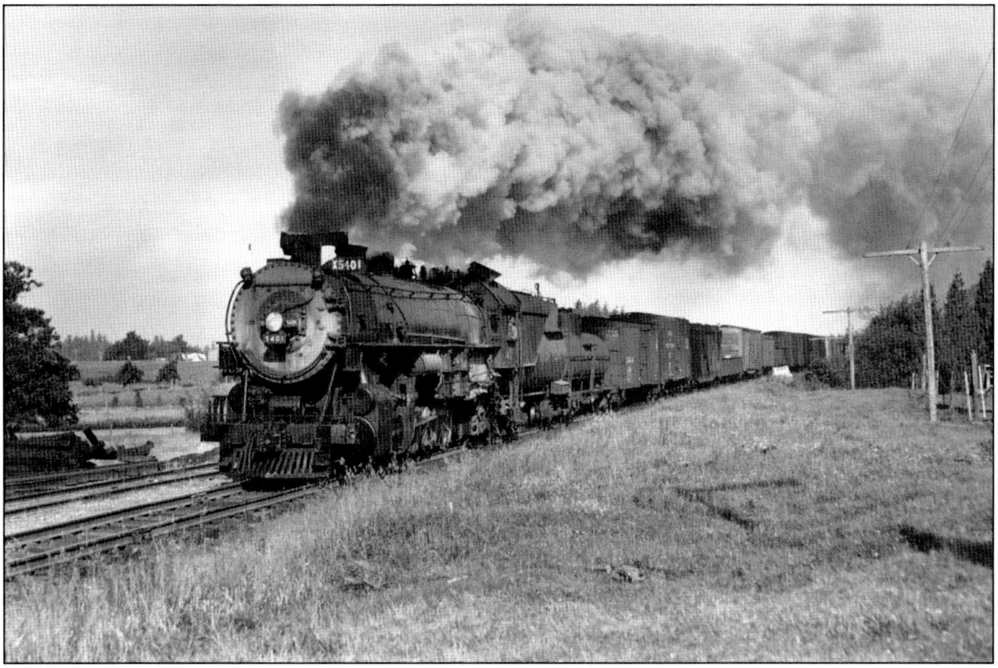

A Union Pacific X5401 2-10-2-type engine with 80 cars nears the Troutdale depot from the east in 1949. At the peak of rail travel, the depot was open three shifts around the clock.

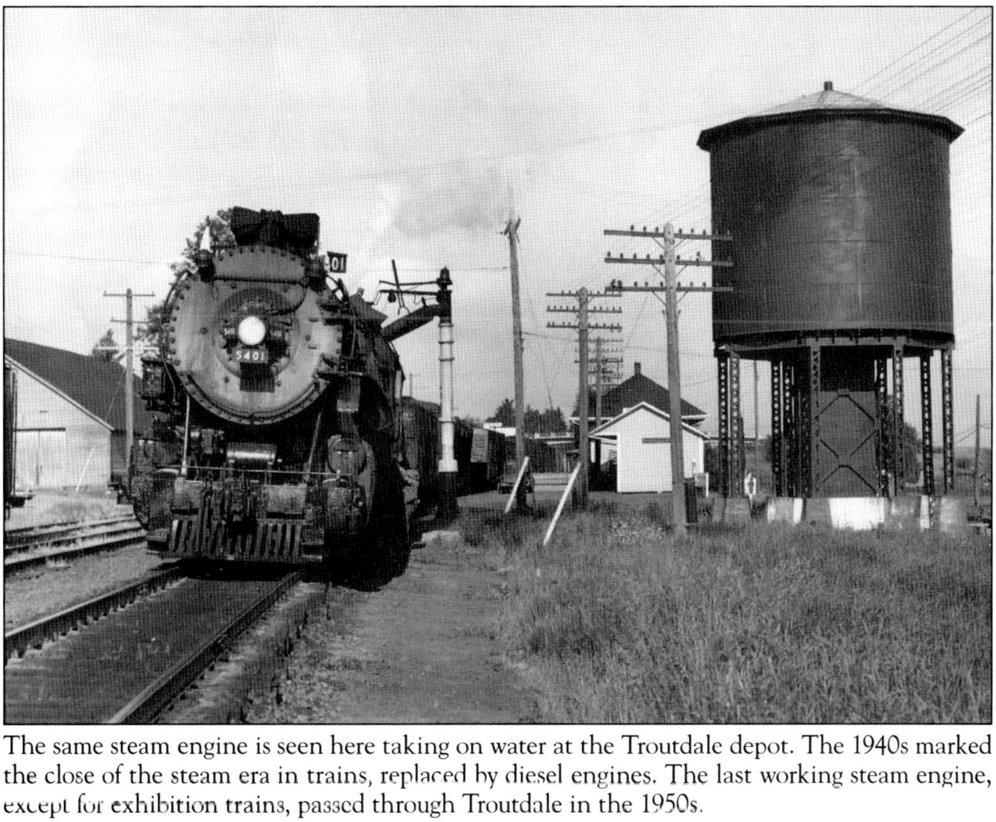

The same steam engine is seen here taking on water at the Troutdale depot. The 1940s marked the close of the steam era in trains, replaced by diesel engines. The last working steam engine, except for exhibition trains, passed through Troutdale in the 1950s.

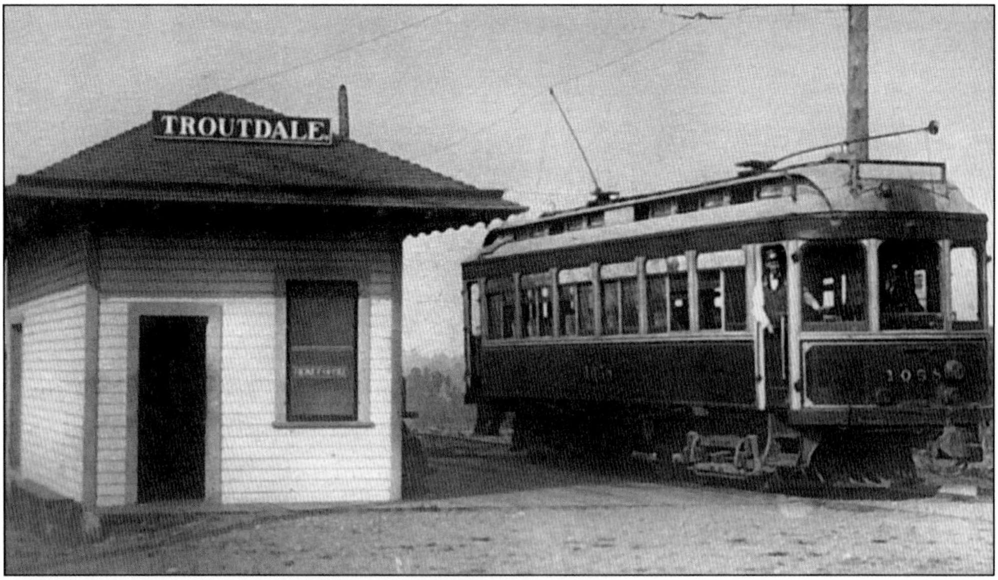

The interurban rail line ran along what is now Halsey Street into Troutdale. Local trains between Troutdale and Portland carried day-trippers, who used the train much like modern-day passengers use the MAX light rail to commute into the city. (Photograph courtesy of Troutdale Historical Society.)

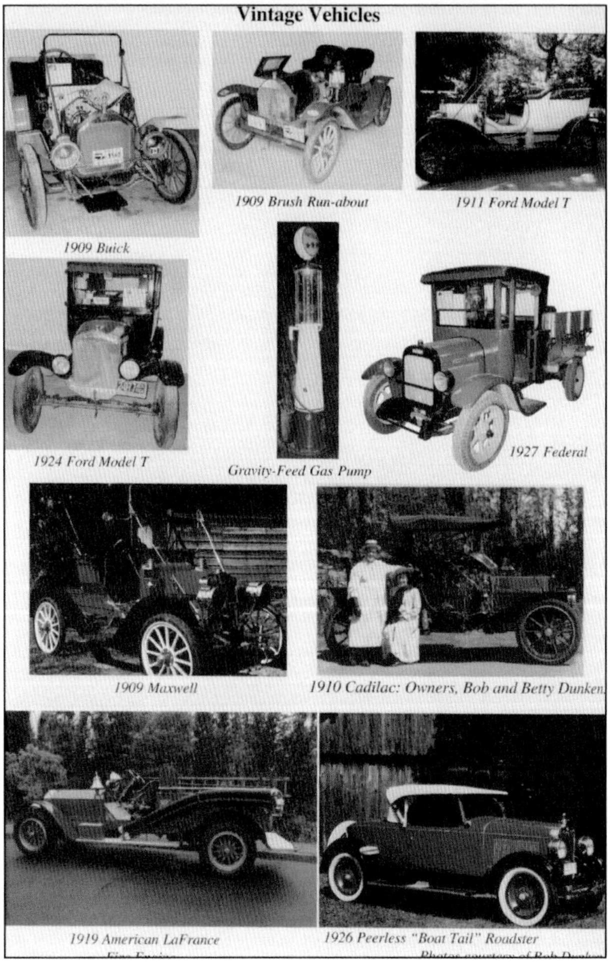

Vintage vehicles like these traversed the early roads and highways. Seen here are a 1909 Buick, a 1909 Brush Run-About, and a 1926 Peerless "Boat Tail" Roadster. The gravity-feed gas pump was common at the time. (All photographs courtesy of Bob Dunken.)

Three

The Historic Columbia River Highway

Lewis and Clark camped along the banks of the Columbia River in 1805 near the present Historic Columbia River Highway. During subsequent years, the river served as the only mode of transportation between towns on the south side of the Columbia. Later, travelers used the narrow ribbon between the Columbia and the basalt cliffs to its south to get beyond the Cascades. When the railroad ran a line from Portland east to The Dalles in 1881, the original wagon road was eliminated. Not until the advent of the first automobiles did the idea of an actual highway that would both move automobile traffic and provide scenic views of the gorge became a reality, connecting Portland to the west and the network of small communities to the east, become a reality.

Lewis and Clark could not have imagined that the steep and treacherous land that lay beside the "River of the West" would become the "King of Roads" by 1916. Samuel C. Lancaster, the engineer in charge of the design and construction of the Columbia River Highway, was determined that "none of this wild beauty should be marred where it could be prevented," and the highway was "built that not one tree was felled, not one fern was crushed, unnecessarily." To accomplish that goal, Lancaster surveyed and mapped out the most scenic viewpoints and ran the road through them, subtly blending it with the environment while meeting the highest engineering standards of the age. His design required no greater than a five-percent grade at any point along the road and no curve with less than a 200-foot turning radius.

Using 2,200 workers, horse-drawn "Fresno" graders, and steam machines, road crews gouged and carved the new highway eastward, laying out the graded roadbed that would eventually join Portland and Hood River, Oregon, on July 6, 1915, for a cost of $223,000. Because automobile traffic and long-distance travel in the United States were in their infancy, long paved stretches of highways did not exist in America at the time. However, by June 1915, the paving of the roadway had begun in Multnomah County. By the time the highway was officially dedicated on June 7, 1916, paving extended only 18.7 miles, but the roadway is considered to be the first major paved highway in the northwest.

Today, the National Scenic Area along Interstate 84 and the Historic Columbia River Highway draw over two million visitors a year.

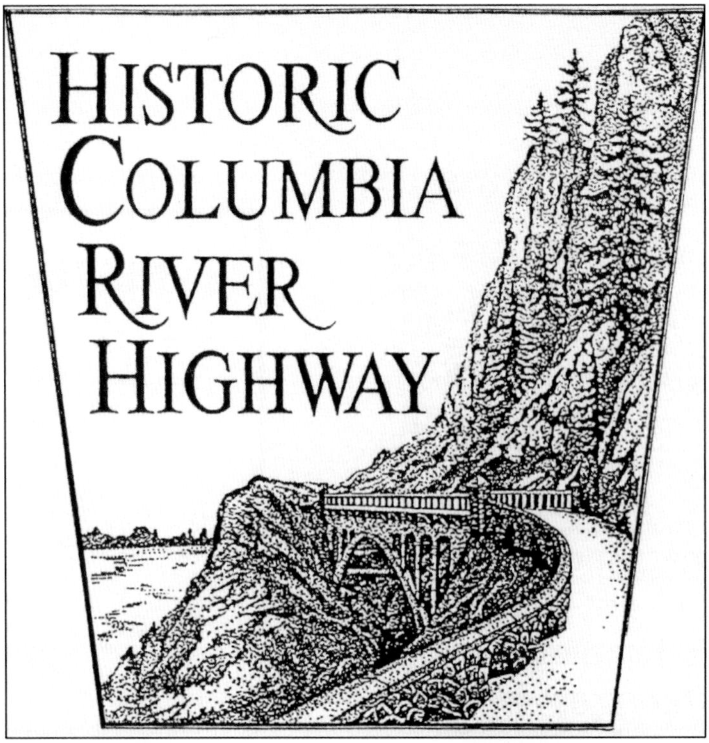

The Historic Columbia River Highway keystone sign was adopted to signify the importance of the highway being designated part of the Columbia River Gorge National Scenic Area and as a historic district. It is still considered to be one of the great scenic highways in the country. In 1996, the Oregon Department of Transportation proposed a master plan to rehabilitate sections of the highway and to construct a connection of trails along the abandoned sections of the original roadway. (Original drawing by Teresa Kasner.)

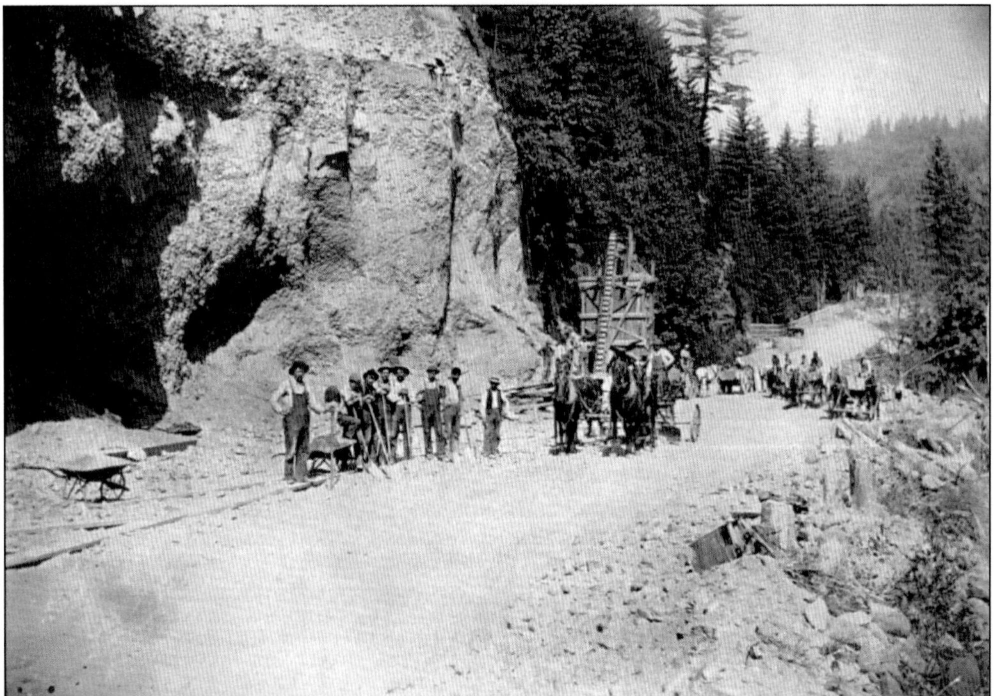

Construction of the Historic Columbia River Highway began in 1912, before the advent of modern machinery. This required using mules and horses to pull the "Fresnoes," or primitive road graders, which were dragged across the earth to level and prepare it for the gravel roadbed.

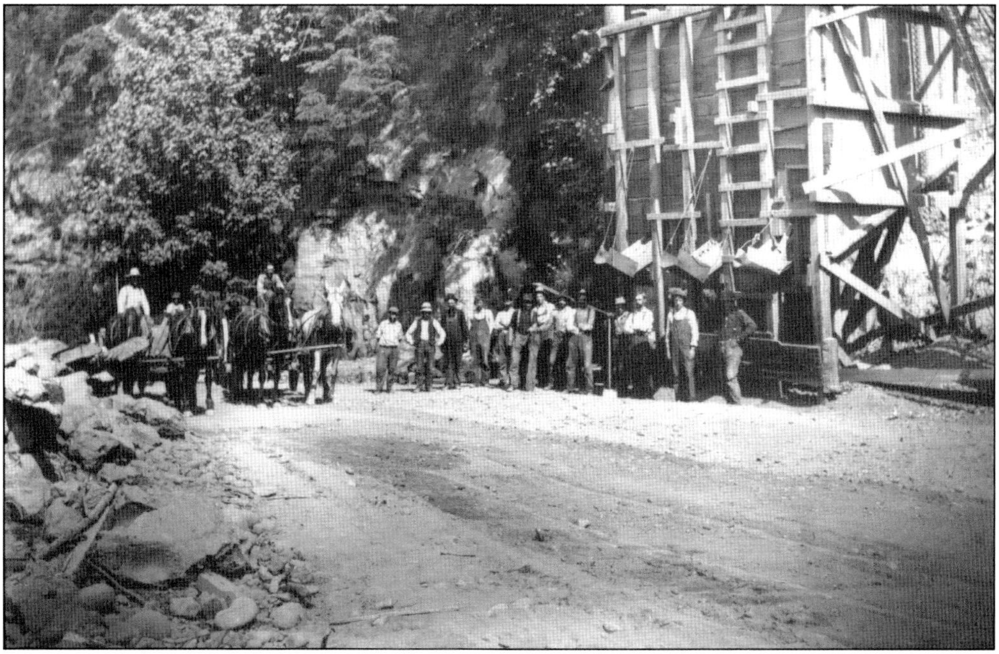

Local residents along the new Historic Columbia River Highway route were hired to help build the roadway. Since the road was begun just as Henry Ford began to mass-produce automobiles, many of those workers and the people who lived alongside the road did not realize its significance.

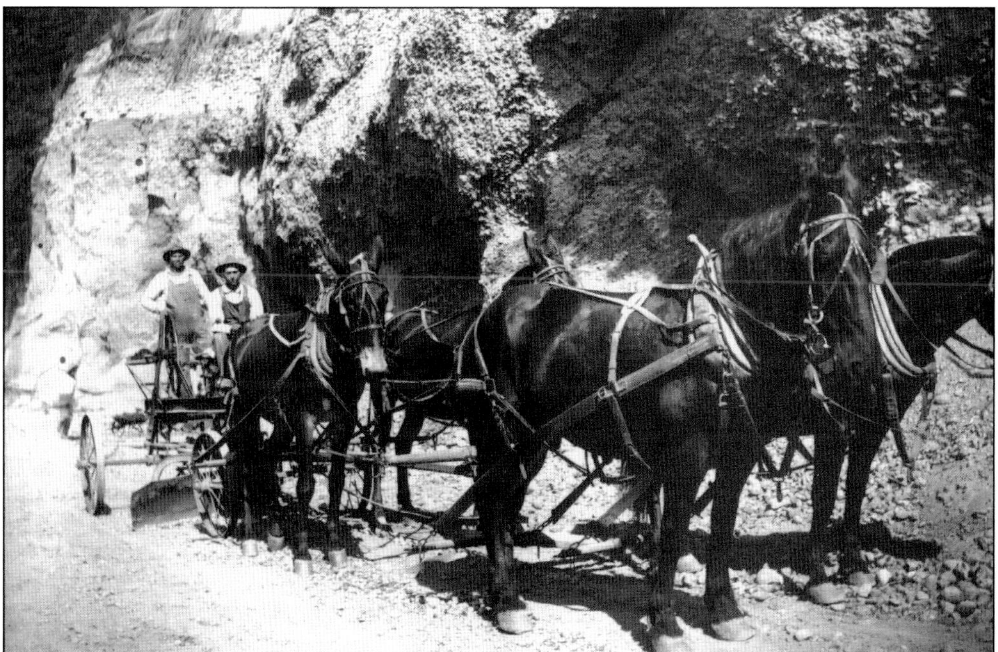

Local residents hired out their mule teams for the road construction. In 1915, laborers earned $2.50 for a 10-hour day and a man with a team earned $5 per day. The money was a welcome supplement to the incomes of struggling farmers and loggers.

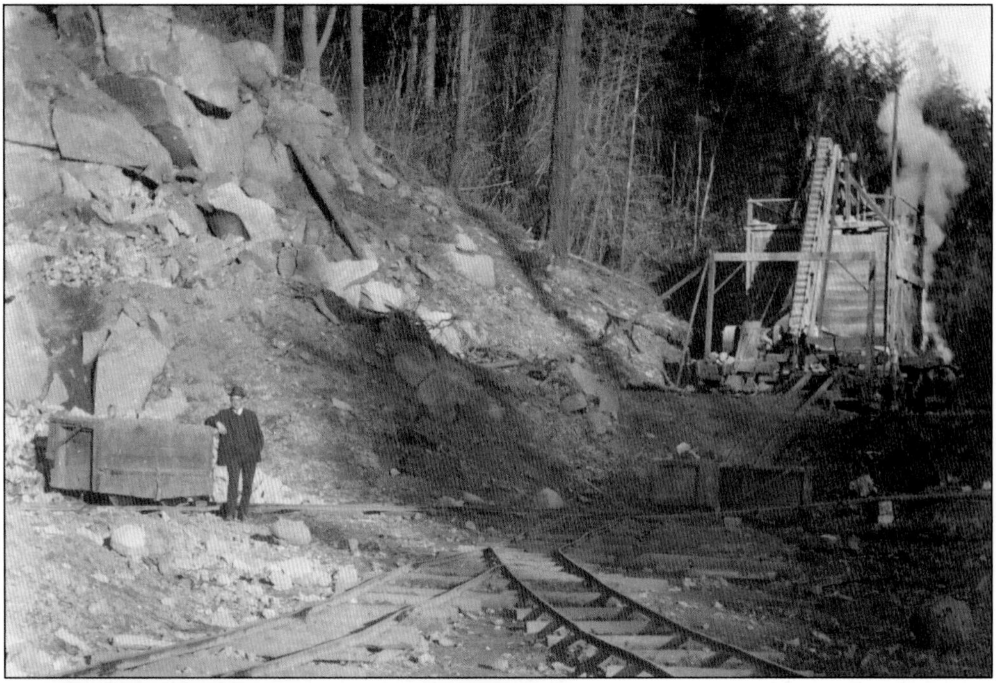

Gravel for the roadbed was loaded onto wagons from the steam-powered rock crusher seen in the background and then moved along the roadway by mule teams to be spread. Local farmers went from digging winter crops to working on the road in a matter of days.

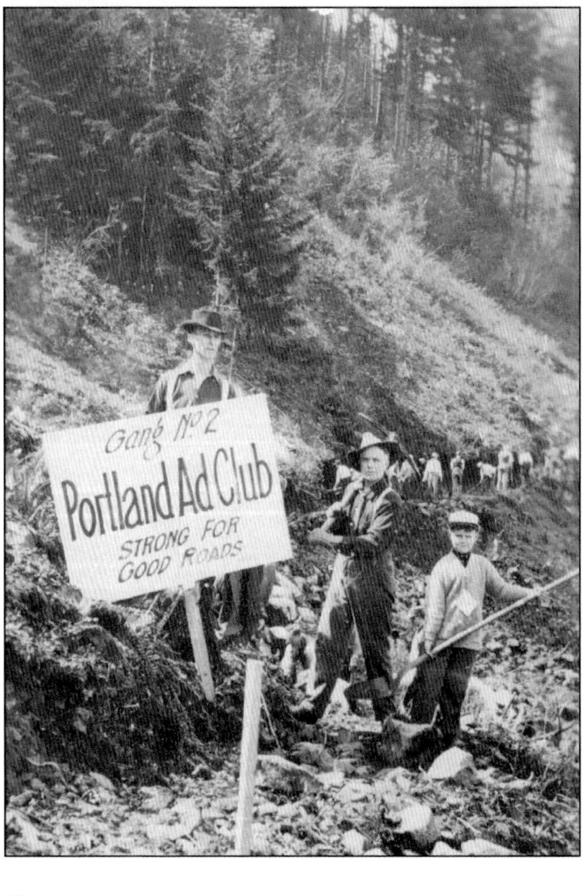

Employees from Portland businesses volunteered a symbolic day of work to help keep the road building ongoing and in the public eye. The man in the middle of the photograph is Alfred P. Goss, a banker, and the young man is his son, James Goss, who later became an attorney.

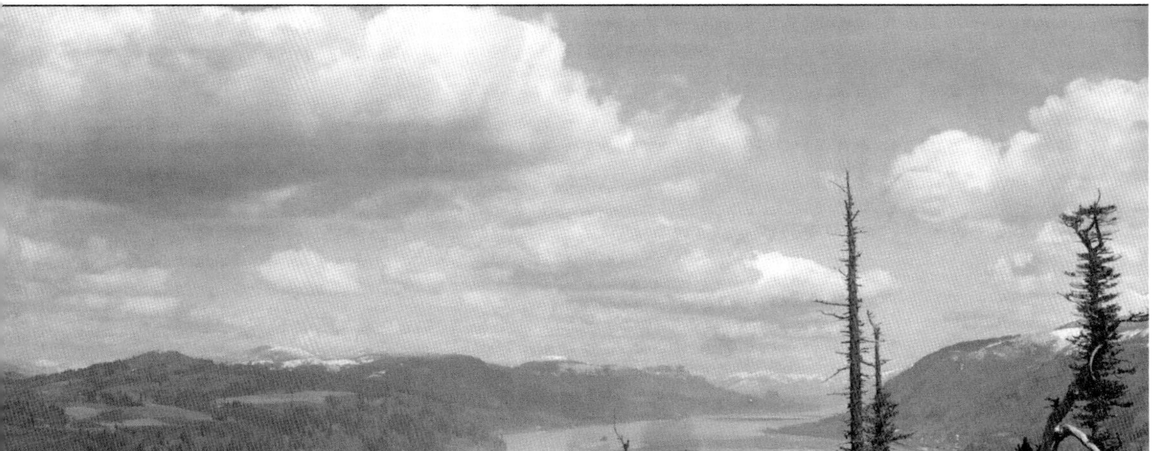

Two portions of the initial construction of the Vista House at Crown Point are shown in this 1917 photograph. Original plans for the Historic Columbia River Highway did not include the Vista House, which was built as a memorial to early pioneers of Oregon. Dedication ceremonies for the new highway were held at Multnomah Falls and Crown Point in 1916. Rose petals were scattered and loganberry juice—Oregon's "temperance beverage"—was served before Pres. Woodrow Wilson touched an electric button in the White House at 5:00 p.m., unfurling the "flag of freedom" at Crown Point.

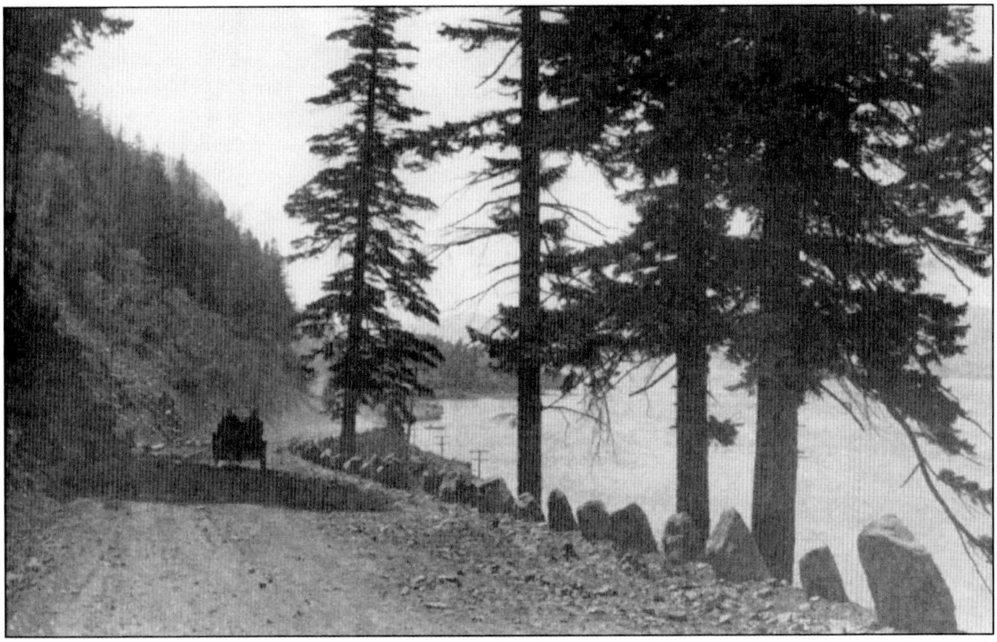

Initial sections of the highway were not paved, but by the spring of 1916, residents of east Multnomah County had a Warrenite-paved—a combination of crushed rock and bitumen—road into Troutdale. Paving continued east to Multnomah Falls for the highway's formal dedication in June 1916. (Photograph by Charles W. Post.)

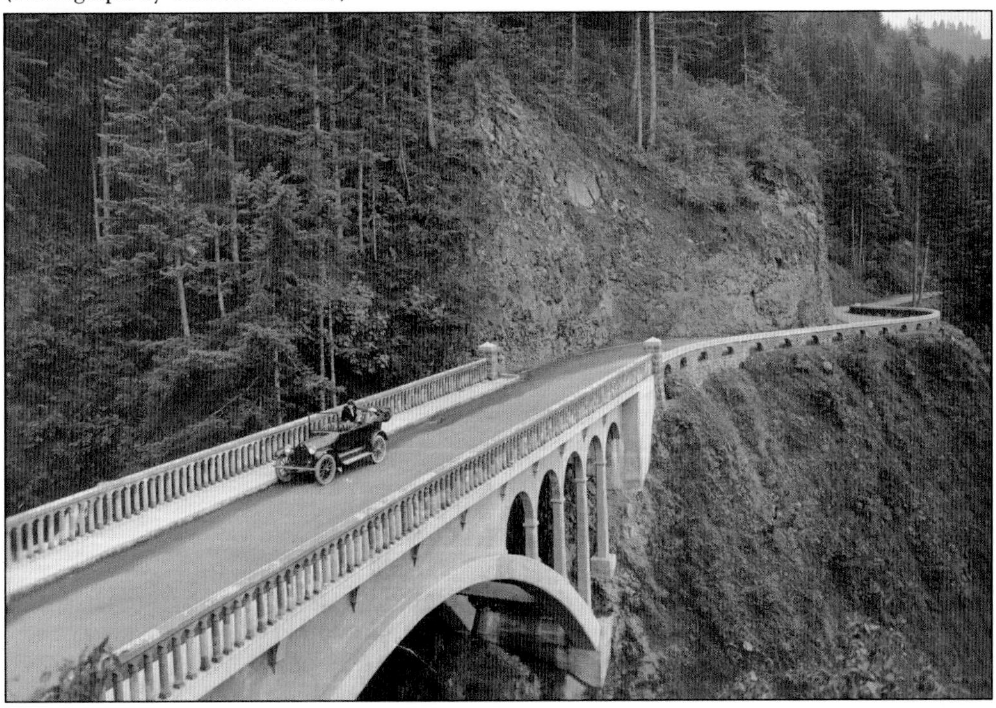

After touring the Swiss and German Alps in 1908, engineers Samuel Hill and Samuel Lancaster chose to design bridges on the Columbia River Highway to resemble the passageways they had seen in Europe. The structures were intended to reflect the forward-thinking ideal of the highway itself.

Multnomah Falls, with its origins on Larch Mountain, plummets 620 feet down the cliff face—the second-highest year-round waterfall in the nation. The waterfall makes two "leaps" with a walking bridge between them and is one of seven waterfalls along the Columbia River Highway.

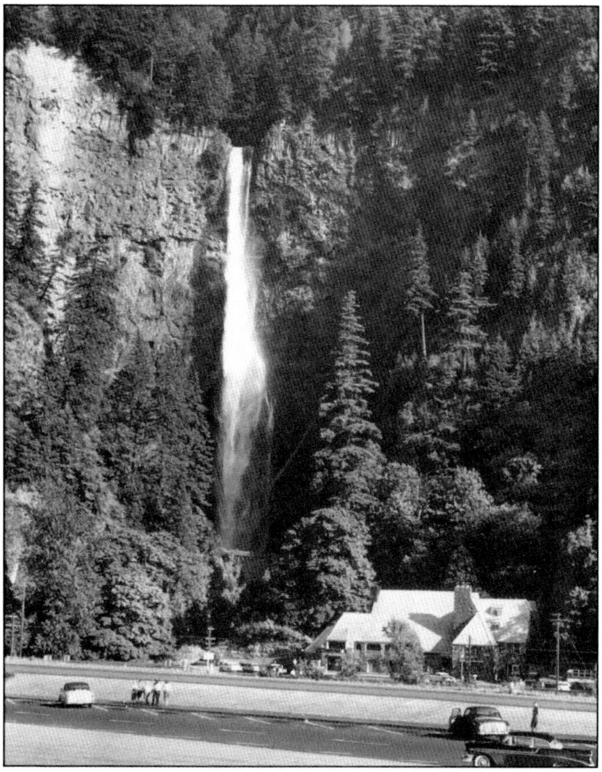

This interior view of the Mitchell Point Tunnel shows the windows cut into the side of the cliff, allowing maximum views of the Columbia River Gorge from within the tunnel. This concept of open tunnels was considered an engineering masterpiece in its day.

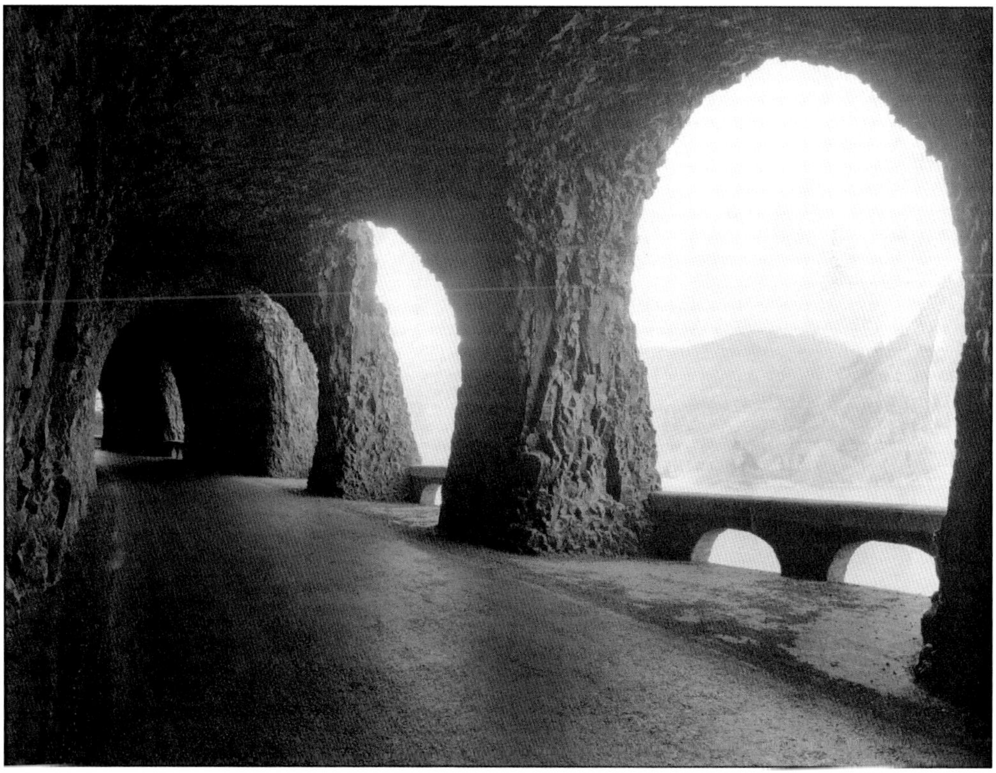

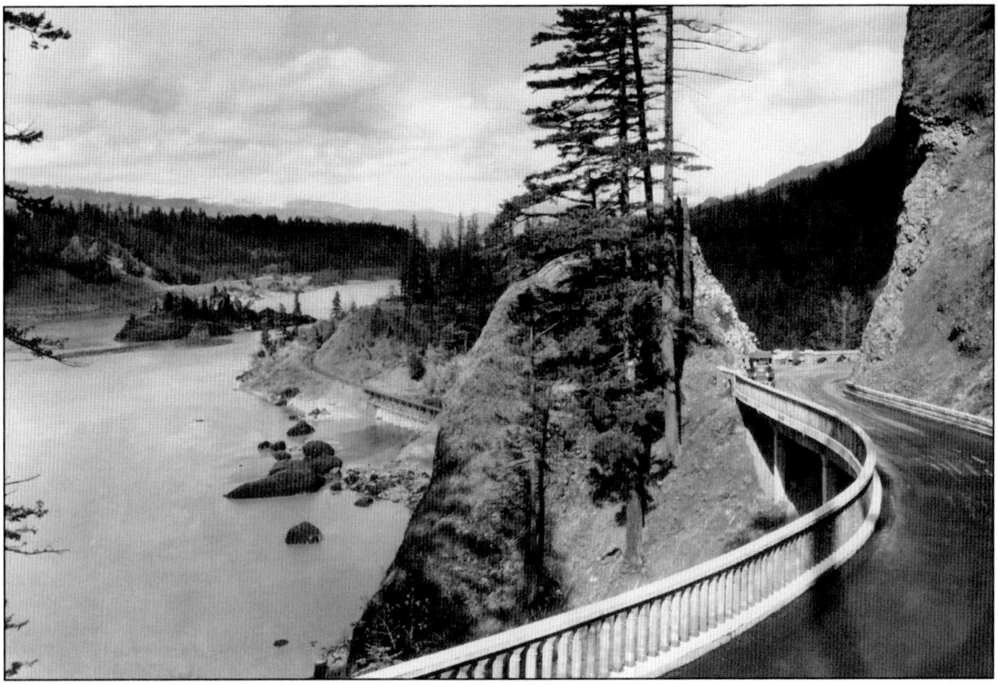

The drive along the south side of the Columbia River Gorge follows the natural curves of the cliffs along the river and was intended to delight the viewer at every turn. Parts of the original highway, which parallels Interstate 84, have been widened to accommodate larger vehicles.

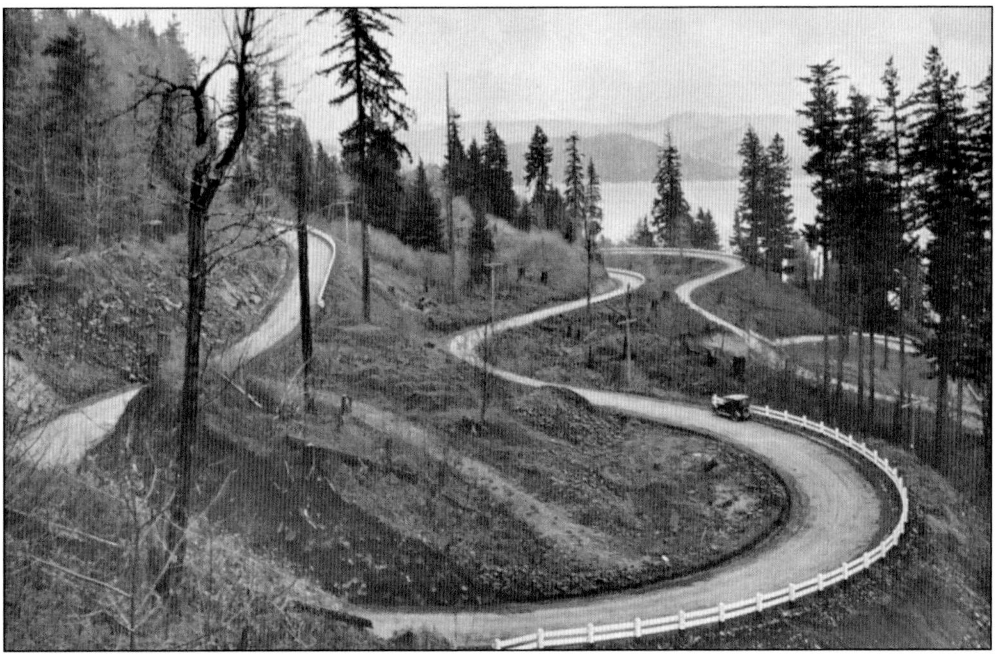

The "figure-eight," also called the loop section, of the Historic Columbia River Highway descends from Crown Point to the small community of Latourell. The roadway runs parallel to itself five times in the course of this 700-foot drop. Although intricately curved, the gentle grades make the descent easier.

Four

LIVING OFF THE LAND IN AGRICULTURE AND LOGGING

The promise of settling on a land grant of 320 acres in a lush, rain-soaked area of Oregon was one of the lures drawing pioneers westward on the Oregon Trail. Although the land had to be initially cleared of trees before crops could be planted, the settlers had faced similar hardships in other parts of the country where they had farmed. They had cleared hedgerows, plowed under prairie grass, and pulled stumps. These folks were as tough as the territory they were settling, and they would need that hardiness.

Mother Nature could be fickle in the Troutdale area, offering up cold, wet springs that left fields sodden until early June, followed by cloudy days and fall rains that began before crops could ripen and be harvested. Throw in an ice storm that destroyed fruits trees in the winter and a gale force wind that blew out of the east, and farmers felt like they were playing with loaded dice.

Families who settled the land along the Columbia River near what is now Troutdale developed their stakes with dairy farms, chicken ranches, and food crops of prodigious variety, as well as ornamentals like flowers and bulbs. The rolling hills on the western end of the Columbia River Gorge became a network of farms that would eventually produce not just enough to feed the families that owned the land, but also people in Portland, and, eventually, "back east" after refrigerated railroad cars allowed farmers to ship their produce beyond the local area.

Those same towering coniferous trees that stymied the first plantings by farmers also proved to be one of the major sources of employment for early settlers in the Troutdale area. The trees, some of which surpassed 200 feet in height, were hewn by men using axes, saws, and wedges. Once the trees were felled, crosscut sawyers cut the trees into manageable lengths, and barkers "dressed" (stripped) the trees so they could "yard" (transport) them to a holding area until they could be moved onto an elevated wooden chute, called a flume, and transported as far as three-quarters of a mile into a pond on the lower end of the flume. Sawmills and lumber mills used the choicest of the strong Douglas firs to make lumber and siding for construction. That legacy of fine timber still exists in Oregon today.

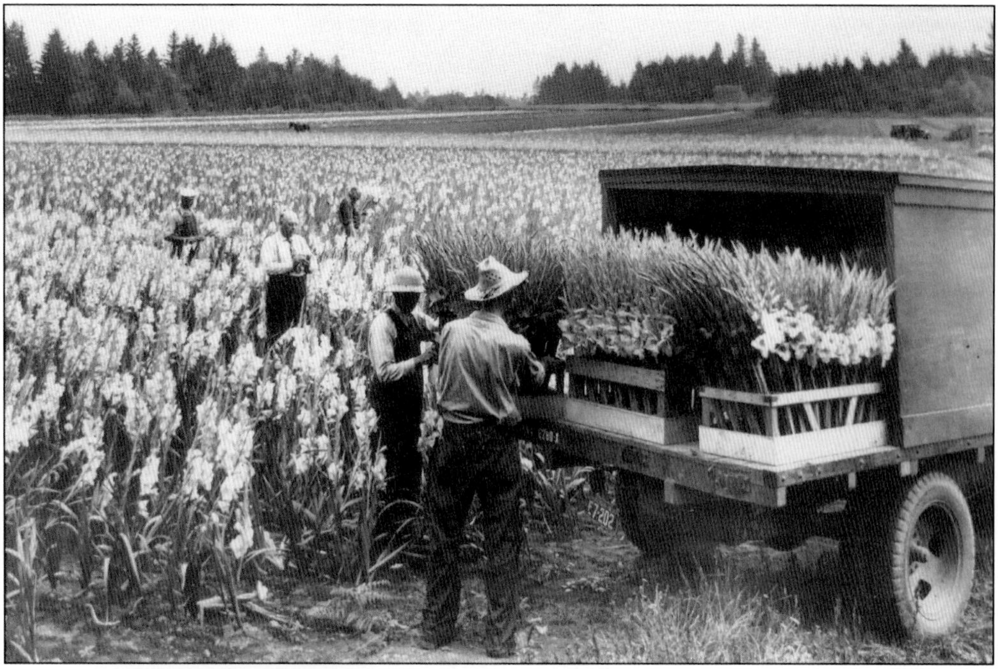

Fields of seasonal specialty flowers are easily found in Oregon, and the area around Troutdale was once a favored spot for bulb varieties such as daffodils and gladiolus. In this photograph, men load a truck with crates of gladiolus picked in September 1937. Gladiolus were planted in the spring after the danger of frost was past. Once they flowered, the bulbs were dug up in the fall, then dried and fumigated for the following year. Individual varieties were kept separated in screen-bottomed boxes and graded by size.

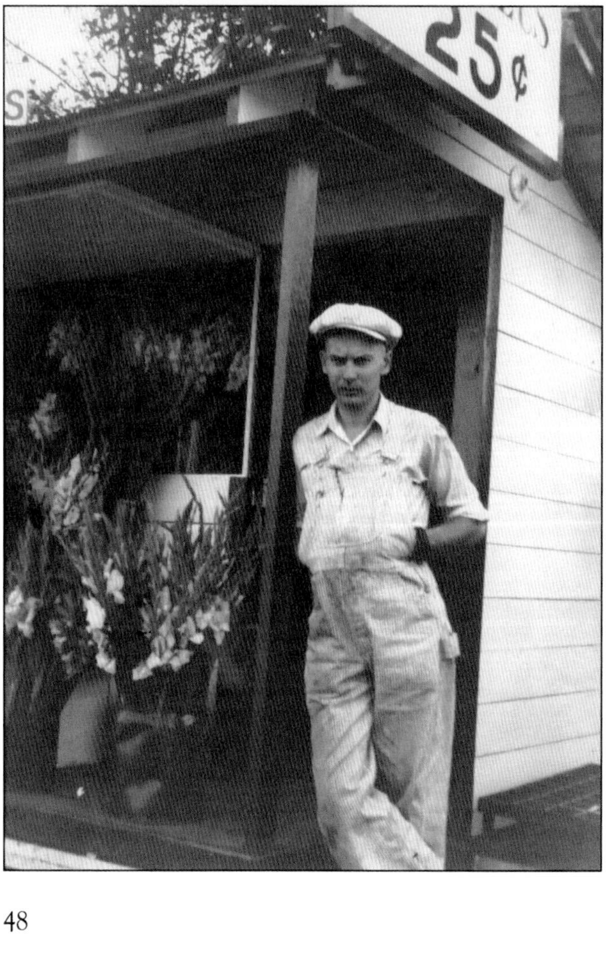

Roadside stands offering gladiolus blooms for sale were a fixture along the Columbia River Highway for many years. Dale Parsons is seen here leaning against Mary Parsons's gladiolus stand on Buxton Street in Troutdale.

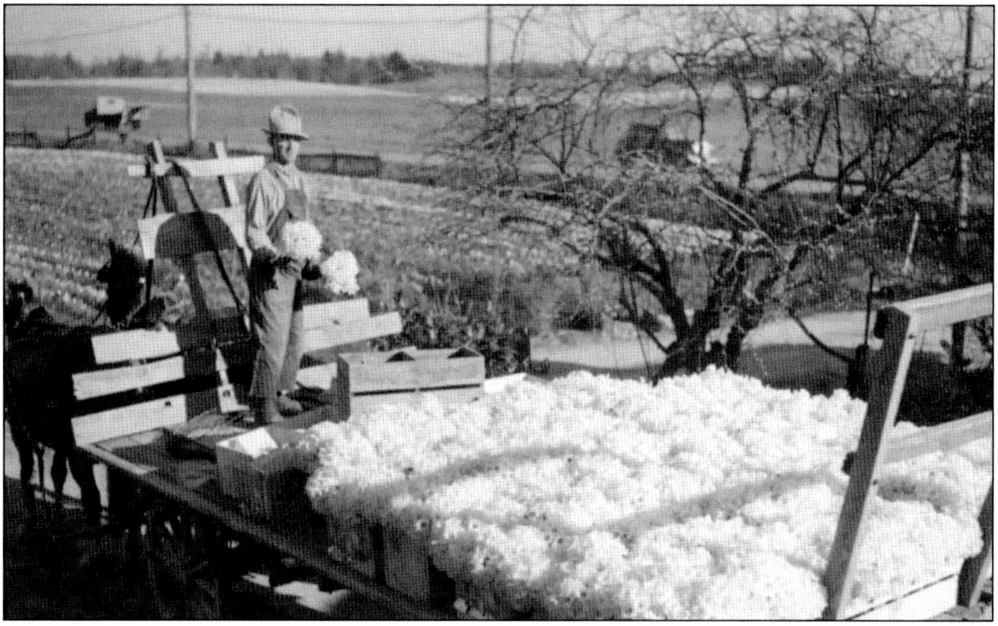

Daffodils and narcissus bulbs were planted in the fall for spring blooms. If the flowers were not sold for their blooms, they were "headed," by removing the blossom to direct growth to the bulbs. One farmer had 80 acres in daffodils in the 1920s, while another began hybridizing the flowers to create new varieties.

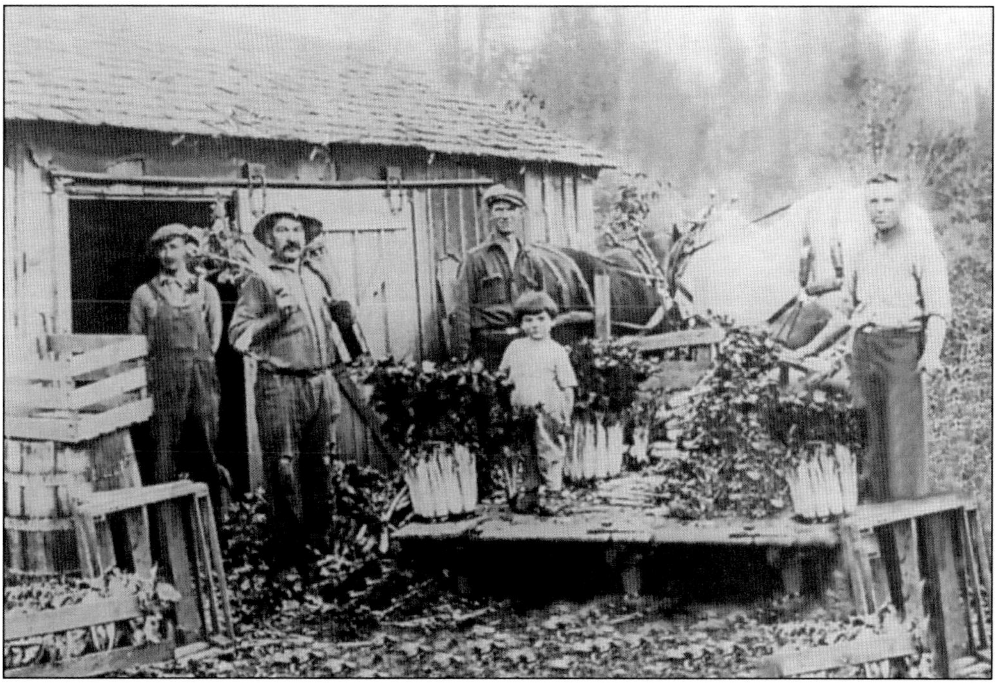

The Laurenzio family's celery operation in the 1930s was on property rented by Maggiorino Laurenzio, seen here. Celery seeds were expensive, costing $30 to $40 a pound, and celery seedlings, planted 30,000 plants to an acre, were started in cold frames and houses. Celery was regarded as a 100-day crop, meaning Oregon farmers could get two crops per year, in spring and fall.

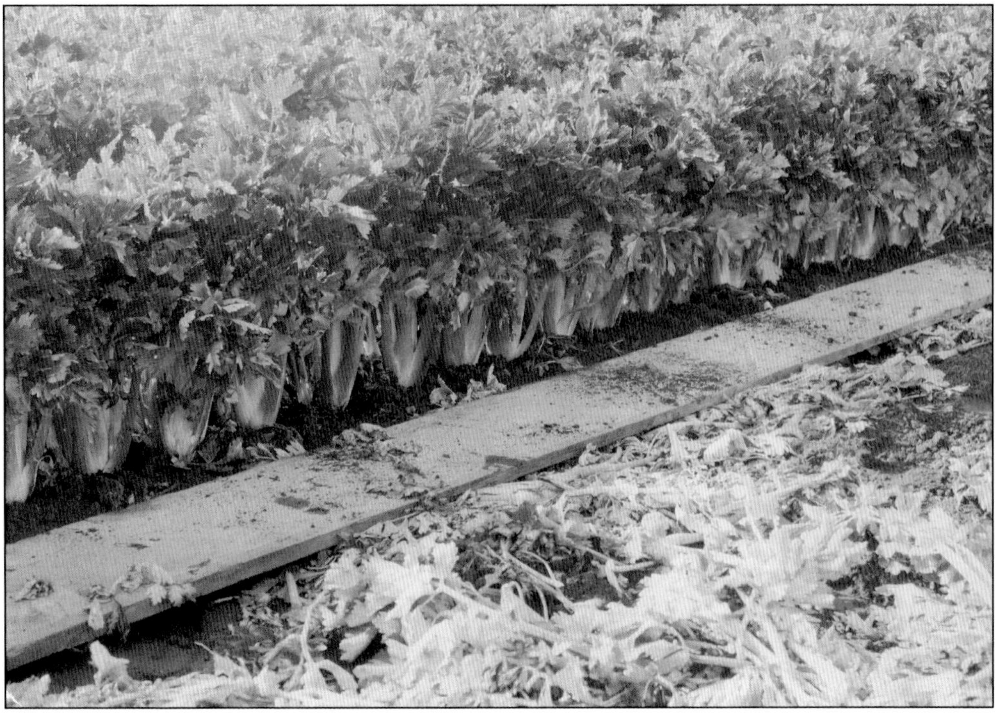

The celery was planted by hand in June or July. When it reached the right height, 12-inch-high boards were placed on either side of the rows to shield the celery from the sun and keep it white. At harvesting, the boards were removed and the celery was cut with a knife by hand and packed into crates.

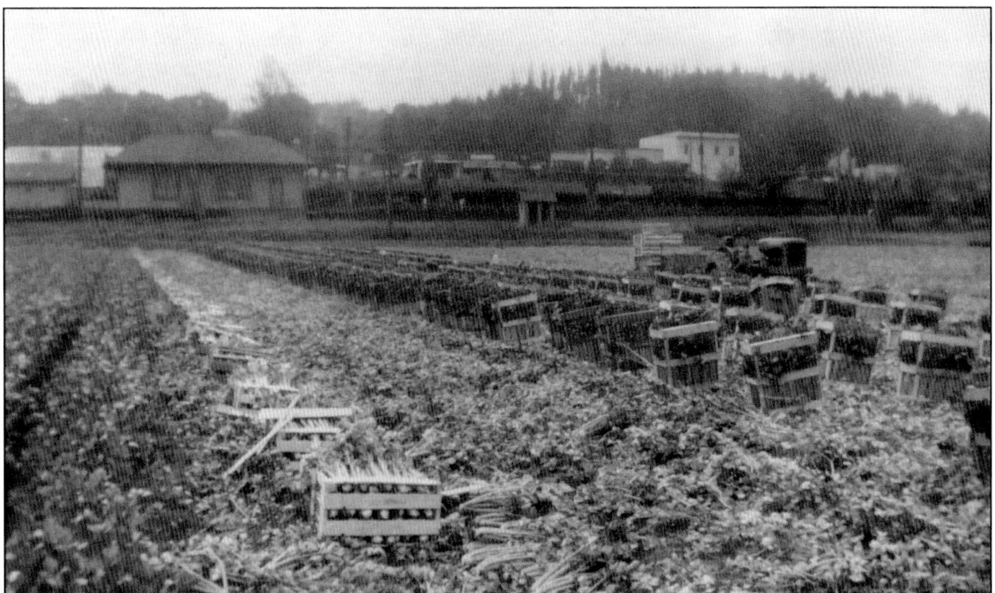

A tractor pulls a flatbed wagon loaded with filled celery crates at harvest time. The crates in the photograph were taken to a celery shed and either sent to local produce markets or cut into celery hearts.

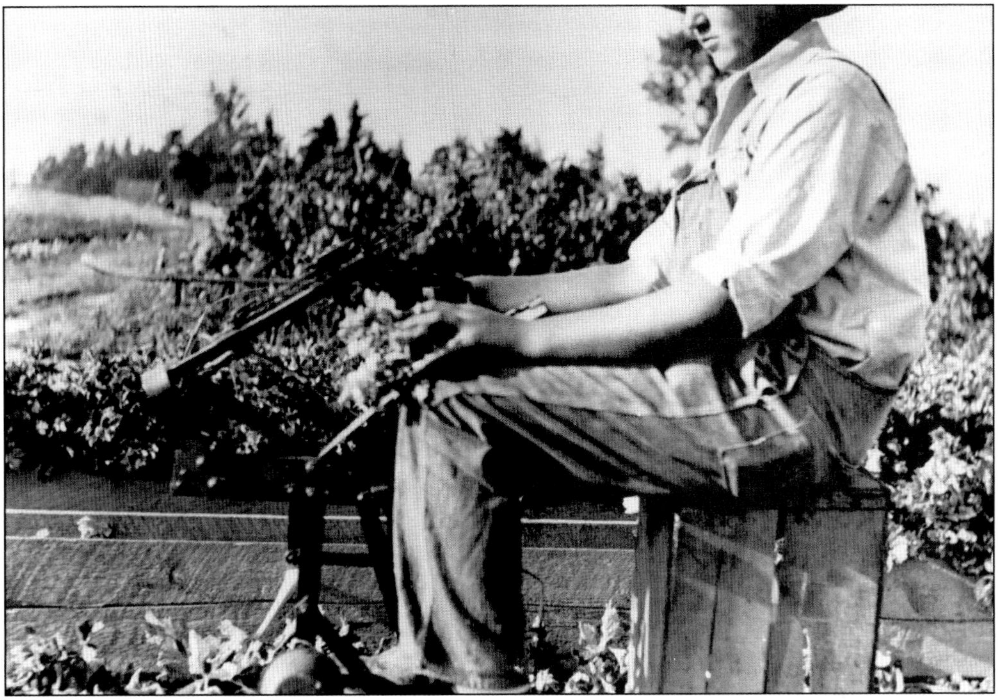

Celery is tied with a machine won in a celery-growing or tying competition. H.C. McGinnis, a local celery farmer, won the world championship trophy in the 1922 Celery King Contest held in Indianapolis. After winning the same award four times, he proudly claimed that Troutdale was the "celery capital of the world" and retired from competition.

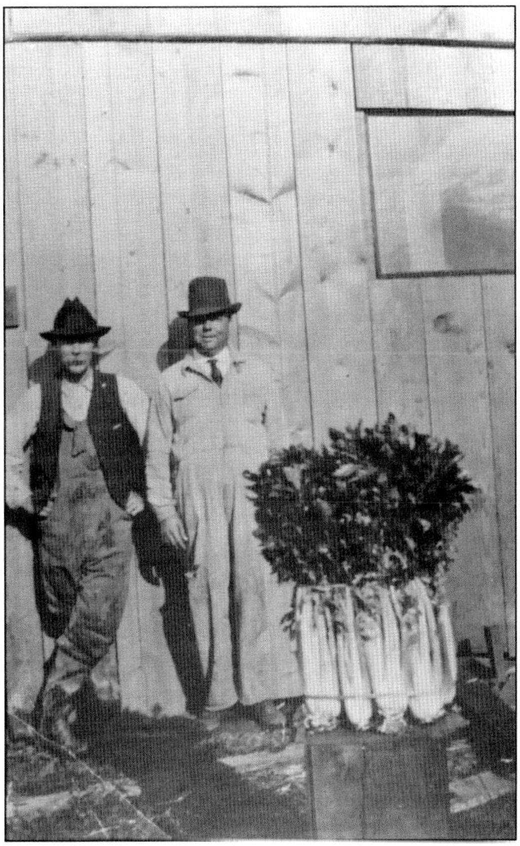

In this photograph from the early 1920s, celery growers Joe McGinnis (left) and A.D. Kendall (right) stand beside a bundle of quality celery. In 1926, McGinnis got $2.75 per crate for his celery. Much of it was shipped out of Troutdale to markets on the East Coast, but it was also sold locally.

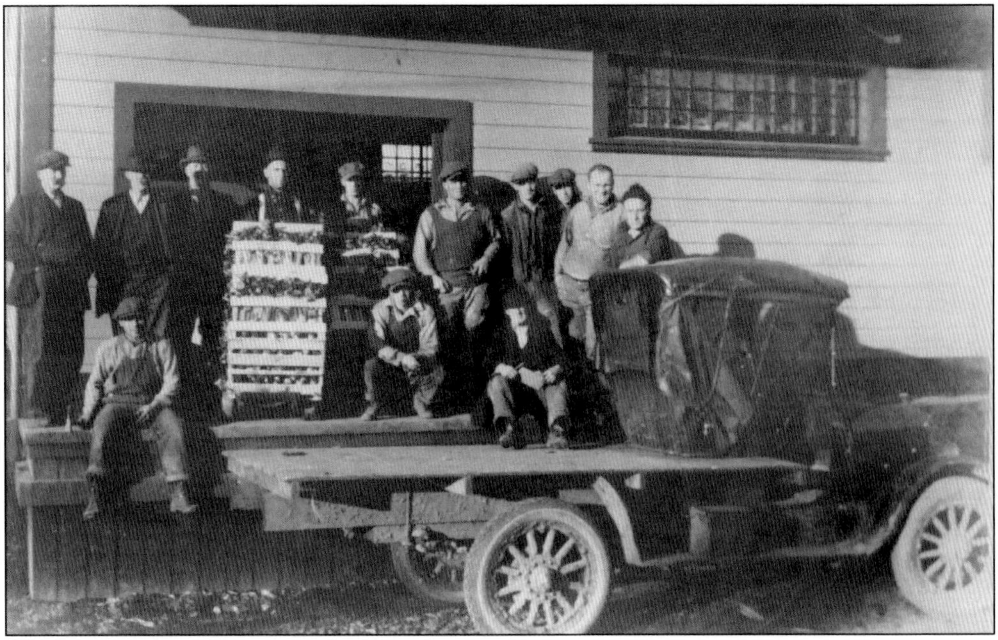

Men stand on the railroad station loading platform behind a depot cart loaded with celery crates. The labor-intensive process of growing the celery was at least partially responsible for ending Troutdale's celery farming tradition at the onset of World War II, when many of the young workers joined the military.

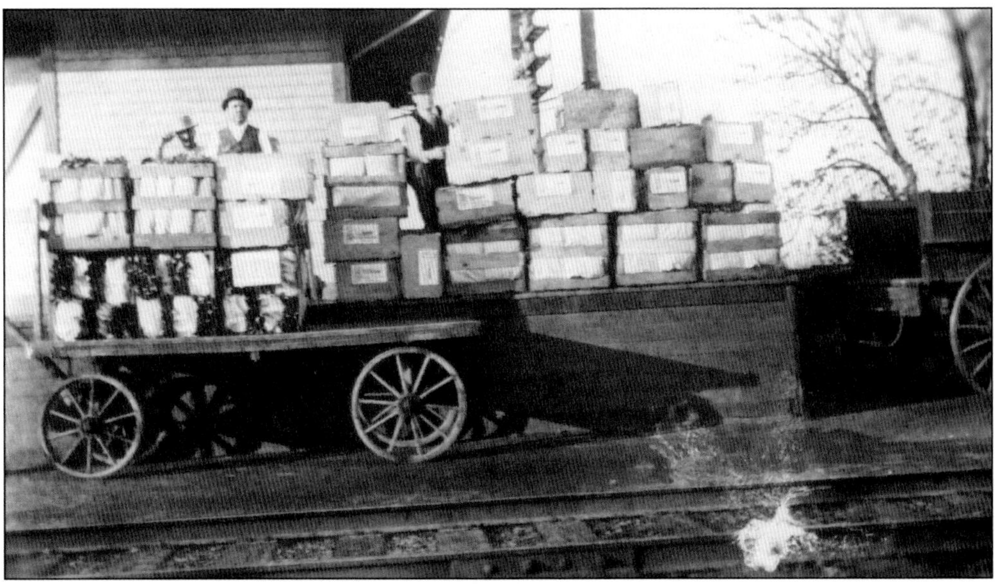

A depot cart is loaded with boxes of celery, ready for shipping. Celery growers in the Troutdale area farmed only 60 acres of the crop, but in 1927, H.C. McGinnis produced 400 crates of celery—at 150 pounds each—on 13.5 acres. A farewell celery stew was served to soldiers departing to World War II.

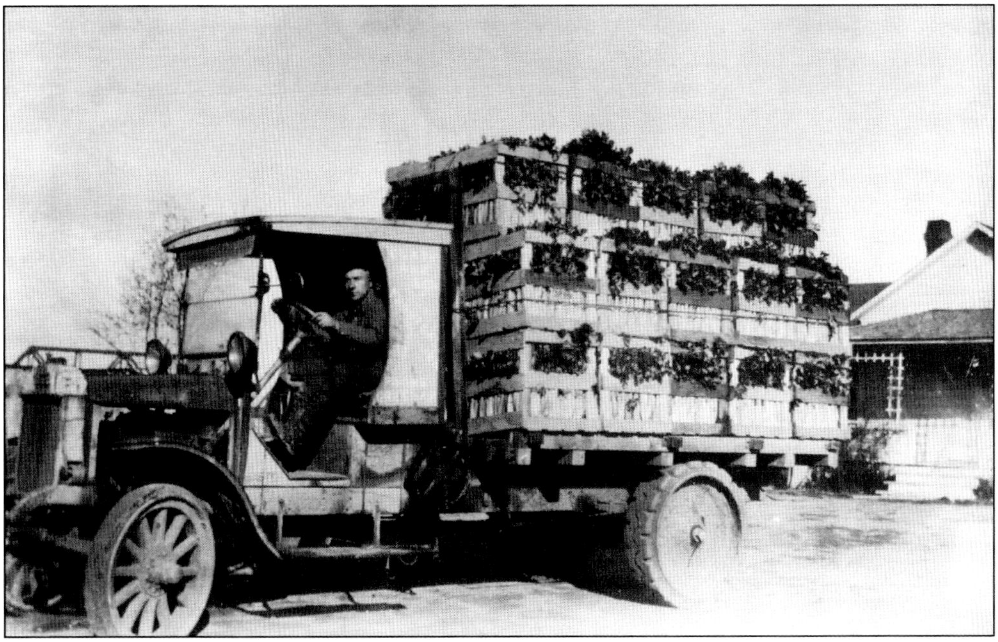

James Knarr drives a load of celery in this 1923 photograph. White celery, instead of the green eaten now, was preferred at the time. The bleaching process of the celery was labor intensive and costly, thus making celery a special treat served only at fine dinners or parties.

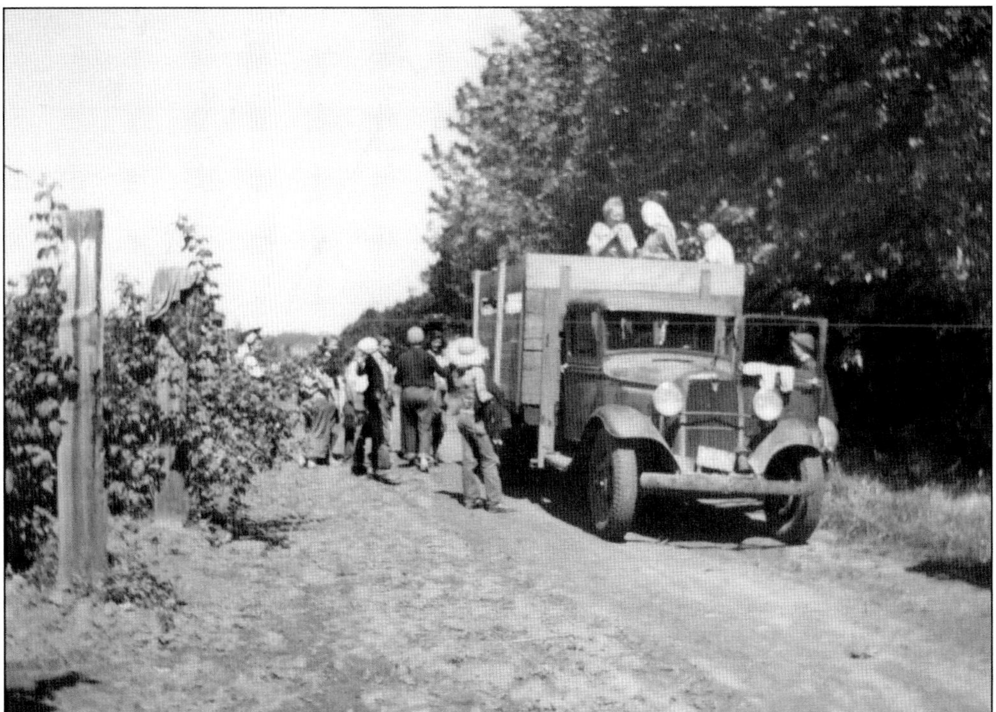

Large-scale farm operations, particularly during planting and harvesting, required extra laborers. During the Depression, Dust Bowl migrants landed in Oregon, looking for work. They found jobs in the berry fields of Oregon farmers as temporary laborers, earning 25¢ per 12-box crate.

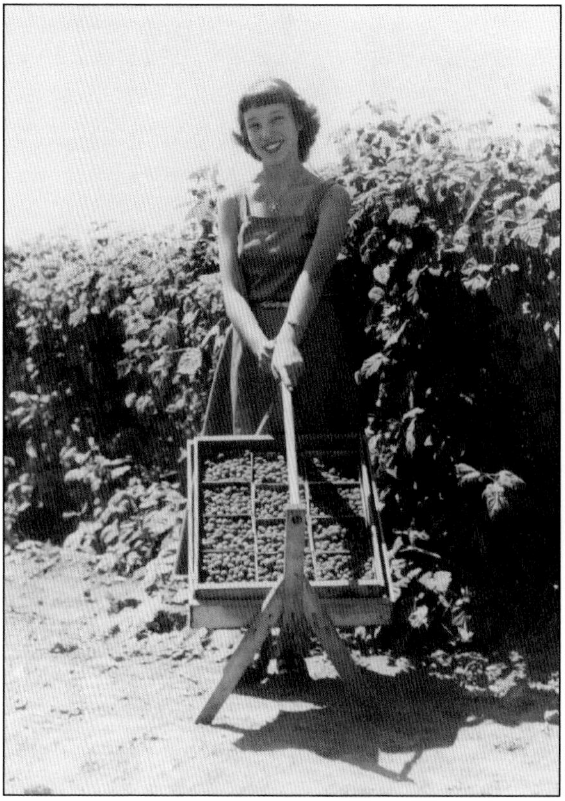

Young people became part of the summer work crews, particularly in the cane berry and strawberry fields around Troutdale. Here, Donna Burlingame holds the end of a berry carrier. The carrier holds a 12-hallock(12-boxes) retail crate. Cannery crates held 15 hallocks.

Bob Baker stands on the running board of a 1926 Model T truck loaded with berry crates. Although the boy was much too young to work in the fields, most school-aged youngsters picked berries in the days before local authorities grew sensitive about chemicals and the welfare of children in the fields.

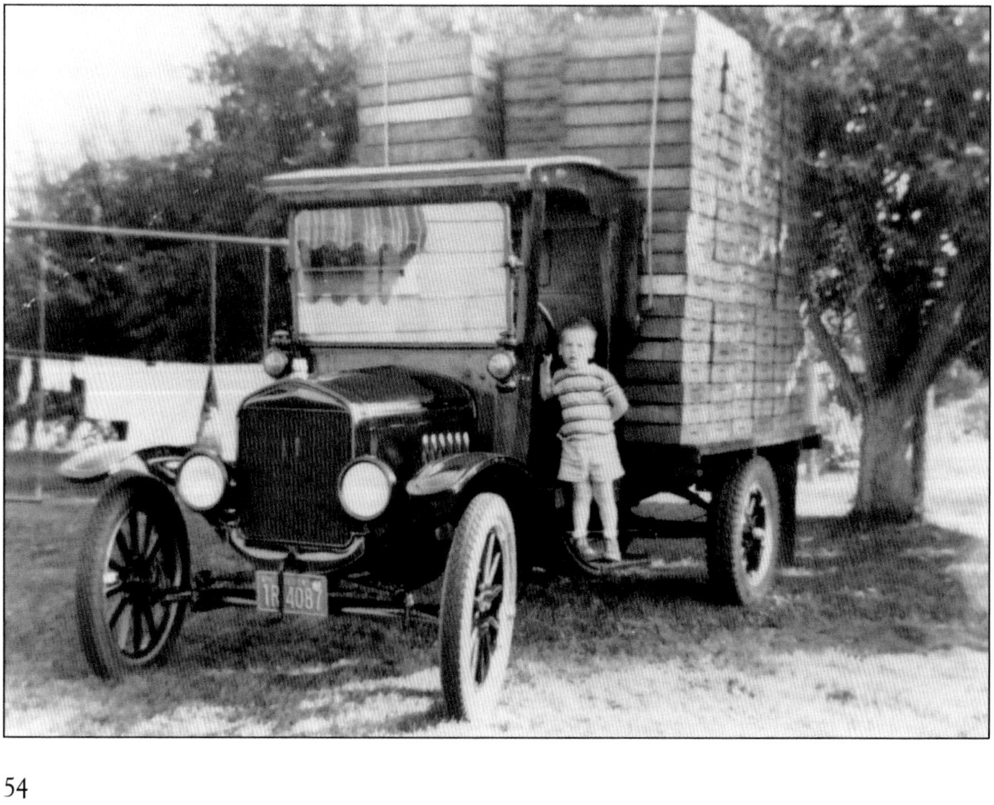

High climbers, as these loggers were called, not only cut down Paul Bunyan–sized trees, but they thumbed their noses at danger and stood atop the trunk in daredevil fashion once they had cut off the branches. (Photograph by Harlow Douglass.)

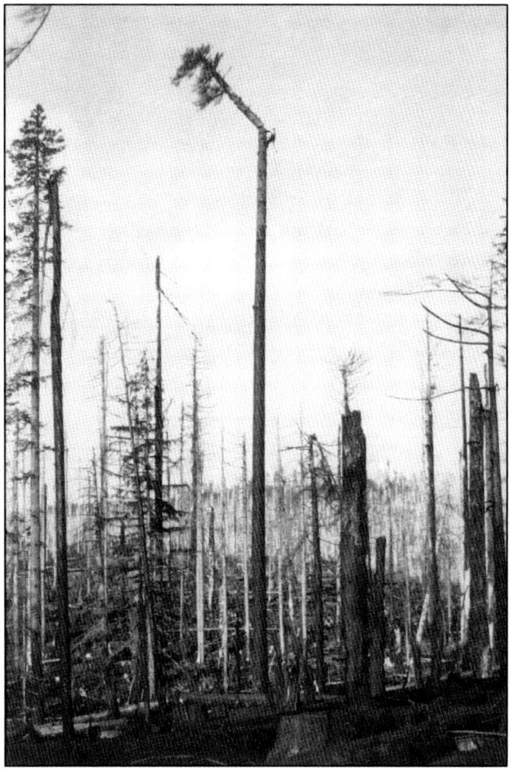

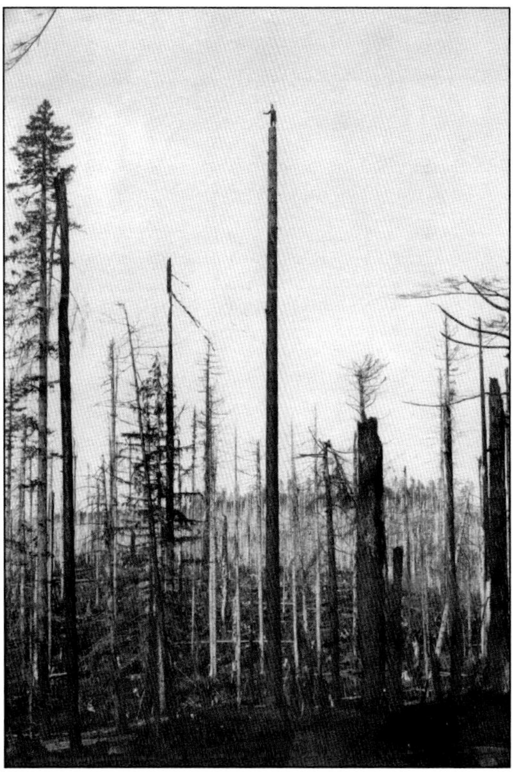

This logger balances on a spar tree that is likely more than 100 feet tall after he has cut off the top. Working that high was akin to being a tightrope-walker working without a net. This photograph was taken at Larch Mountain, east of Troutdale, following a fire. (Photograph by Harlow Douglas.)

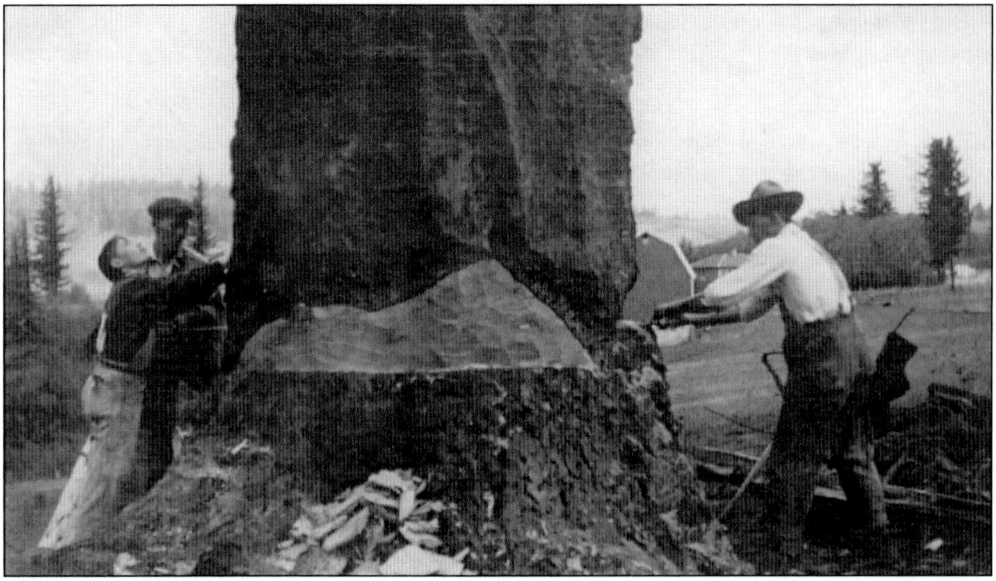

Timber fallers used 12-foot crosscut—or drag—saws, wedges, and axes to fell the giant Douglas, silver, and noble firs. Loggers had colorful titles for their jobs: bull skinners, skid greasers, high climbers, and donkey punchers, to name a few.

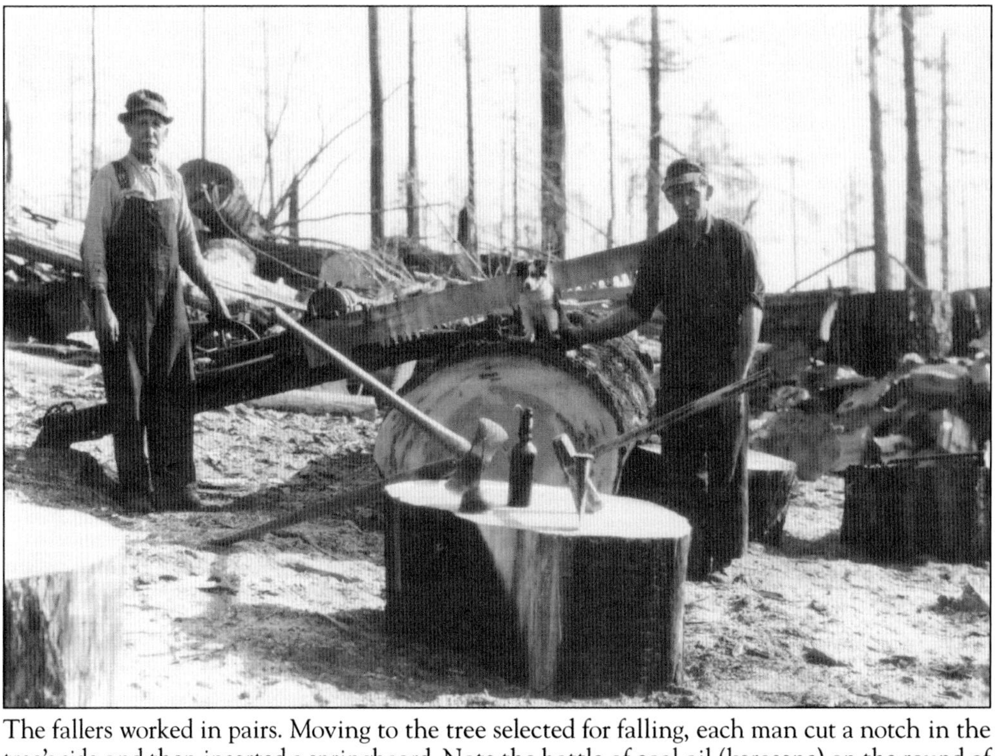

The fallers worked in pairs. Moving to the tree selected for falling, each man cut a notch in the tree's side and then inserted a springboard. Note the bottle of coal oil (kerosene) on the round of wood. The oil lubricated the blade of the saw to prevent pine pitch from bogging down the blade as the saw moved through the wood.

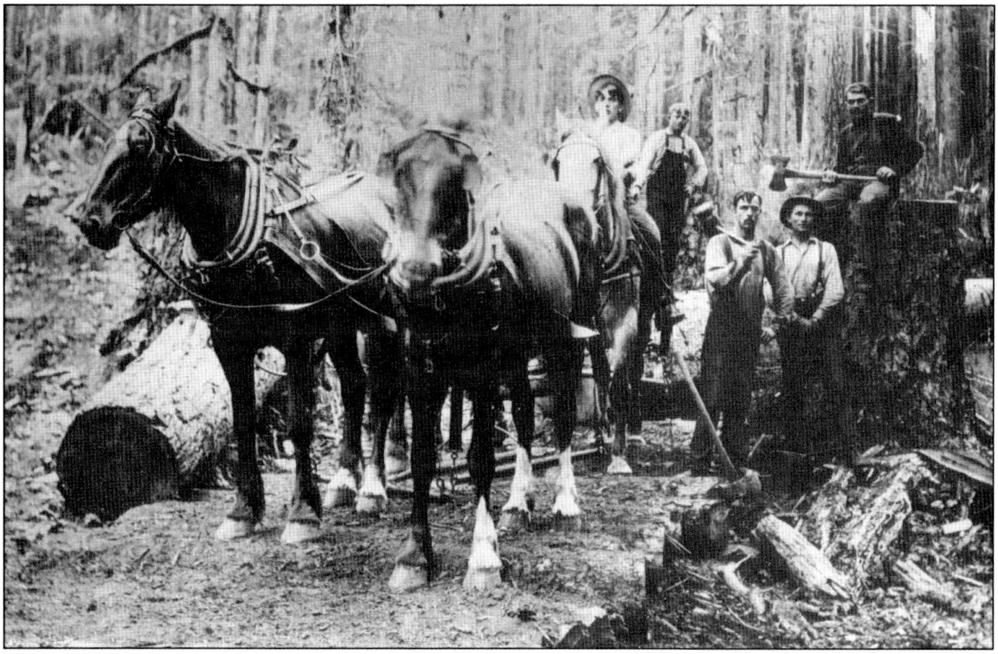

Once the trees were on the ground, the crosscut sawyers and barkers went into action. The trees were cut into proper lengths, and the barkers took the bark off with a "spud," or ax. After the logs were barked, they had to be dragged to a central point where they were made into "trains" ready to be hauled away.

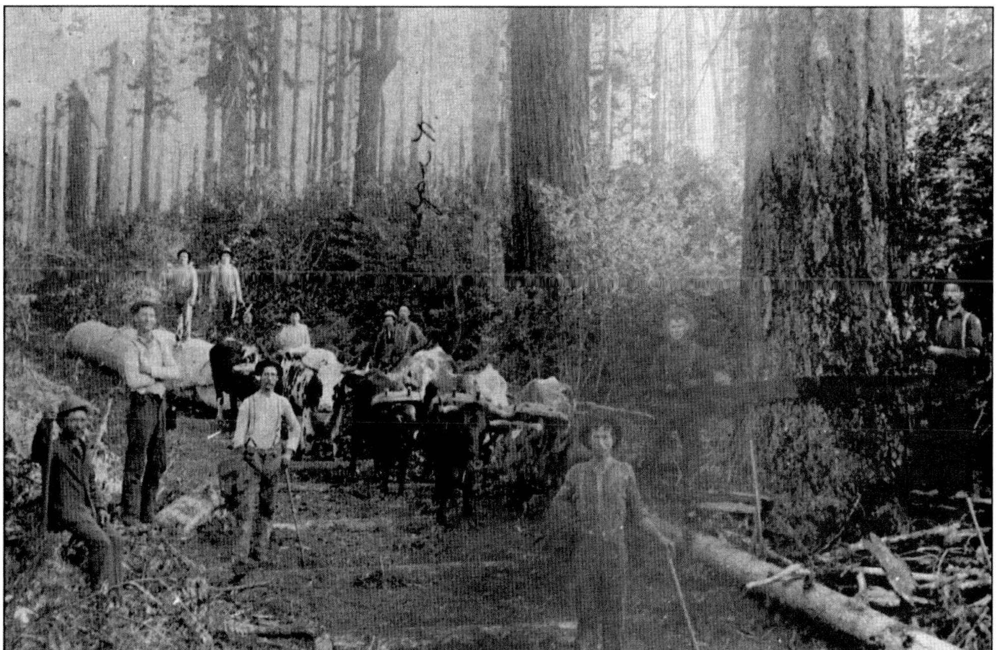

Skid roads were built in straight lines to avoid curves by placing small logs about every five feet and raising them above the surface. The sawn tree trunks were then dragged by oxen or horse teams to the central receiving area.

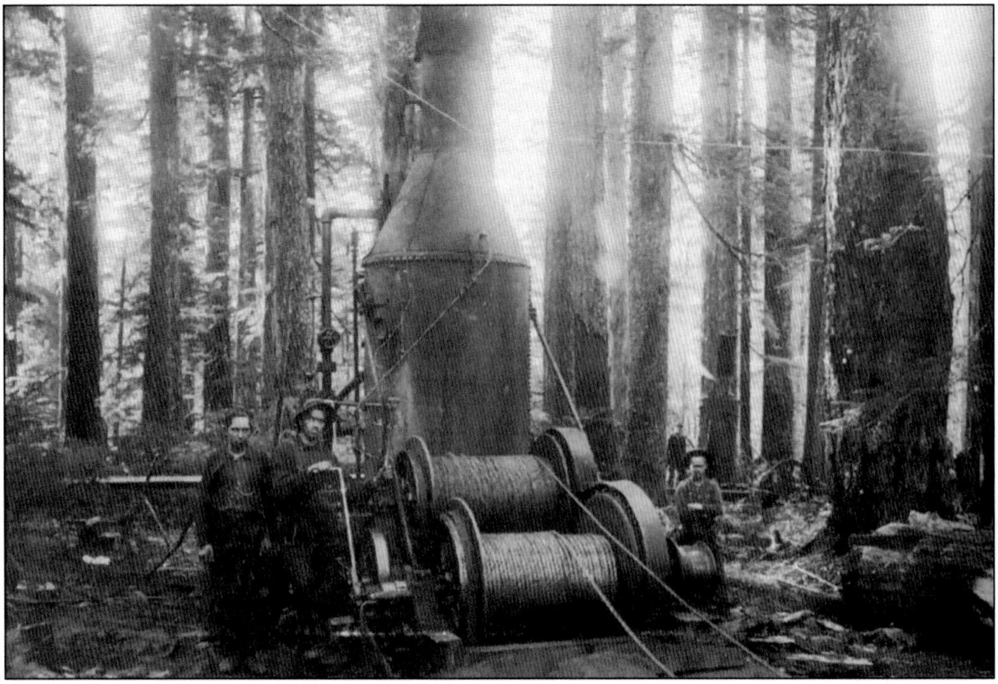

J.S. Munday built a steam-powered machine called a bull donkey, which replaced oxen. The bull donkey dragged immense logs up to 1.5 miles from the forest by a pair of cables attached to large drums. The logs could be pulled along the skid road.

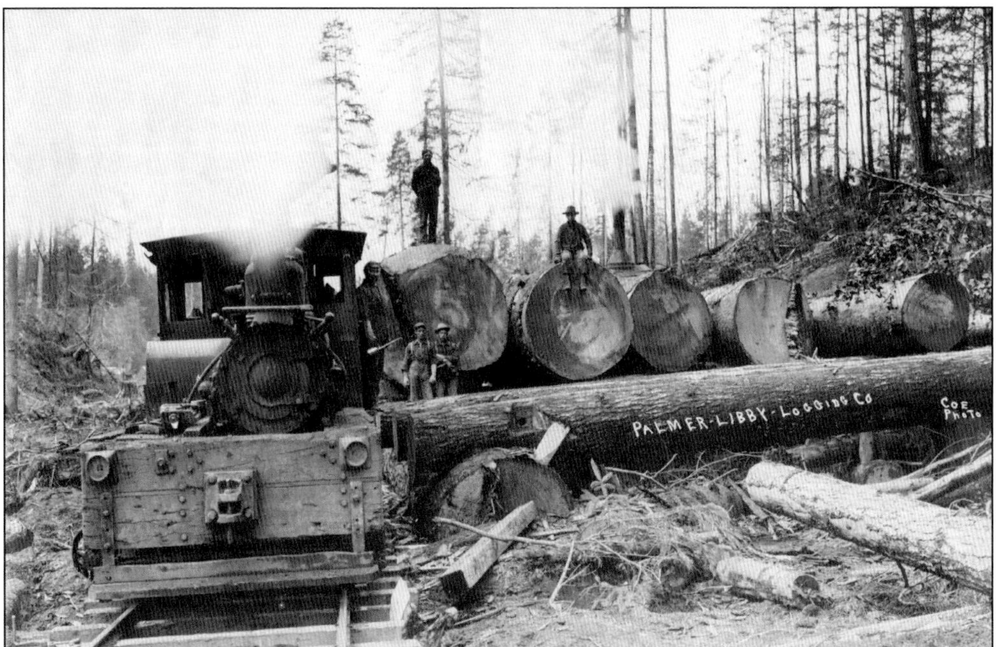

The machine was so powerful that 30,000 feet of logs—about 120,000 pounds—could be moved at one time. The logs brought to the landings by the "donkey" were then skidded along ties by railcar.

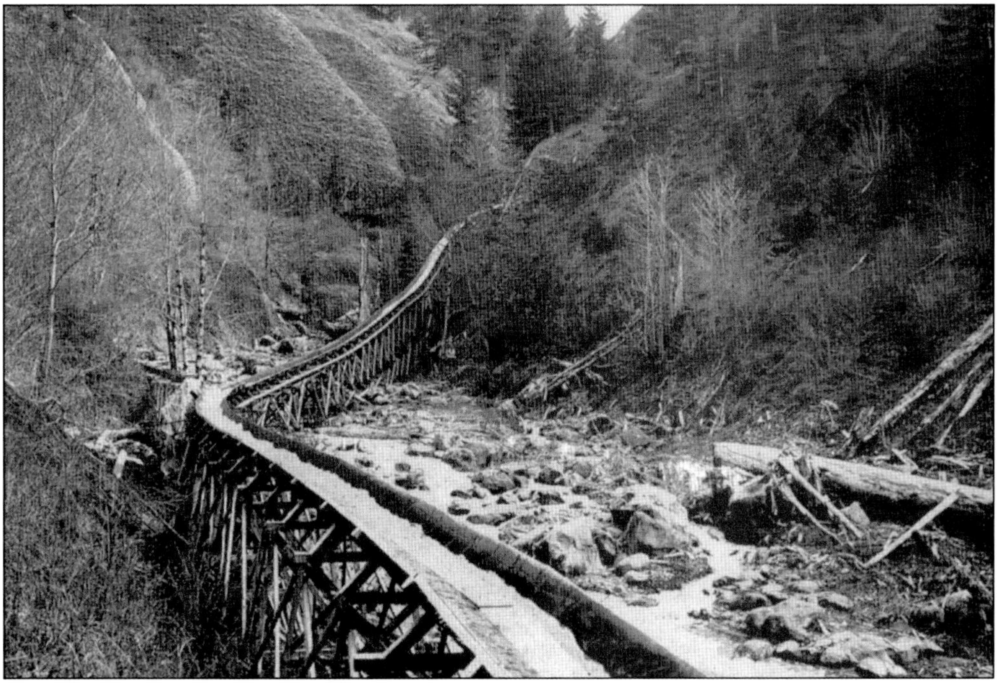

Once the logs were at the central point, a cable pulled them to the top of a hill, where an aboveground timbered chute, built on a six-percent grade, allowed the logs to slide down nearly a half mile to a holding pond at the bottom.

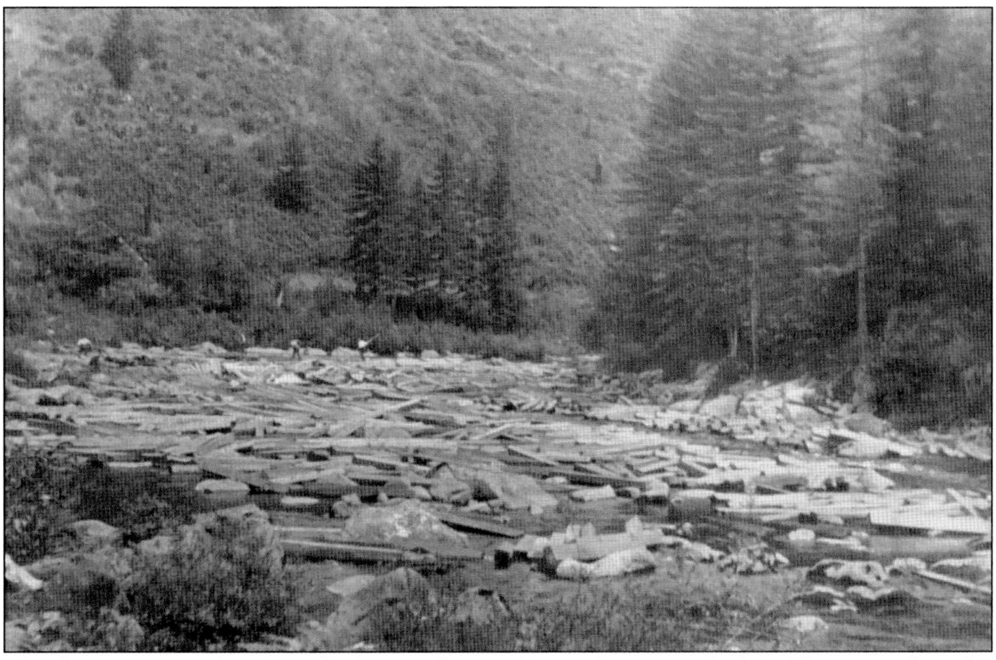

The dangerous "tie drives" took place each year during the spring freshet. The men riding the logs kept them from snarling up on the banks of the river and becoming an unmovable pile. A boom captured them at Troutdale and lifted them onto railroad cars to be shipped. One former logger remarked that the ties resembled giant French fries floating down the river.

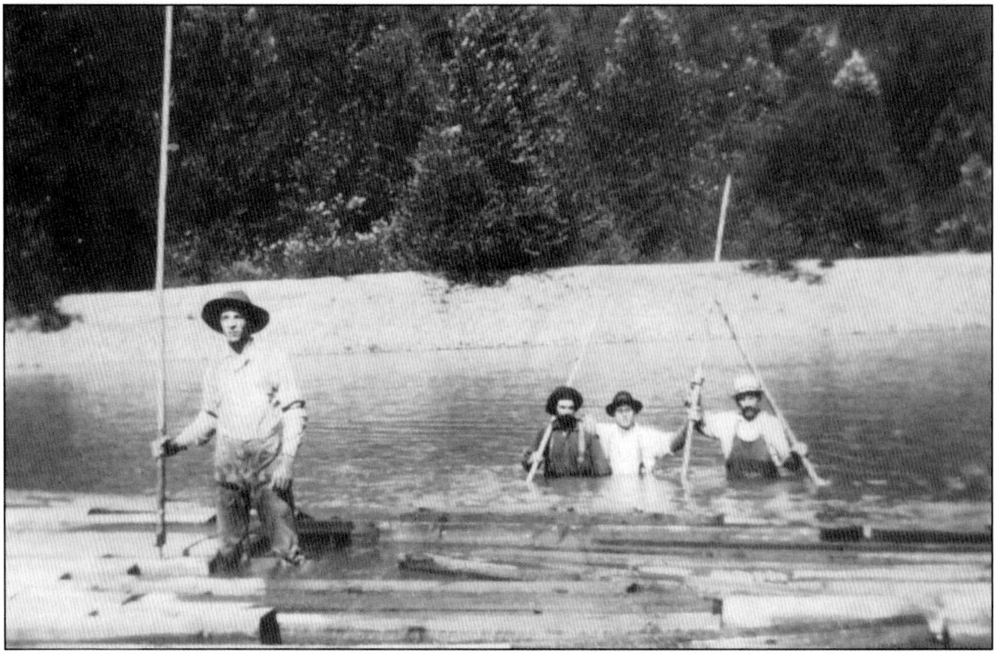

Making crossties for building railroad lines was part of the logging operations in the Pacific Northwest. The task of getting the milled ties down the river was given to tie drivers, who rode precariously atop the ties or stood armpit deep among them in the river, always in danger of being crushed between the ties or knocked under them.

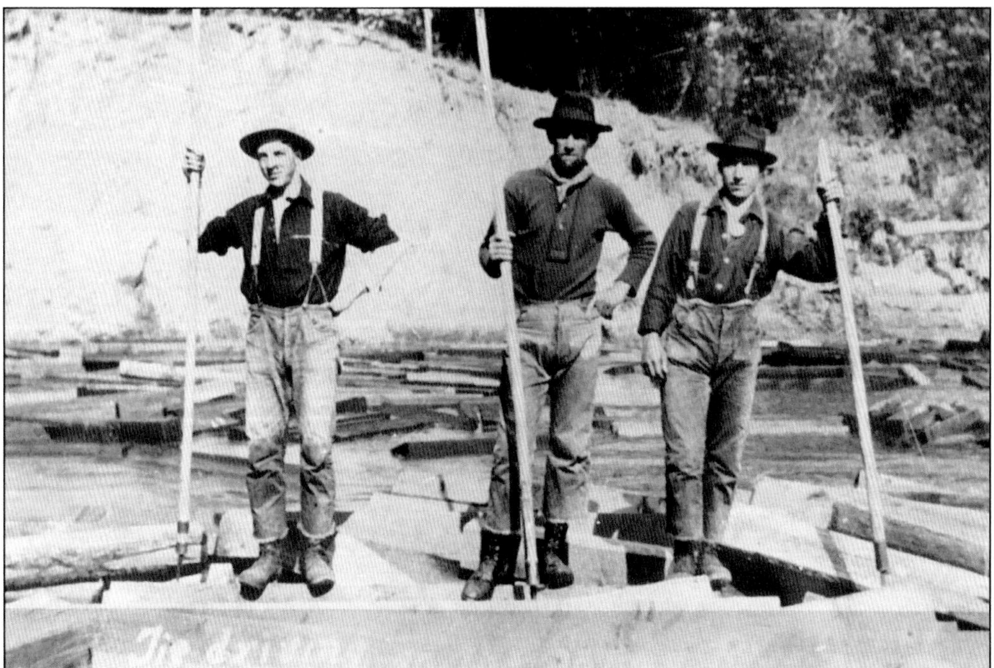

Using peaveys—poles with long hooks on the ends—and wearing caulked boots with holes punched through them to let the water drain out as fast as it poured in, they rode the ties ski-fashion down the river.

Five

Schools and Churches

Schools form the lifeblood of any community, especially small ones, and Troutdale was no different. To quote Sharon Nesbit, the resident historian and columnist in town, "School is a people place. It is where Olive Parsons saw the East Wind blow so hard that it swayed the clock on the wall. It is where people shook their heads when Chim Howell came to school barefoot on icy days. It is where the Troutdale Rod and Gun Club practiced target shooting in the basement, and where mothers canned beans to serve at those first school lunches."

Schools in Troutdale can be enumerated as the first, second, and third Troutdale Schools, the first, second, and third Cedar Schools, and a military academy for boys that few could afford to attend. From the first shake-and-cedar log schools, built in 1855 or 1857, the schools in Troutdale comingled with adjacent communities, enlarging and relocating buildings as school enrollments increased in size.

As in most schools, the PTA was active in Troutdale, starting its own hot lunch program in 1923 on a gas plate in the school, while also assuring parents that "the schoolyard would be closed to chickens . . . and mules" and helping with the funeral expenses of a local Indian woman.

Unlike most towns, Troutdale was the "least churched community in East County." For more than 60 years in early Troutdale, only one church served the community with any continuity. The Methodist Episcopal Church was established in 1895, and the Ladies Aid Society kept the church running, with sermons delivered by a circuit-riding minister. Faced with mounting bills and few funds, the Ladies Aid Society sold the building to the Presbyterian congregation in 1924. Not all religion took place in a church, however. One local resident recalls an elderly man from the "County Farm," who set up a makeshift pulpit alongside the highway east of the Sandy River and led weekly sermons to an imaginary flock of parishioners.

Troutdale's lineup of community organizations has boasted a Lions Club, Masonic Lodge, a garden club, the Troutdale Rod and Gun Club, a chamber of commerce, and the Troutdale Historical Society. All have provided havens for civic-minded folks in Troutdale. Community spirit has flourished over the decades, from holding Easter egg hunts, hosting tent revivals, sponsoring fishing contests, and championing interest in local history.

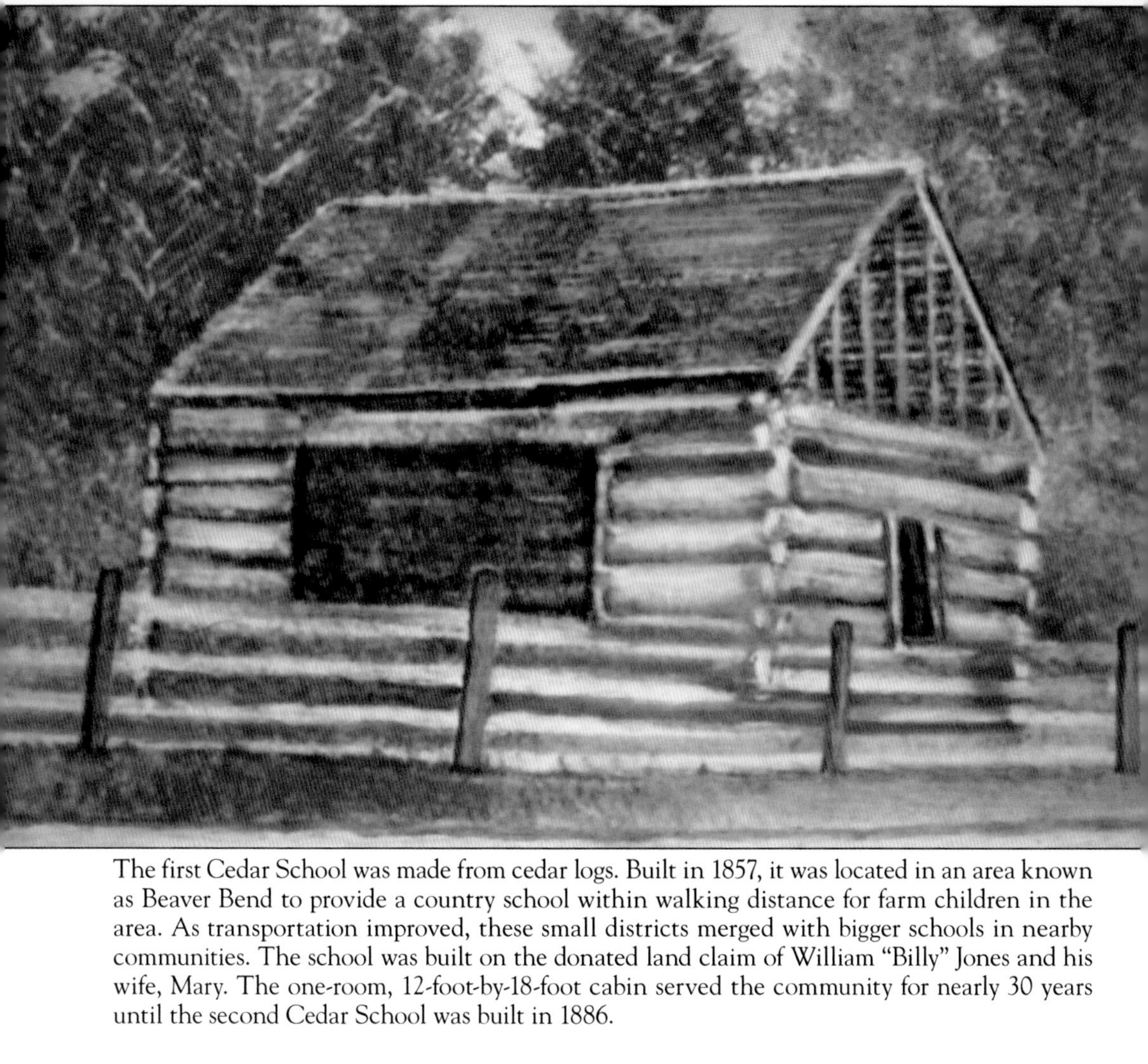

The first Cedar School was made from cedar logs. Built in 1857, it was located in an area known as Beaver Bend to provide a country school within walking distance for farm children in the area. As transportation improved, these small districts merged with bigger schools in nearby communities. The school was built on the donated land claim of William "Billy" Jones and his wife, Mary. The one-room, 12-foot-by-18-foot cabin served the community for nearly 30 years until the second Cedar School was built in 1886.

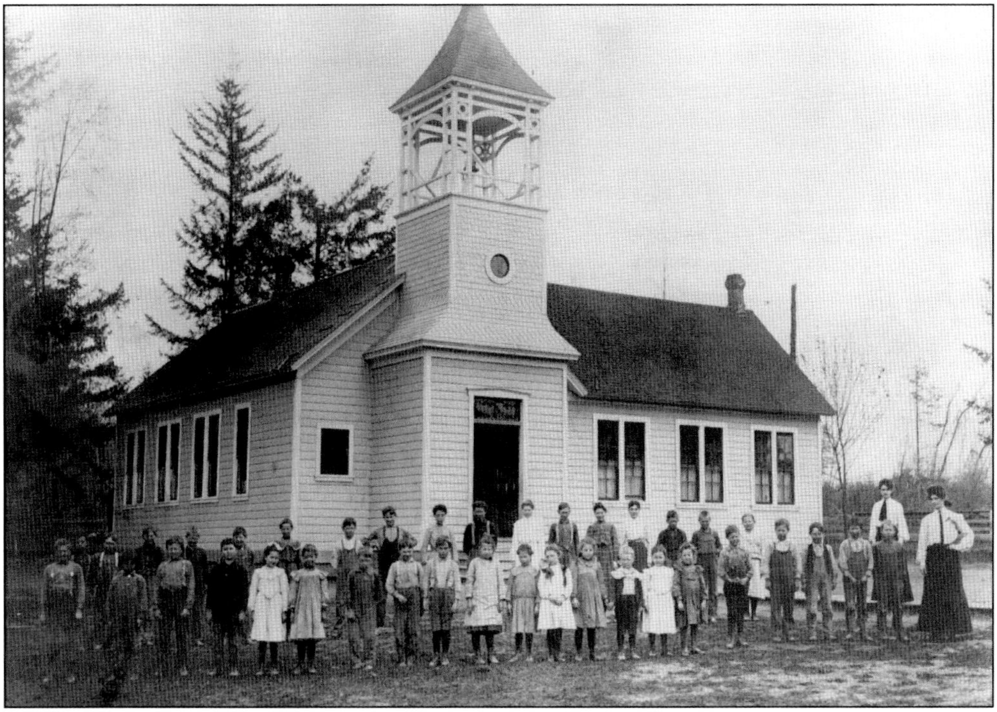

The second Cedar School was a frame building with an openwork belfry built on the same property as the first, but in a different location. In 1904, students of teacher Lulu Massey planted a seedling maple tree on the school grounds, placing at its roots a glass-jar time capsule containing their written work. The school closed in 1908 when the school district was divided to form Victory School. Enrollment at the time of the closing was 66 students.

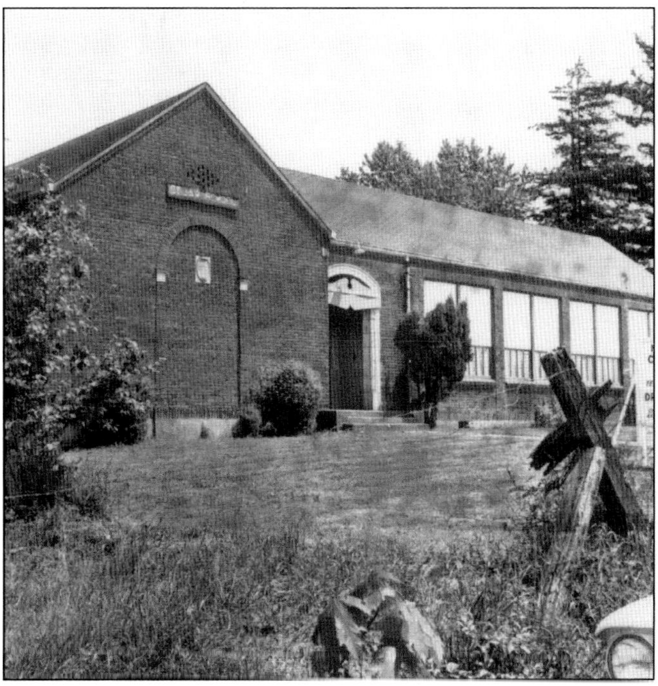

The third Cedar School was built of brick in 1926 at a cost of $10,000. The school was used throughout World War II, when Troutdale School overflowed with children of wartime workers. In 1955, the school patrons decided to join the Gresham Grade School District, and the building was later used by Mount Hood Community College for drama productions. Today, it is privately owned.

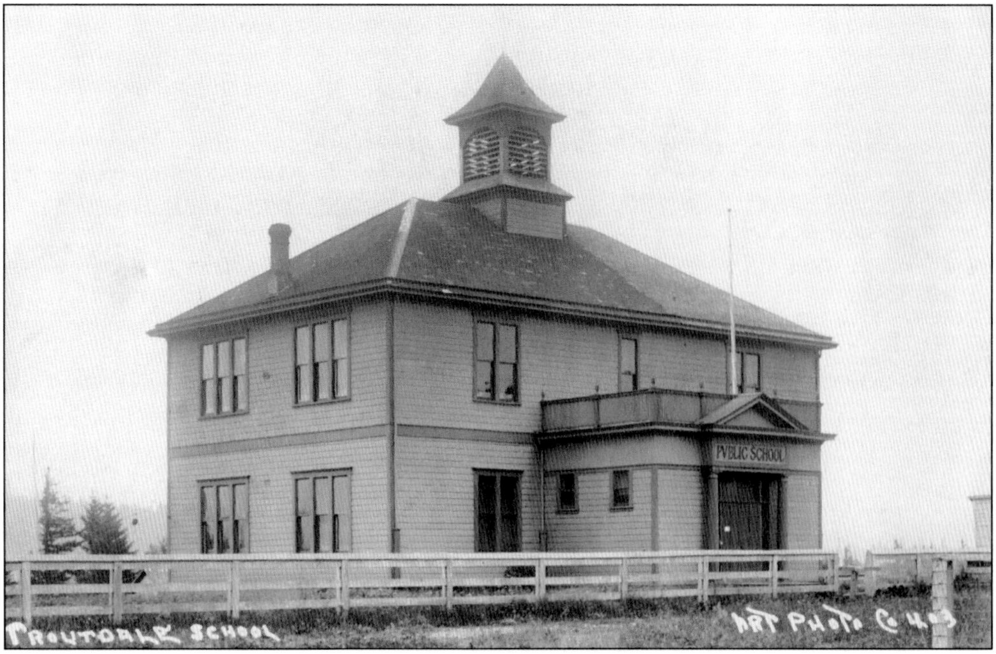

The second Troutdale School was built on a hillside above the new town in 1892, atop 40 acres known as the "Harlow Forty," by the county road master. In that first year, 78 pupils were enrolled, though only about 45 attended on a daily basis. The teachers were R.H. Thomas and Ida D. Sabin, and the school was a two-story, four-room building with a library. It served the community until 1926 when a new, sturdier, concrete-and-stucco school was constructed.

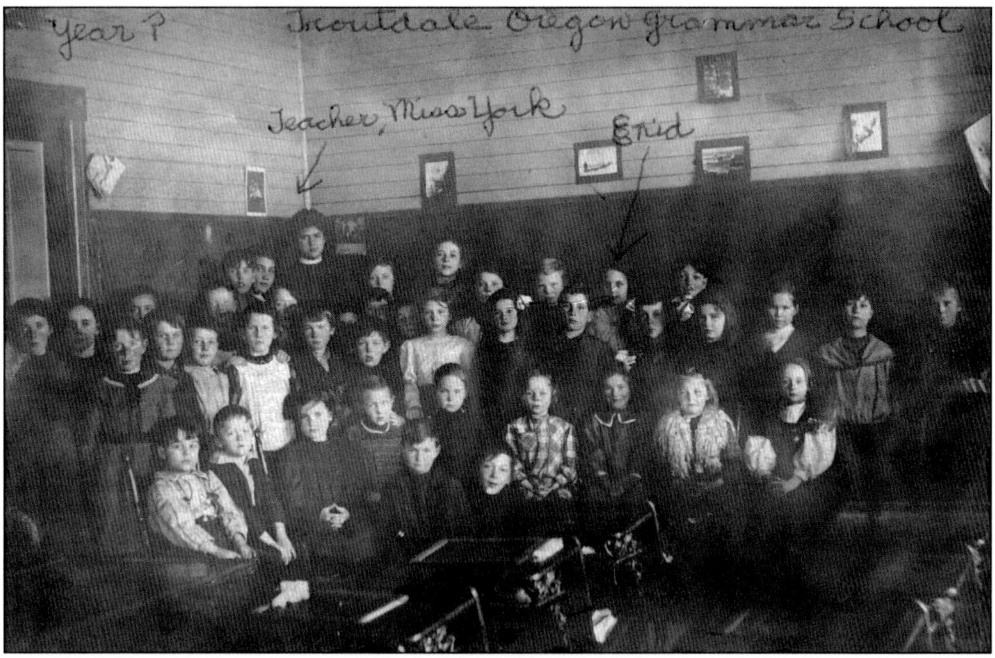

A classroom photograph from 1905 shows the teacher, Miss York, with her 42 pupils at the Troutdale School. Notice the chalkboards on each student's desk and the fixed seats attached to the desks behind them. The school had four rooms—two upstairs and two downstairs.

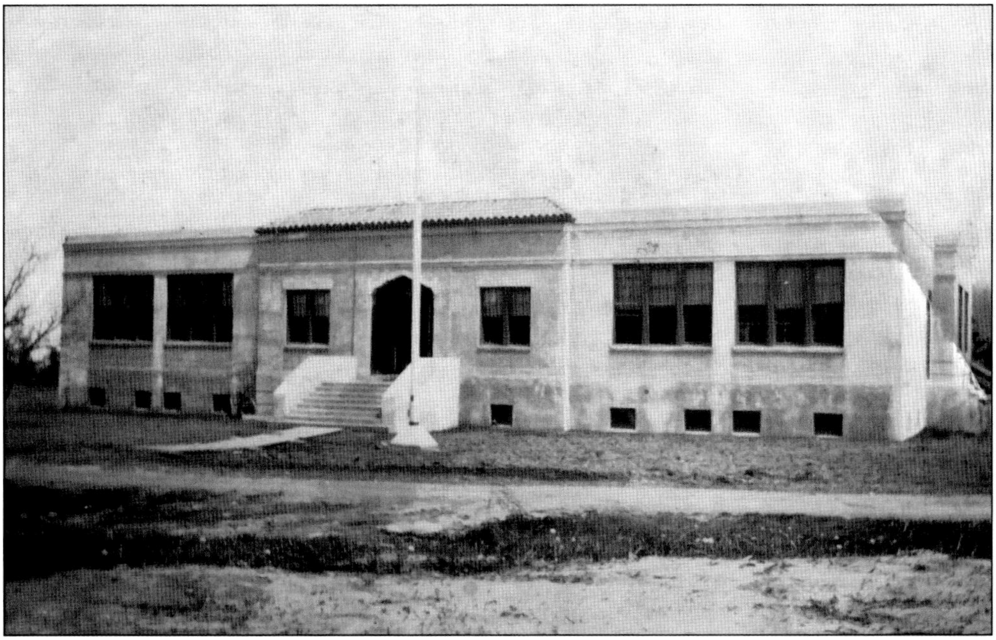

The new Troutdale School was built in 1926, just south of the second school. The building, costing $29,000, included a gymnasium and a full cement basement that was used as a play area in the winter. When the school opened, there were only three classrooms in use for the 72 children.

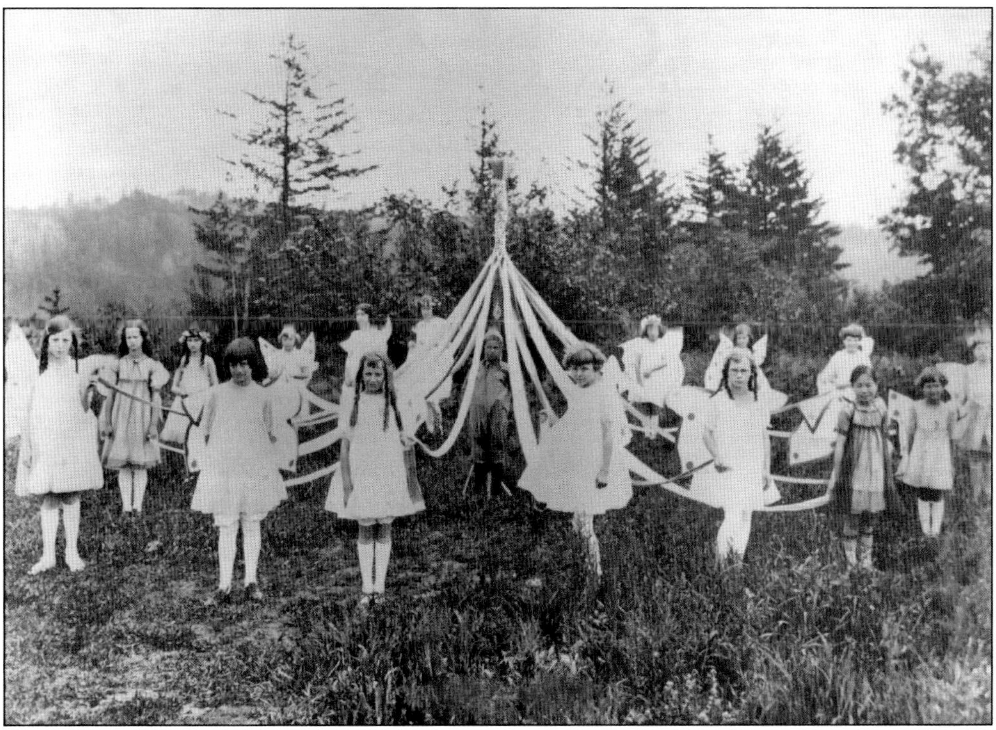

Girls wearing similar dresses, bloomers, knee socks, and butterfly wings hold ribbons attached to a central May Pole while a boy keeps the pole upright in this 1923 photograph. Such activities were popular at that time, and fun filled May Pole festivities were conducted at many schools.

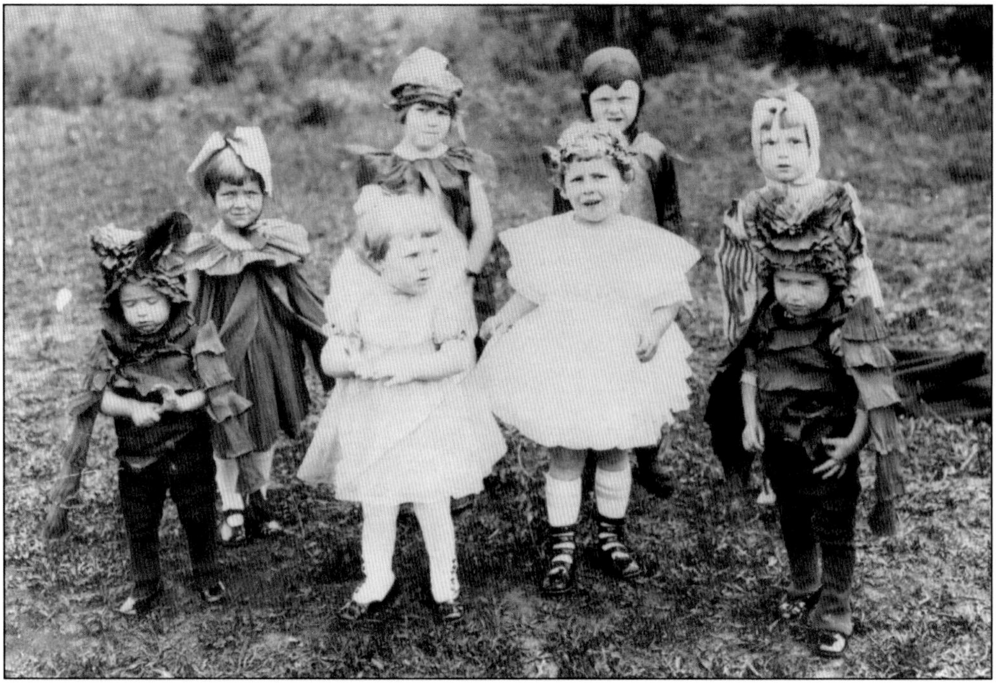

These eight kindergarteners, dressed as elves and fairies, pose for a photograph at the Troutdale School in the 1920s. The school district's parents were actively involved in school programs, even before the advent of PTAs, and offered a variety of events for the children, including costumed parties like this one.

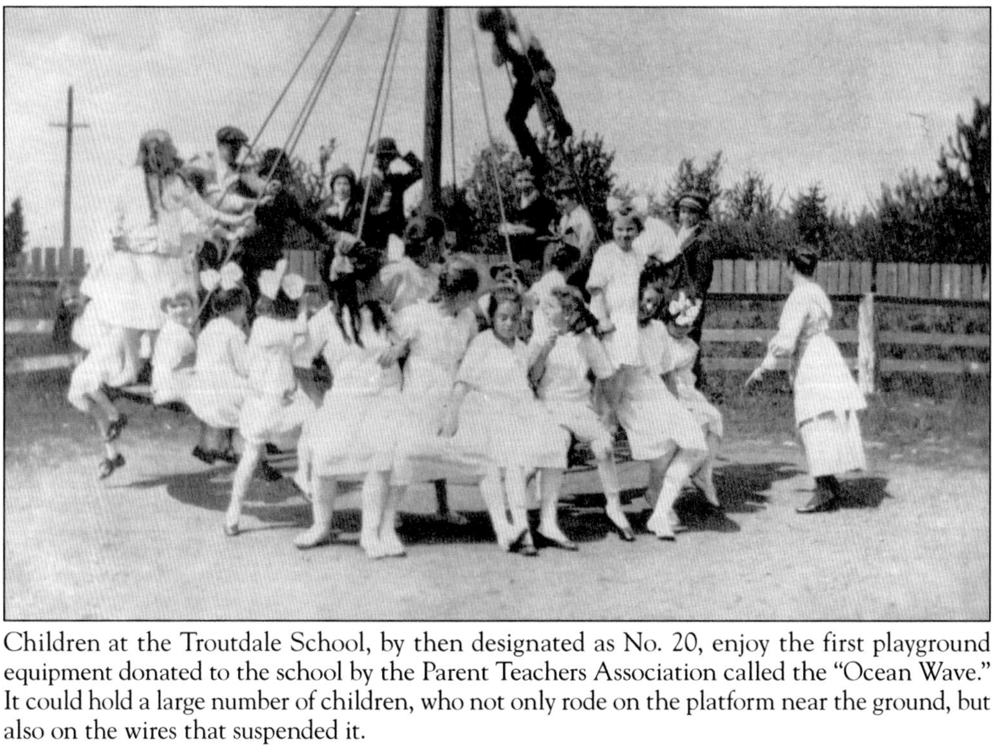

Children at the Troutdale School, by then designated as No. 20, enjoy the first playground equipment donated to the school by the Parent Teachers Association called the "Ocean Wave." It could hold a large number of children, who not only rode on the platform near the ground, but also on the wires that suspended it.

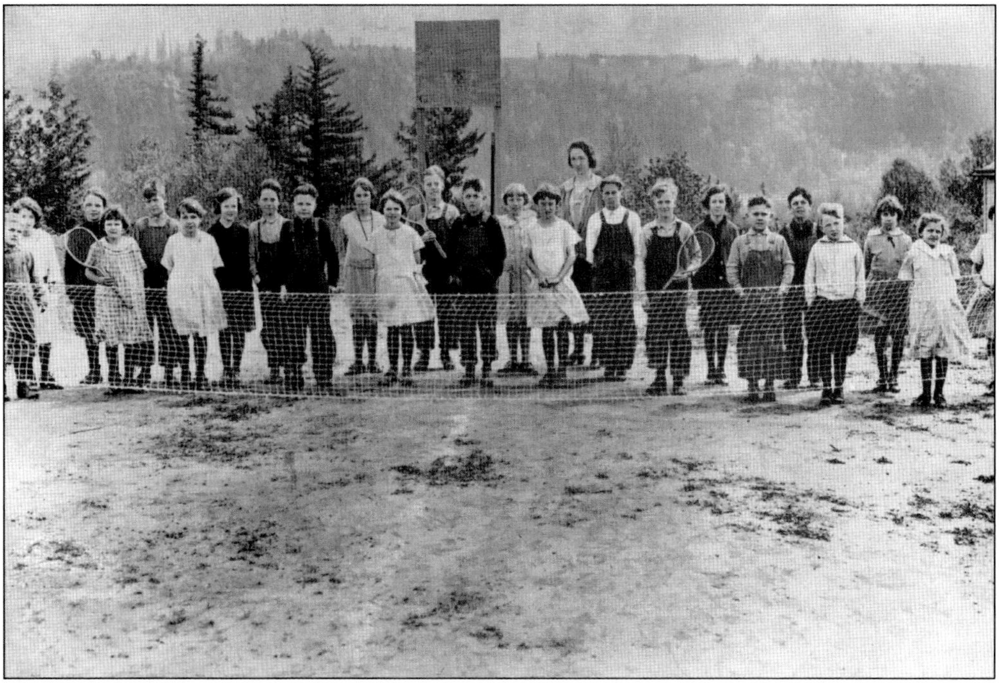

Mrs. Otto's third-, fourth-, and fifth-grade Troutdale School badminton team poses behind the net. The idea of having a badminton team would have been an innovative one for the time period, and the court was probably built by volunteers near the school's playground.

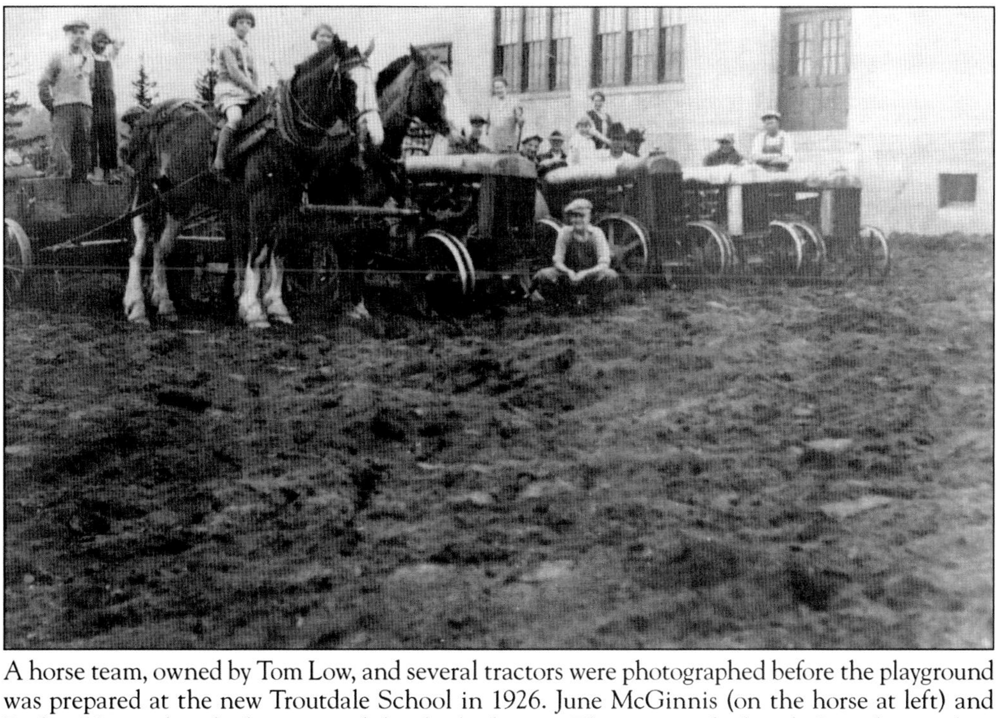

A horse team, owned by Tom Low, and several tractors were photographed before the playground was prepared at the new Troutdale School in 1926. June McGinnis (on the horse at left) and Evelyn Hewitt (on the horse at right) ride the horses. The men worked each Saturday, grading and leveling the playground, and afterwards, the women fixed a large meal for them.

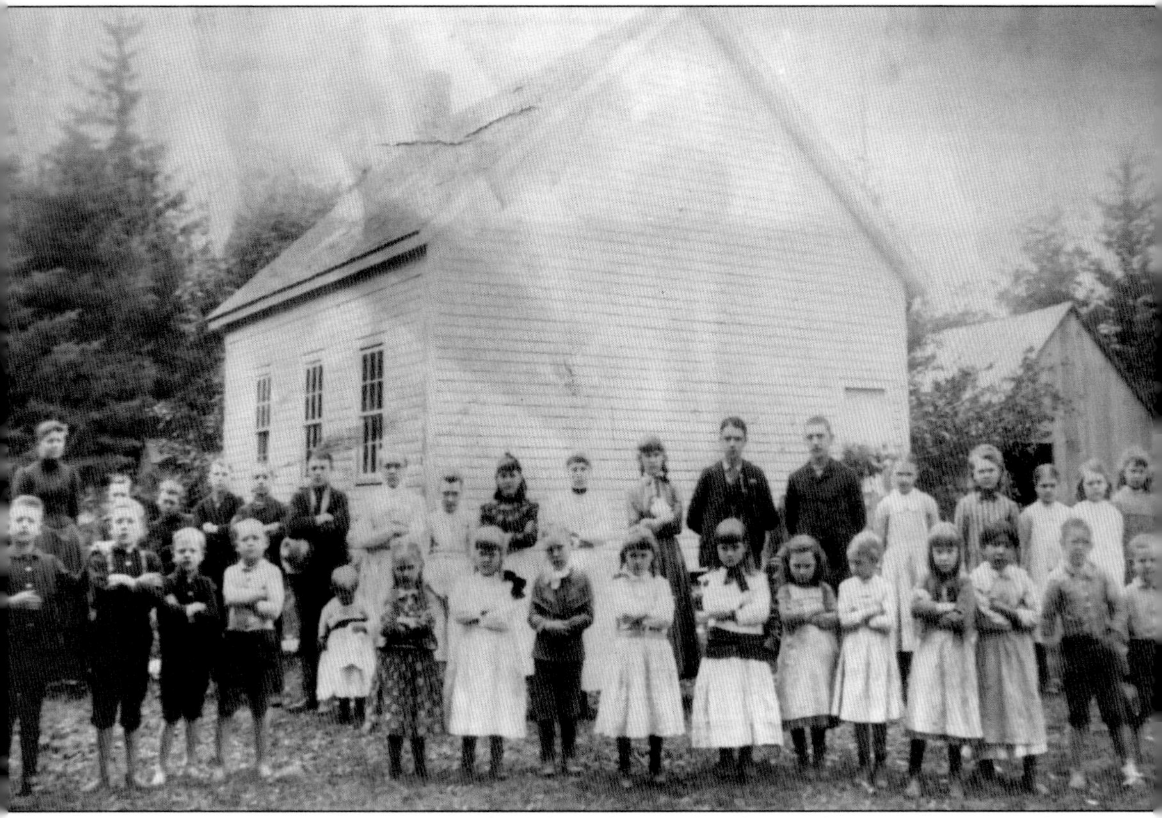

For more than 60 years in early Troutdale, only one church served the community with any continuity. The Troutdale Methodist Episcopal Church was built on a lot purchased for $125 in 1895 and was completed sometime between 1895 and 1900 for $250. It stood three blocks uphill from the row of saloons in downtown Troutdale. Here, children pose outside the church in 1910. It is now an apartment building and is in the National Register of Historic Places.

Six

LOCAL NOTABLES

Capt. John Harlow, formerly of Bangor, Maine, arrived in the Pacific Northwest in 1851. By 1860, he was listed in the census records as a farmer in the Sandy precinct, later called Troutdale. He purchased a donation land grant owned by his son-in-law John Kibling who was married to Harlow's daughter Dora.

By 1870, John Harlow and his third wife, Celeste, had purchased additional property in the Troutdale area from David Buxton, another Troutdale pioneer. Harlow widened an existing stream that ran through his property, creating a fishpond; it is from that trout farm that Troutdale got its name. While he initially stocked the pond with trout, he later purchased 35 German carp in California and brought them to his fishponds in Troutdale with hopes of promoting them to local restaurants and citizens as a new fish delicacy. Instead, the fish were renounced as too soft-fleshed. Thousands of the carp in Harlow's fishpond unfortunately escaped into the adjacent rivers in a flood and became one of the nuisance fishes of the Columbia system.

Thankfully, the town's name came not from Harlow's ill-fortuned carp venture but from his original trout ponds. It was Harlow himself, who, in 1880, requested that the new Oregon Railway and Navigation Company station be named Troutdale.

Aaron Fox, the proprietor of a general merchandise store, served as Troutdale's first mayor, from 1907 to 1909. While there have been two-dozen mayors since Fox, two especially stood out, not for their policies but for their gender. Clara Latourell Larsson, who was one-quarter Yakama Indian, was 40 years old when she was elected by a margin of only five votes as Troutdale's first female mayor in December 1913, only a year after Oregon granted suffrage to women. Laura Bullock Harlow, who married into the founding Harlow family, was mayor from 1925 until 1930.

In 1966, Glenn Otto, a restaurant owner and electrician, was elected mayor. Otto embodied the "Mr. Smith Goes to Washington" image at its best, serving as Troutdale's mayor until 1972. Later elected to the Oregon state senate, he became one of Oregon's most beloved state senators during his 20 years in office.

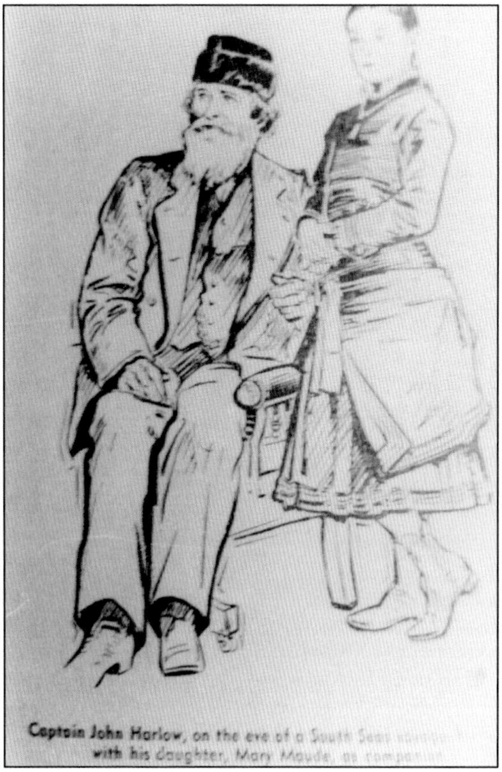

John Harlow arrived in Portland after sailing his ship to San Francisco for the Gold Rush. He made his money operating a coastal ship service and starting a box company in Portland. He built a farm retreat in Troutdale and is credited with persuading the Oregon Railway & Navigation Company to build a rail depot at Troutdale. This drawing of him and his daughter Mary Maude appeared in Ben Hur Lampman's book *The Coming of the Fish Ponds*.

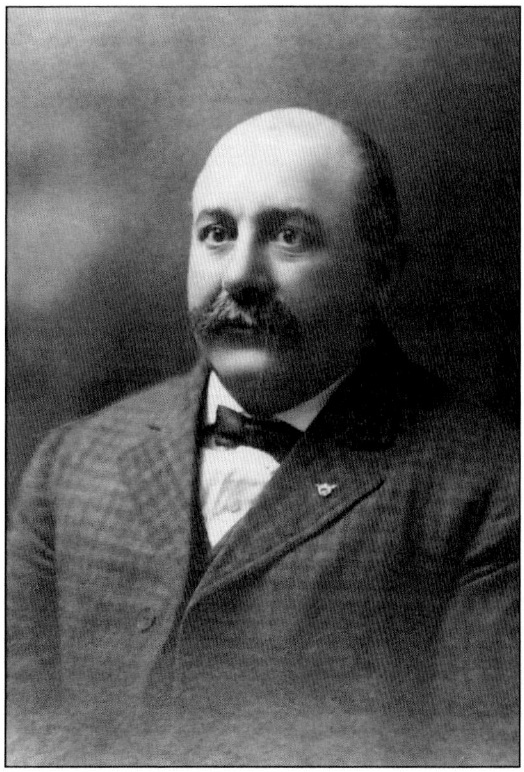

Aaron Fox figured prominently in Troutdale's early years. He owned and operated Fox's general store for 26 years on what is now the historic highway in Troutdale and served as Troutdale's first mayor and postmaster.

Clara Latourell Larsson was the granddaughter of a Native American woman named Betsy Ough. A housewife, she ran for mayor in 1914 against the incumbent mayor and won the election by five votes, becoming one of Oregon's early women politicians.

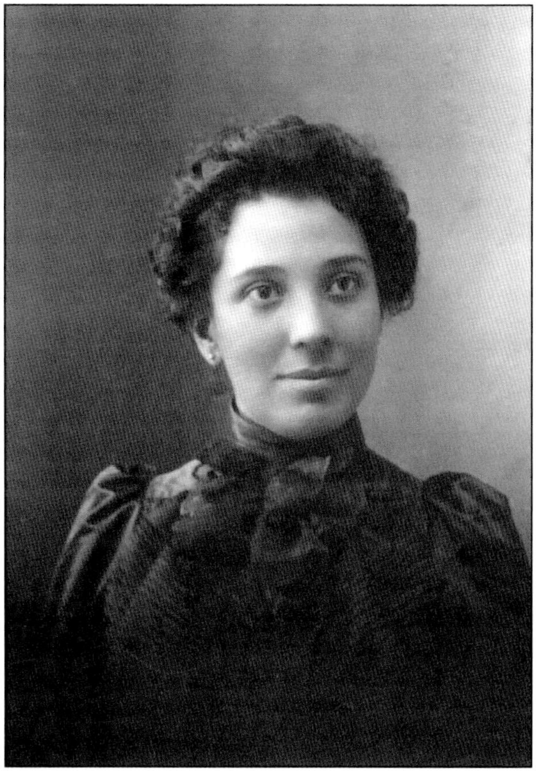

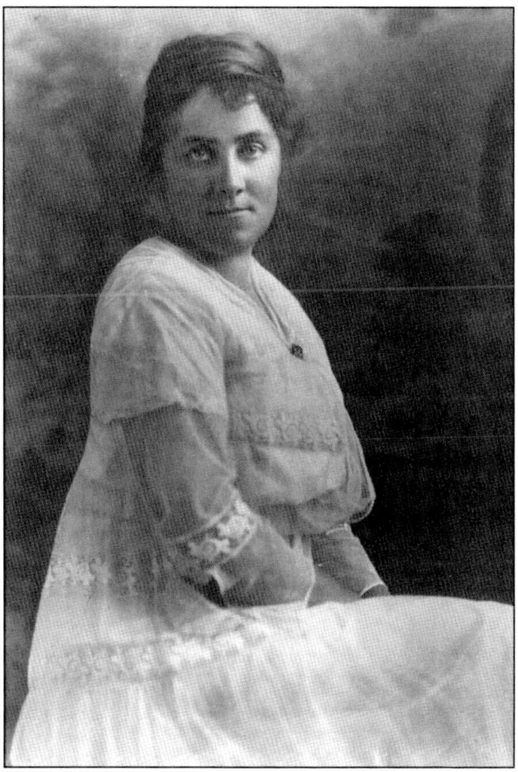

Laura Harlow, the wife of Louis Harlow, of one of the founding families of Troutdale, was Troutdale's second female mayor, from 1925 to 1930, just prior to the end of Prohibition. A friend of the previous female mayor, Clara Larsson, Harlow was a leader in school and civic activities.

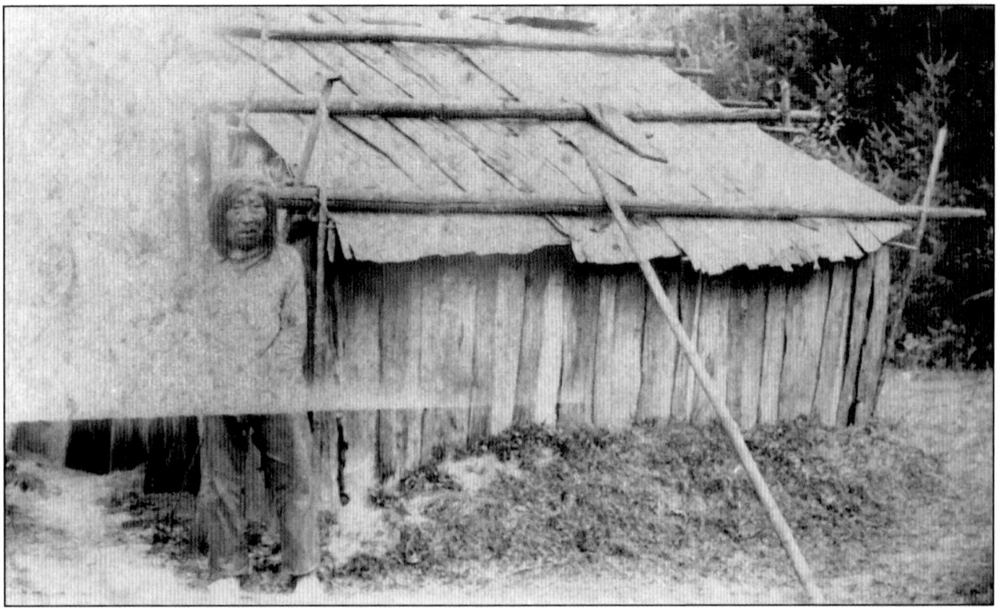

Indian John, also known as "Old John," as his historian prefers, was a member of the Multnomah tribe and one of the few remaining Native Americans in the Troutdale area. He was well known and respected by area residents. He died in 1893, when he was reputedly more than 100 years old.

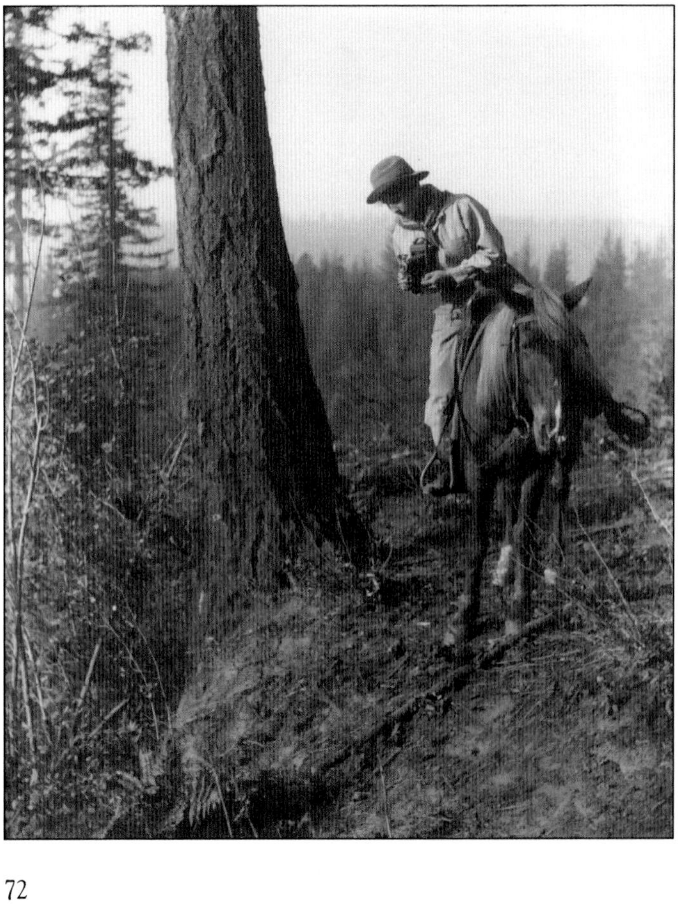

Mary Bourgeois Wright was one of 11 children in one of the first families to settle in the Troutdale area. Largely self-taught, she took candid photographs of everyday life and people. While she traveled widely to photograph her subjects, she never learned to drive a car.

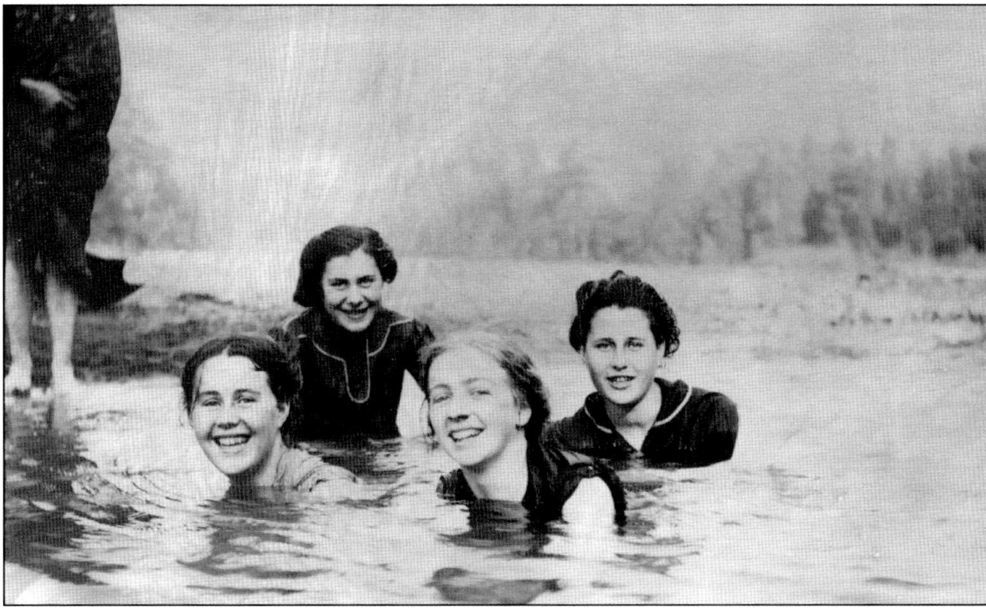

Mary Bourgeois Wright (far right) swims in the Sandy River with three friends in 1914. From a typical farm girl, Wright went on to become one of the best-known photographic chroniclers of the Troutdale area, preserving historical scenes on her glass-plate negatives.

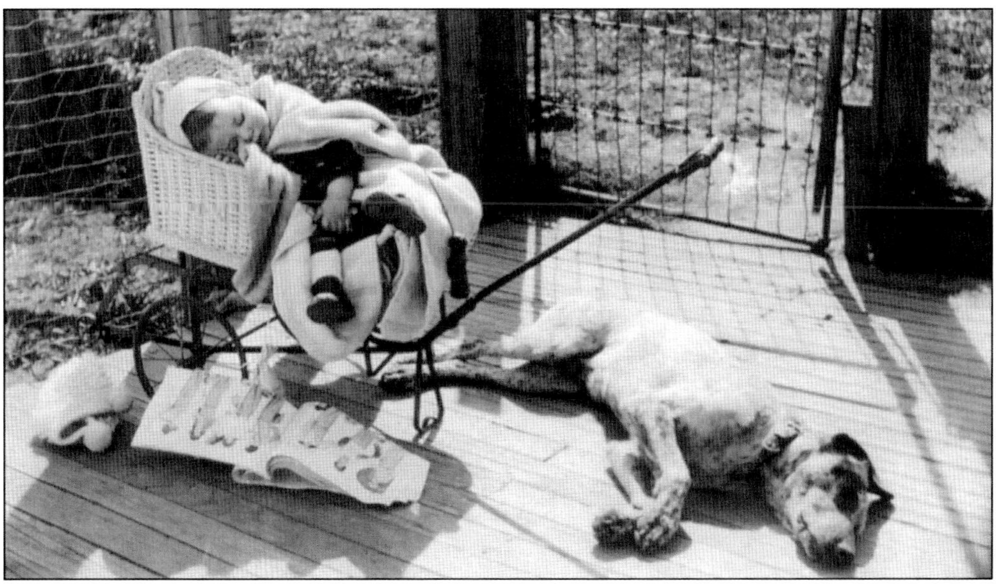

This photograph by Mary Bourgeois Wright shows the simplicity of her subjects: a sleeping baby and the family dog, Rowdy. Always with an eye toward seeking the pure essence of the moment, Wright photographed still-lifes, family scenes, the timber industry, and the building of the Historic Columbia River Highway.

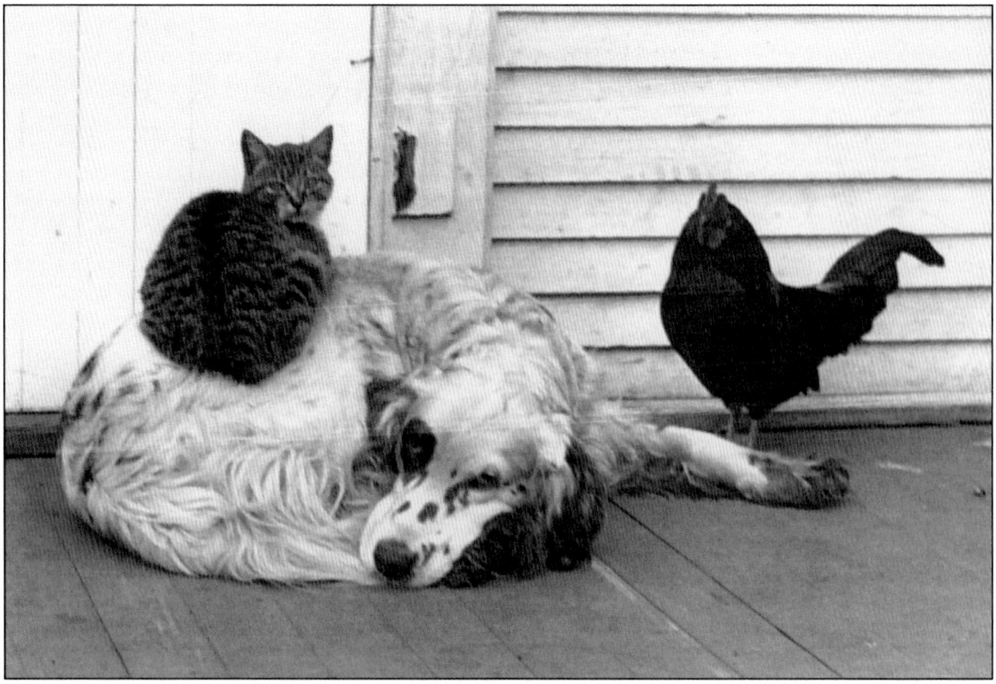

This photograph by Mary Bourgeois Wright illustrates that "strange bedfellows" can still be friends, whether they are furred or feathered. Wright entered several of her photographs in contests and took home awards for her work.

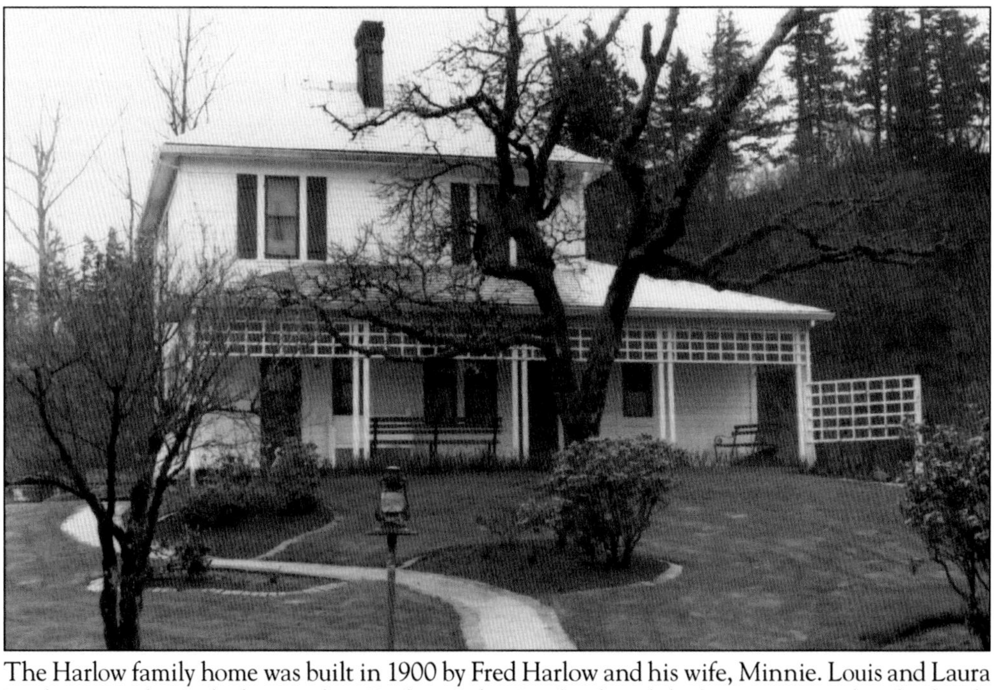

The Harlow family home was built in 1900 by Fred Harlow and his wife, Minnie. Louis and Laura Harlow moved into the house when Fred moved to Portland, and the home remained in the family until 1940, when it was sold to Lee and Mabel Evans. It is currently used as the local historical society's residential museum and is in the National Register of Historic Places.

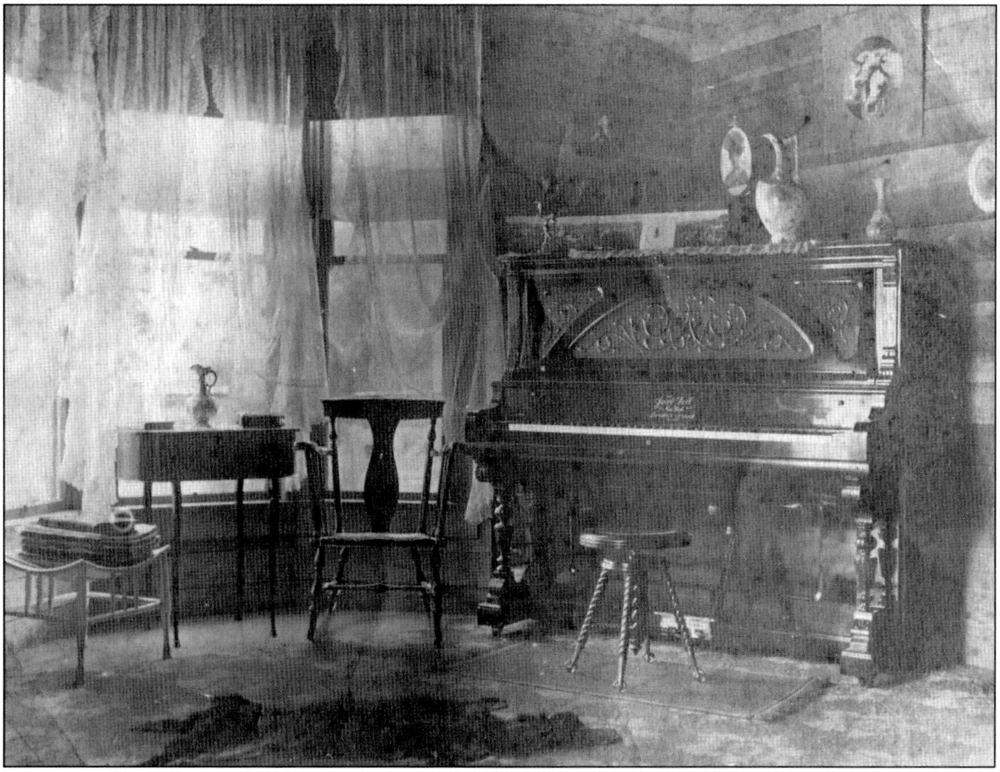

This rare indoor photograph shows the furnishings in Capt. John Harlow's original house, which was located next door to today's Harlow House.

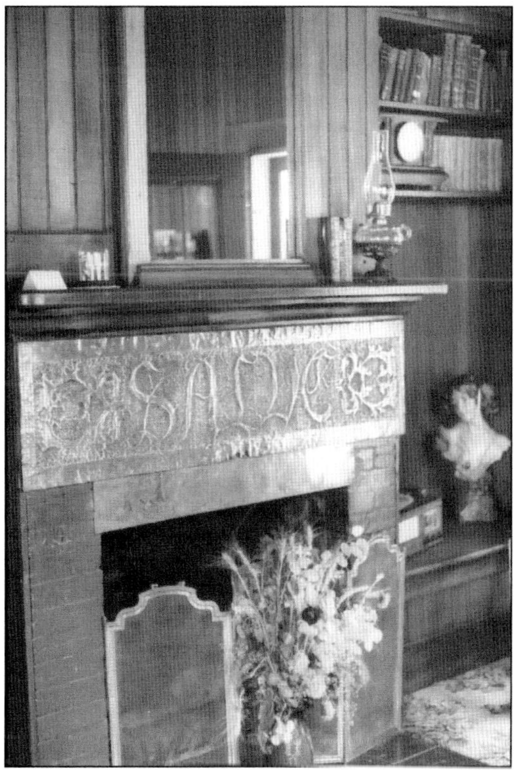

The fireplace at the Harlow House features a copper plate spanning the width of the fireplace with the word "Salve"—Latin for "Greetings" or "Welcome"—hammered into the metal from the back side. Laura Harlow and her sons created this piece with a pattern from a magazine.

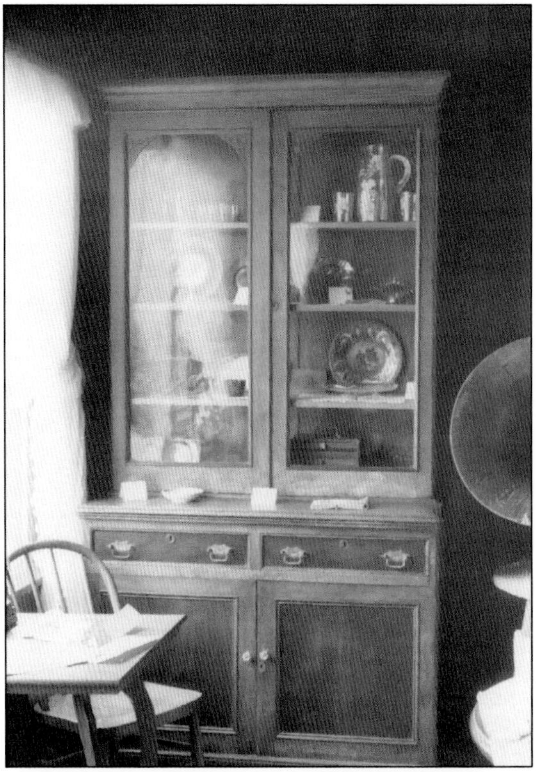

The china hutch in the Harlow House living room is credited as having belonged to the original John Harlow family. One story says that it was built with wood from Harlow's last ship, but that has not been authenticated. It is used to display decorative glassware at the museum.

This photograph, titled "Mayor's Day Off", shows Glenn Otto doing what he loved most: smelt dipping in the Sandy River. An electrician, restaurant owner, and commercial smelt fisherman, he eventually became mayor of Troutdale and went on to serve as an elected member of the Oregon House and Senate. (Photograph courtesy of Len Otto.)

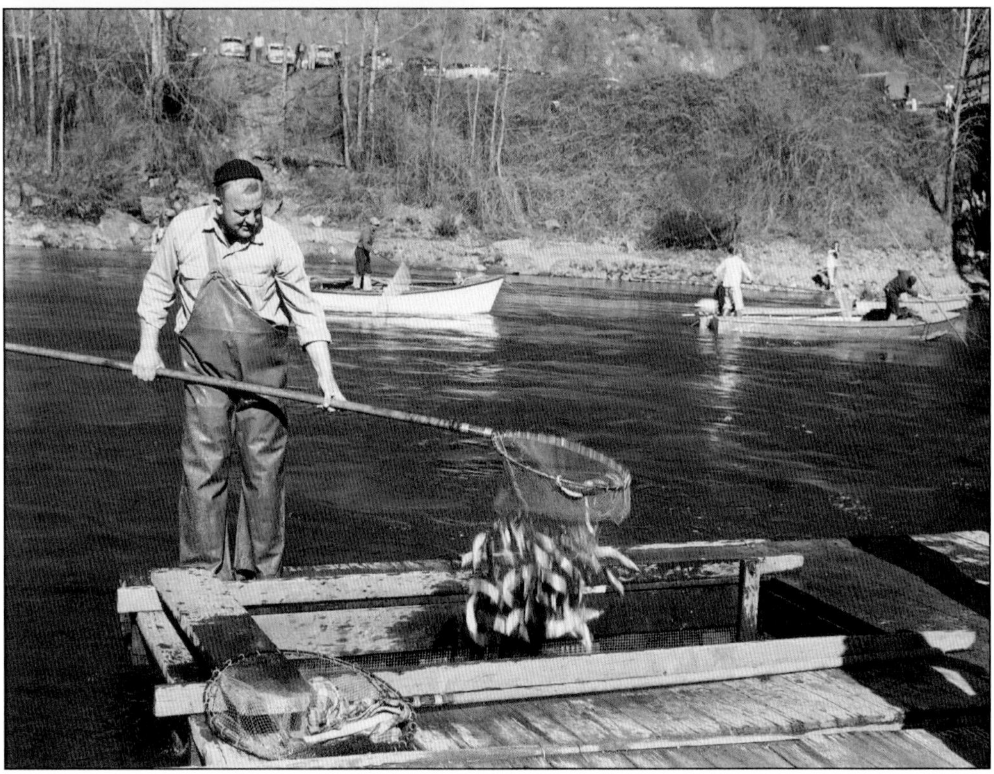

Seven

Mother Nature's Tantrums

The Farmers' Almanac makes long-range predictions for the nation's weather, and the Weather Channel pinpoints local weather when it is happening, but seasoned veterans in Troutdale do not need the National Weather Service to predict the infamous East Wind that creates whitecaps in their toilets and makes the windows in their houses bulge from the force of its blasts on blustery days. Mother Nature has often thrown temper tantrums in the area, creating freak snowstorms, ice storms, and flooding that have paralyzed this river town.

Any person who has lived in the Troutdale vicinity for more than a year or two can tell harrowing tales of the wind. When Portland is experiencing a light zephyr, Troutdale may have steady 50-mile-per-hour winds. Troutdalians shrug off the weather as just another pesky trick that Mother Nature plays on them. Winds as strong as 125 miles per hour have been clocked just a few miles east of town. In the days before insulation in houses, local homeowners used melted paraffin to fill cracks or threw water onto the east sides of their homes in an attempt to seal out the wind when the water froze into a sheet of protective ice. Older homes even had newspapers and felt within the walls to keep the wind out. One of the previous owners of the Harlow House, which still stands on the Historic Columbia River Highway, told of the linoleum on the kitchen and dining room floors "levitating" when the wind blew through the house in the winter.

Crippling ice storms have also been a part of life in Troutdale. Longtime residents can give vivid details of the ice storm that suddenly hit in November 1921, leaving a foot of ice on the Columbia River Highway. Road crews were not able to clear it until they finally punched a one-lane hole through the ice in February 1922. Residents even found chunks of ice in fields the following April.

Lying in close proximity to two rivers and several local streams, Troutdale has also experienced seasonal flooding. In 1948, the Columbia River spilled over its banks, swept away a Portland community, and left Troutdale marooned by floodwaters. Local residents used canoes, boats, and ingenuity to navigate through the waters to do their daily chores, including feeding livestock and delivering newspapers. Living through such circumstances leaves plenty of memories and stories to share with younger generations and new residents who often wonder where their garbage cans rolled to in the middle of a windstorm.

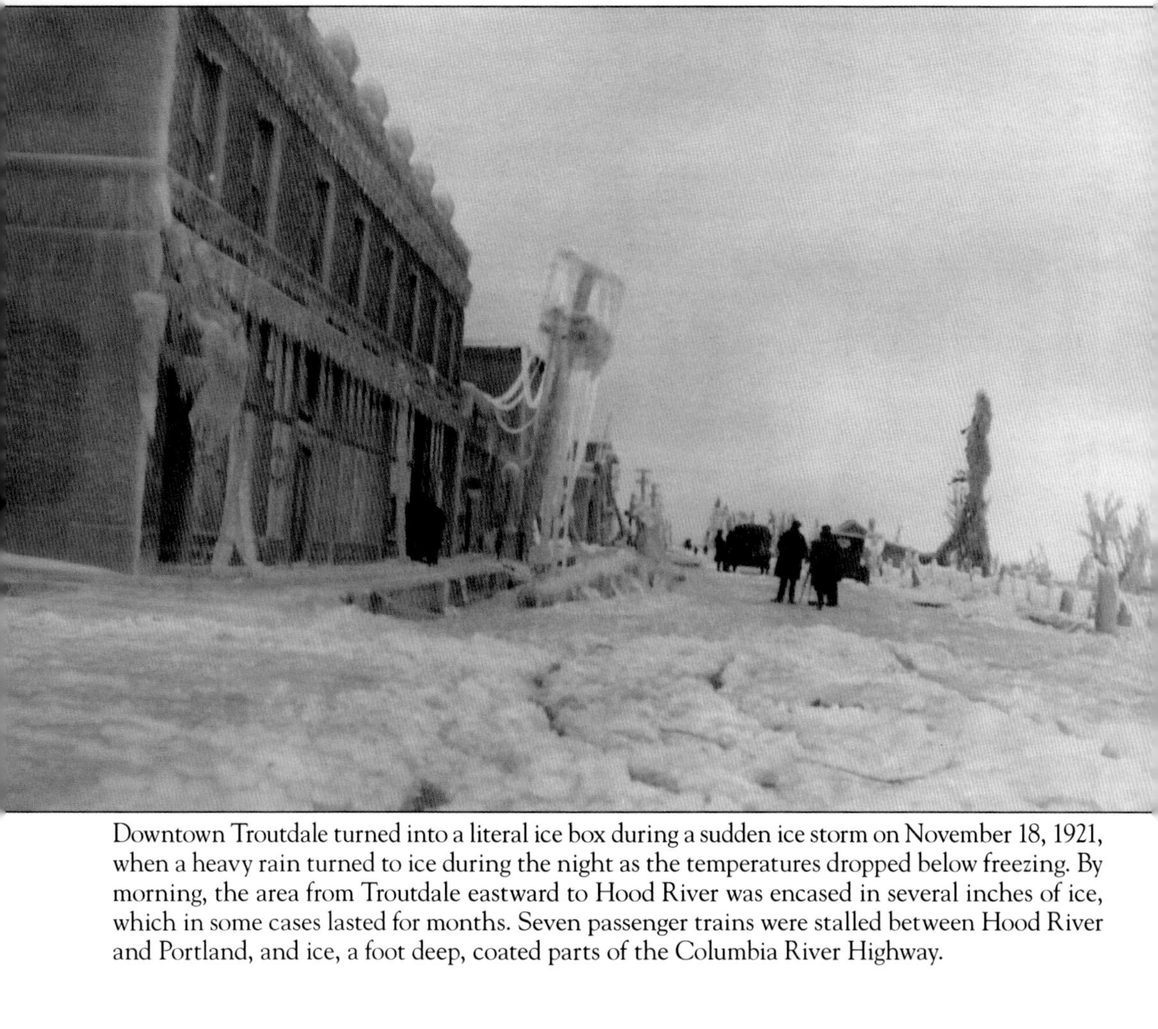

Downtown Troutdale turned into a literal ice box during a sudden ice storm on November 18, 1921, when a heavy rain turned to ice during the night as the temperatures dropped below freezing. By morning, the area from Troutdale eastward to Hood River was encased in several inches of ice, which in some cases lasted for months. Seven passenger trains were stalled between Hood River and Portland, and ice, a foot deep, coated parts of the Columbia River Highway.

This photograph, looking west on the historic highway, shows the chunks of ice that fell to the road. Local residents who remember the sudden storm recall that it was the worst weather event of their lives. Luckily, no deaths were reported during the storm.

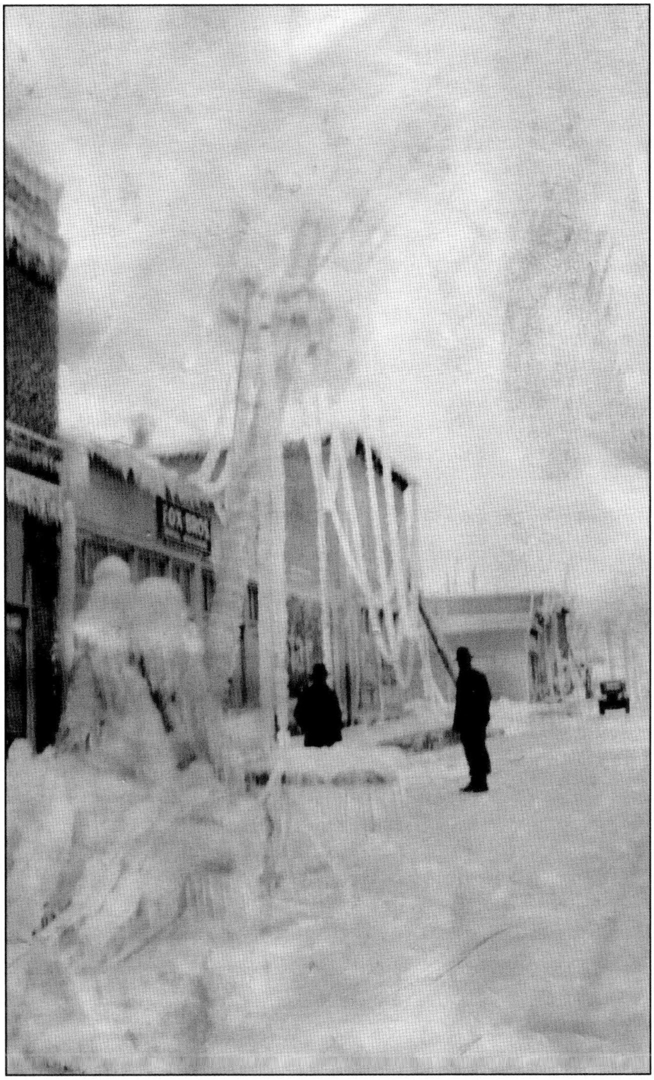

Trees and power lines were no match for the layer of ice and snow that fell in 1921. Telephone poles snapped and, just a few miles east of Troutdale, only the cross pieces of 30-foot-high telephone poles stuck out of the huge drifts of ice and "tapioca" snow.

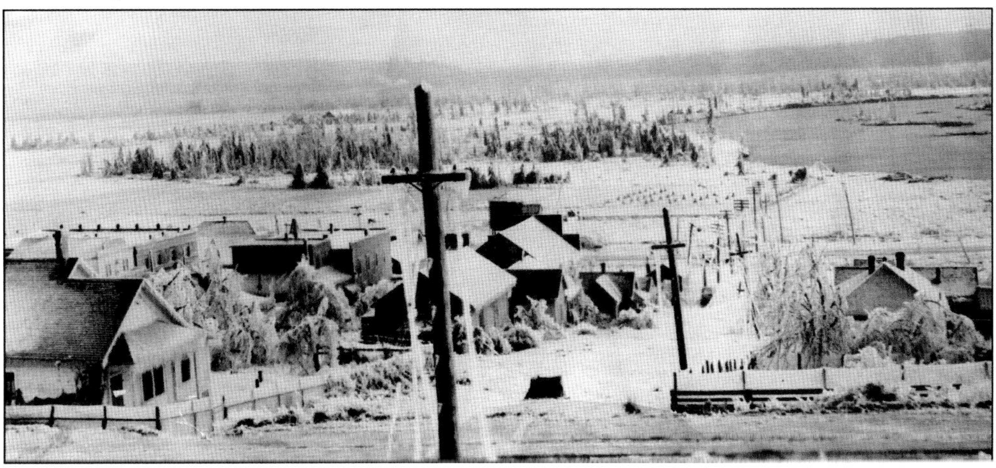

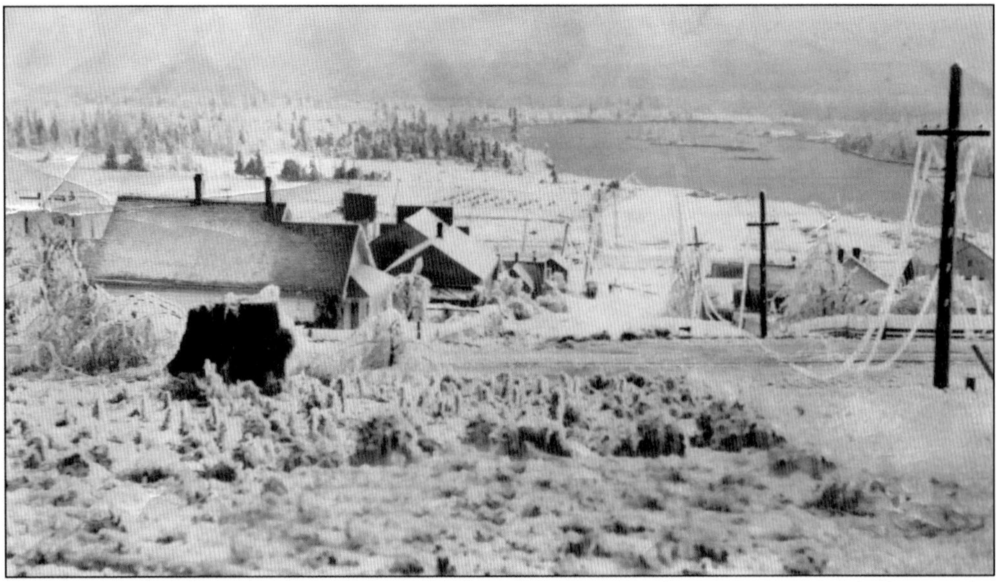

Trees were snapped and orchards in the area were flattened by the ice. So many telephone poles were down that phone company crews laid new phone lines on top of the ice-covered ground to restart communication.

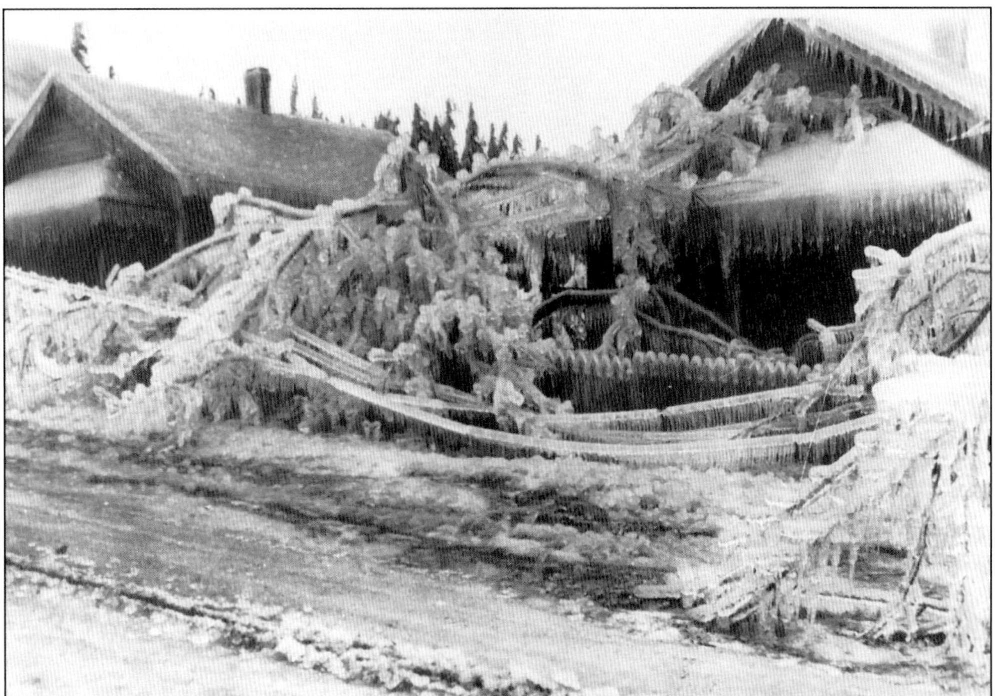

Although Troutdale residents lost their phone service and the ability to drive on city streets and county roads during the storm, rural residents never lost their lights and heat because they had not yet been hooked up to electricity.

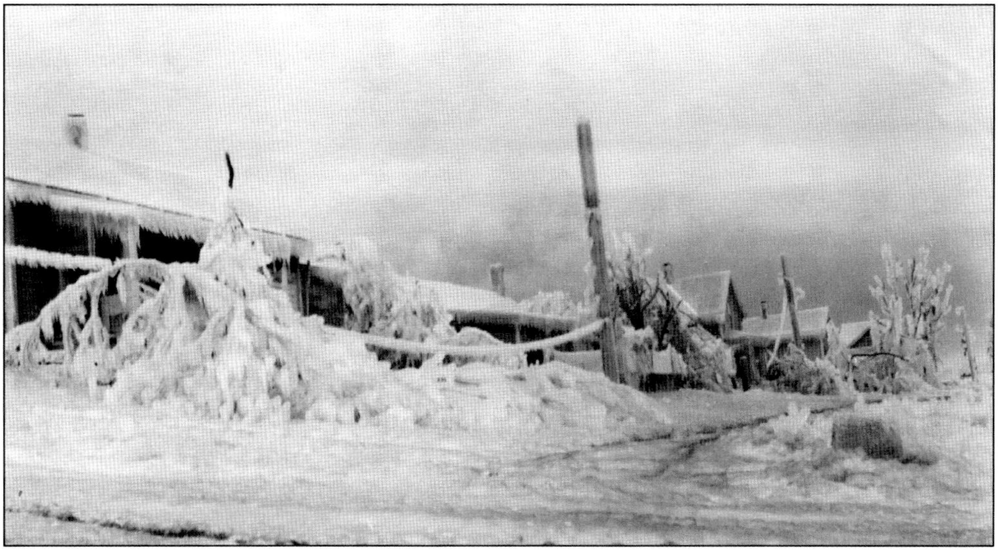

Highway bridges and viaducts collapsed and 174 automobiles were stalled on the highway east of Troutdale. One local resident chose to drive his car home by straddling the railroad tracks, keeping his right wheels between the rails and his left wheels on the outside, between Bonneville and Bridal Veil.

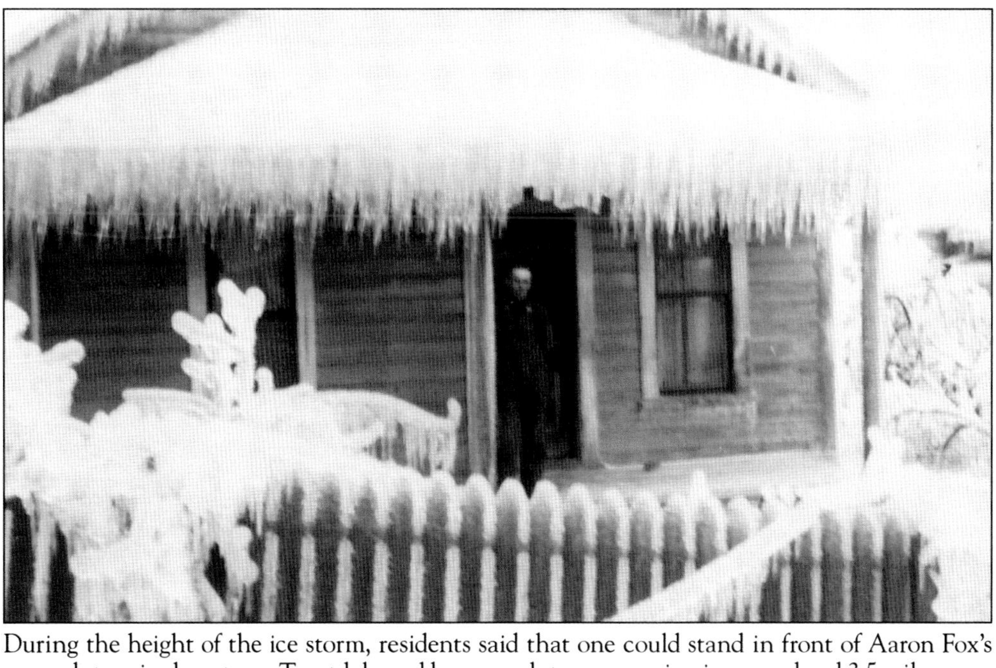

During the height of the ice storm, residents said that one could stand in front of Aaron Fox's general store in downtown Troutdale and hear peach trees snapping in an orchard 3.5 miles away near Blue Lake Park.

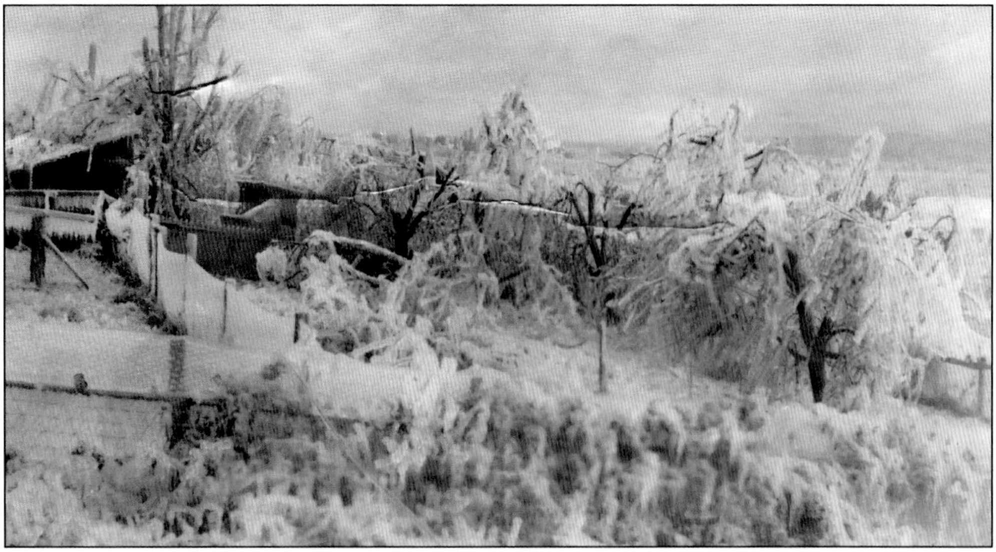

Due to the long-lasting railroad disruptions caused by the snow and ice, Troutdale celery farmers missed their chance to ship their celery back east for the Thanksgiving holiday. A freight train spent nine hours creeping the 40 miles to The Dalles.

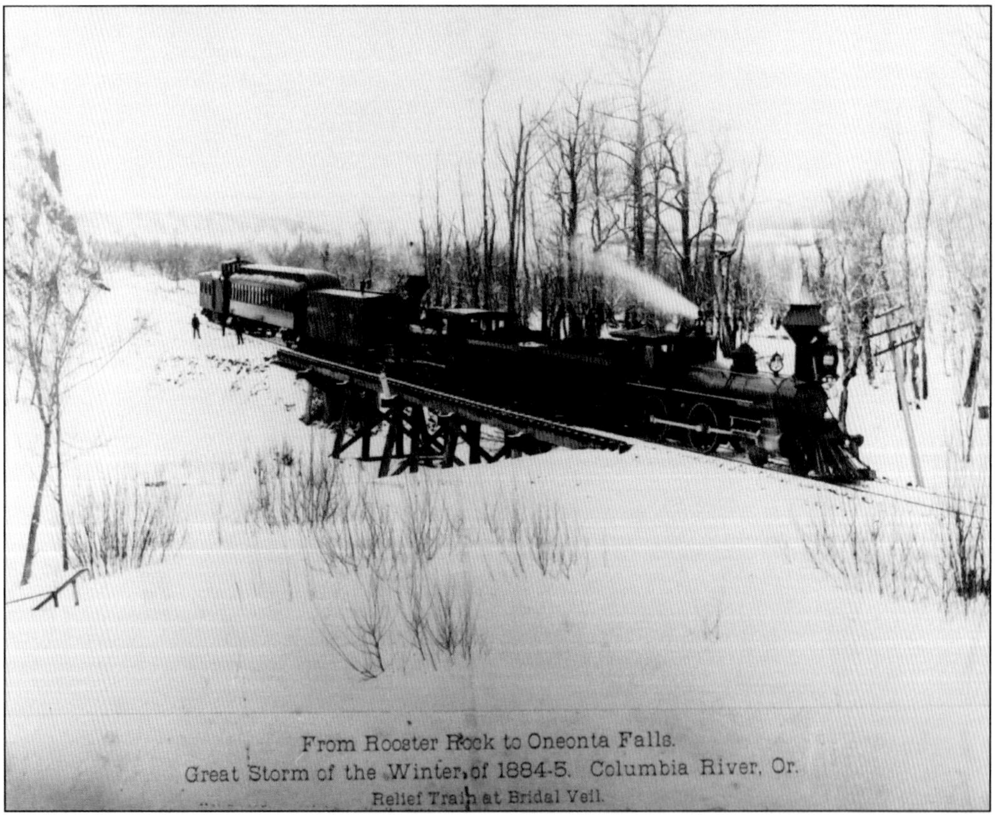

Between the Christmas and New Year's holidays of 1884–1885, a massive snowstorm blew through the Columbia River Gorge, sealing it off from the rest of the world. Transcontinental passenger traffic through the gorge had only been in service for a month when it was halted by the storm.

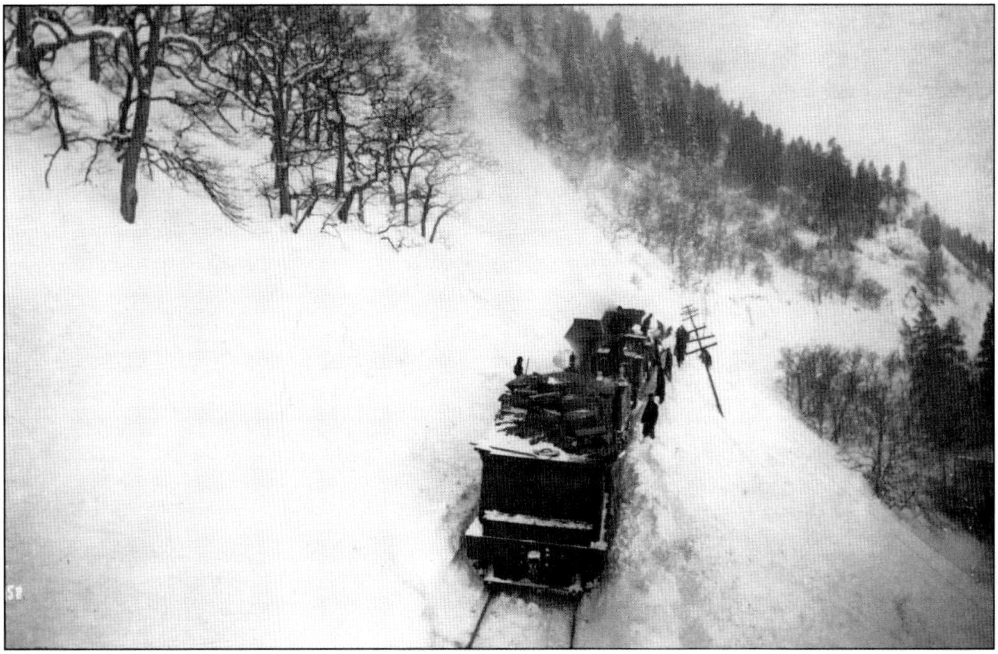

Passengers aboard that Pacific Express train were on their way to Portland for the upcoming Christmas holiday season in 1884, but the storm left drifts 6 to 10 feet deep across the tracks, stranding the 150 passengers for 20 days while rescuers dug their way to the train.

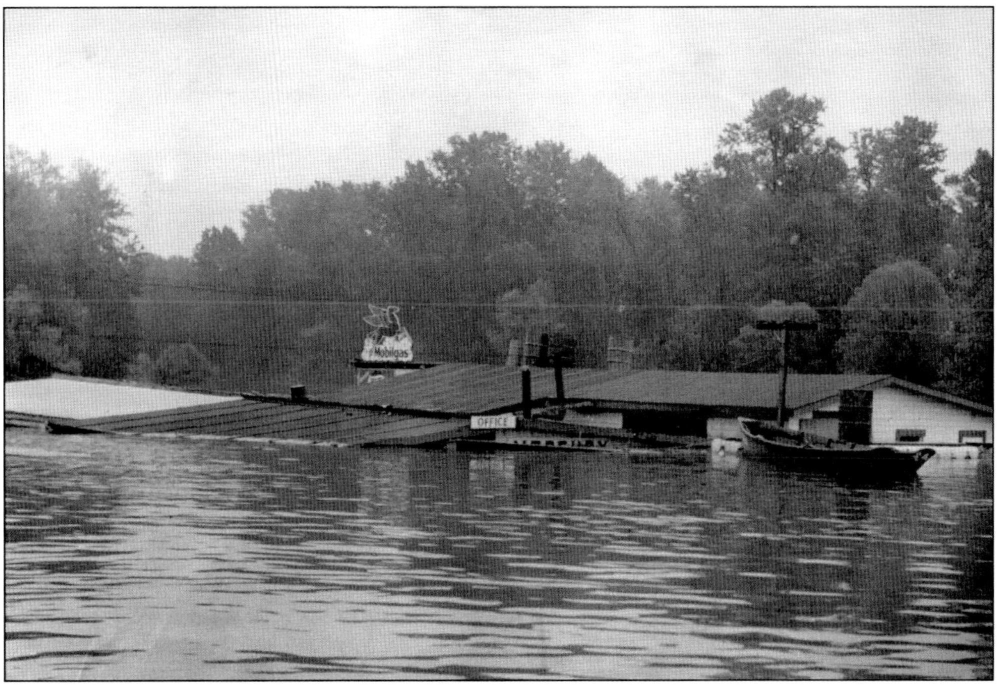

Floodwaters nearly topped the Espenel garage in this 1948 photograph. A boat is tethered to the roof near the submerged office. The Columbia River Highway to The Dalles was closed at Troutdale when the Columbia River backed into the Sandy River, inundating businesses along the road beside it.

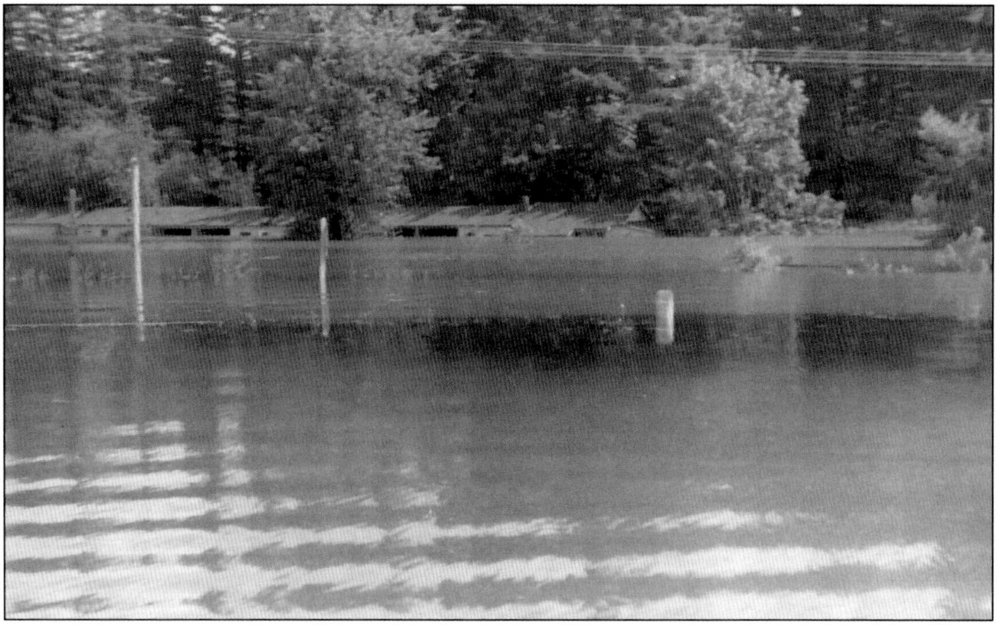

Residents used pioneer-like ingenuity to save their possessions during the flood of 1948. One family moved their household goods onto a floating dock moored to a large tree, while another moved laying hens to a two-story hen house and used a smelt barge to shovel chicken feed to them.

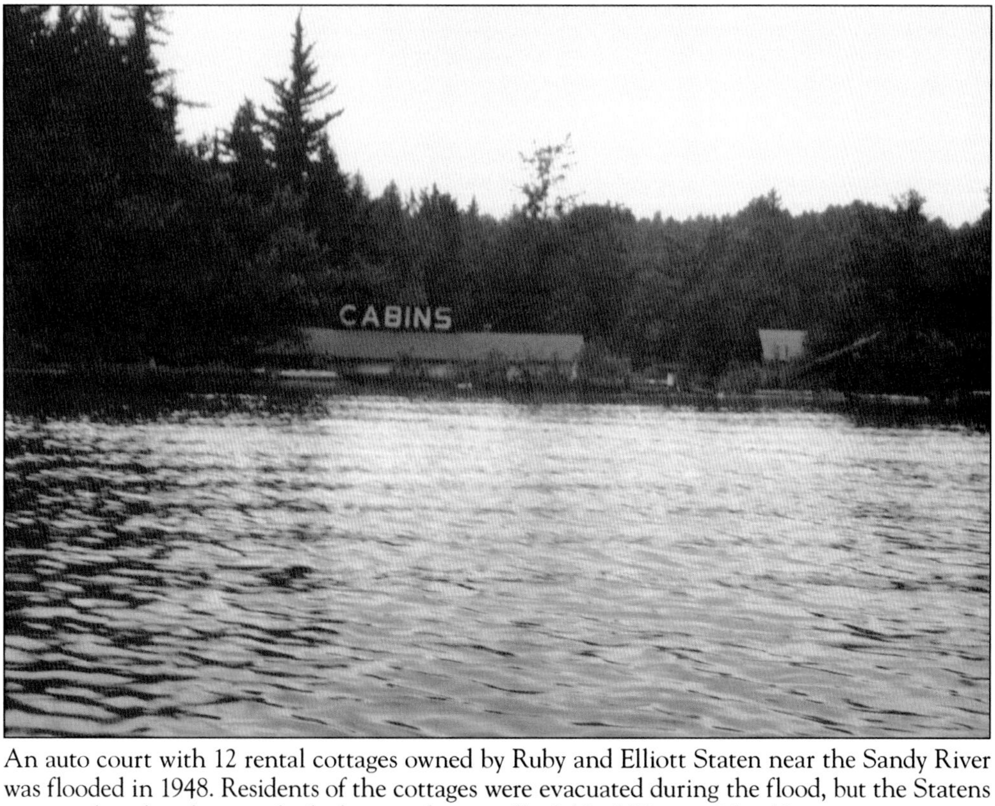

An auto court with 12 rental cottages owned by Ruby and Elliott Staten near the Sandy River was flooded in 1948. Residents of the cottages were evacuated during the flood, but the Statens remained in their home, which they good-naturedly dubbed "Staten Island."

One man looked out the window of his submerged home to see one of John Harlow's infamous carp's descendants eating the grass off his flooded lawn. A flooded home with a "For Sale" sign posted on it by real estate agent Dan Flood was altered to read "For Sale Dam Flood."

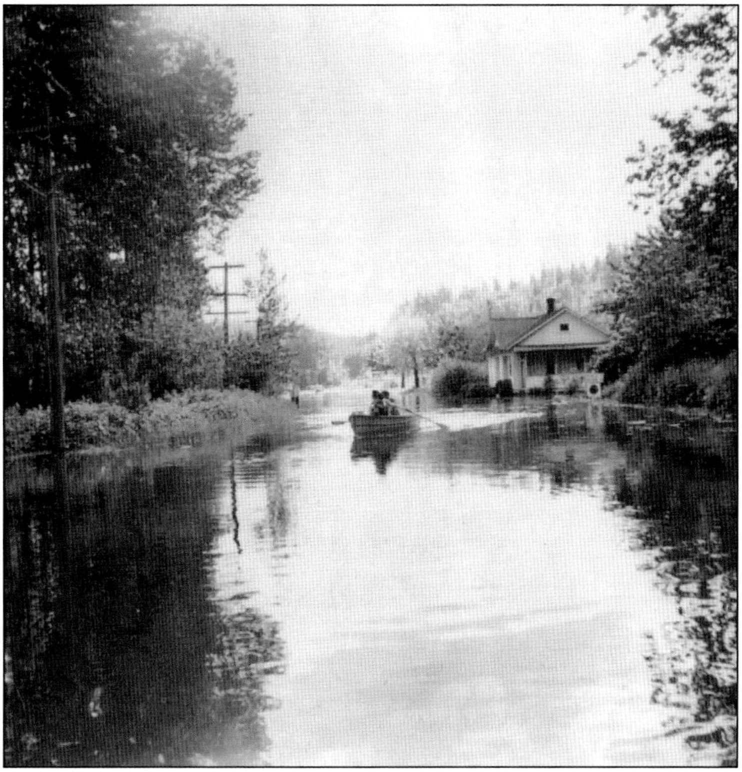

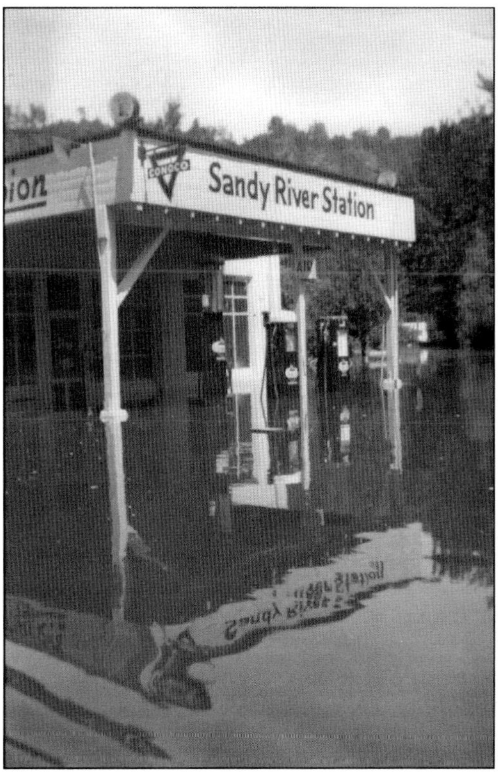

Floodwaters inundated the Sandy River Gas Station on the Historic Columbia River Highway at Beaver Creek in May 1948, reaching to the middle of the gas pumps. The highway at Troutdale was underwater for days, and residents used rowboats, canoes, and skiffs to maneuver around the flooded areas.

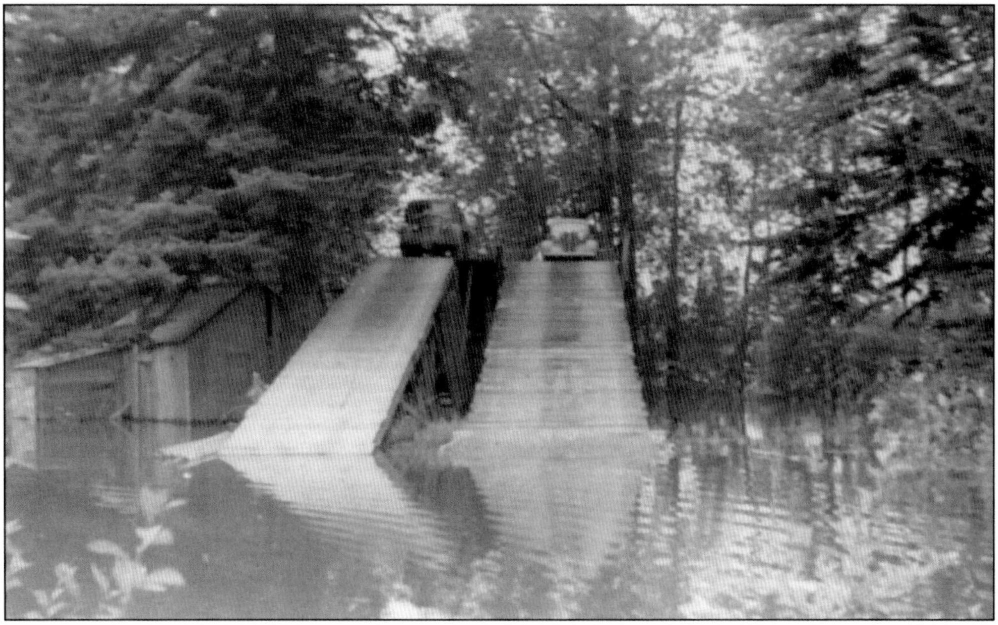

Troutdale residents used the ramps at the Troutdale Sand and Gravel Company to elevate their cars from the floodwaters in 1948. A local car dealer was not as lucky with his stock of new 1949 model Fords, which he had been hiding at a warehouse in Troutdale. Floodwaters forced him to move them to a berry field above the waterline, revealing the new models to onlookers.

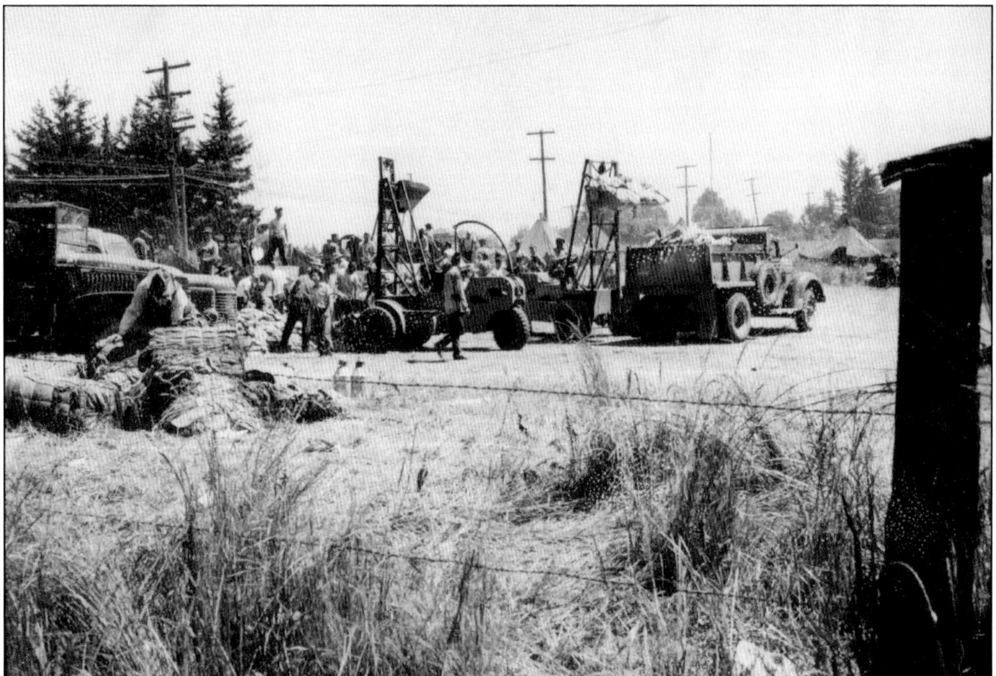

Staging areas were set up by the owners of Reynolds Metals Co. during the 1948 flood to prevent a 10-foot-deep surge of river water from hitting the molten metal in the pot-lines inside, which would have set off a catastrophic explosion.

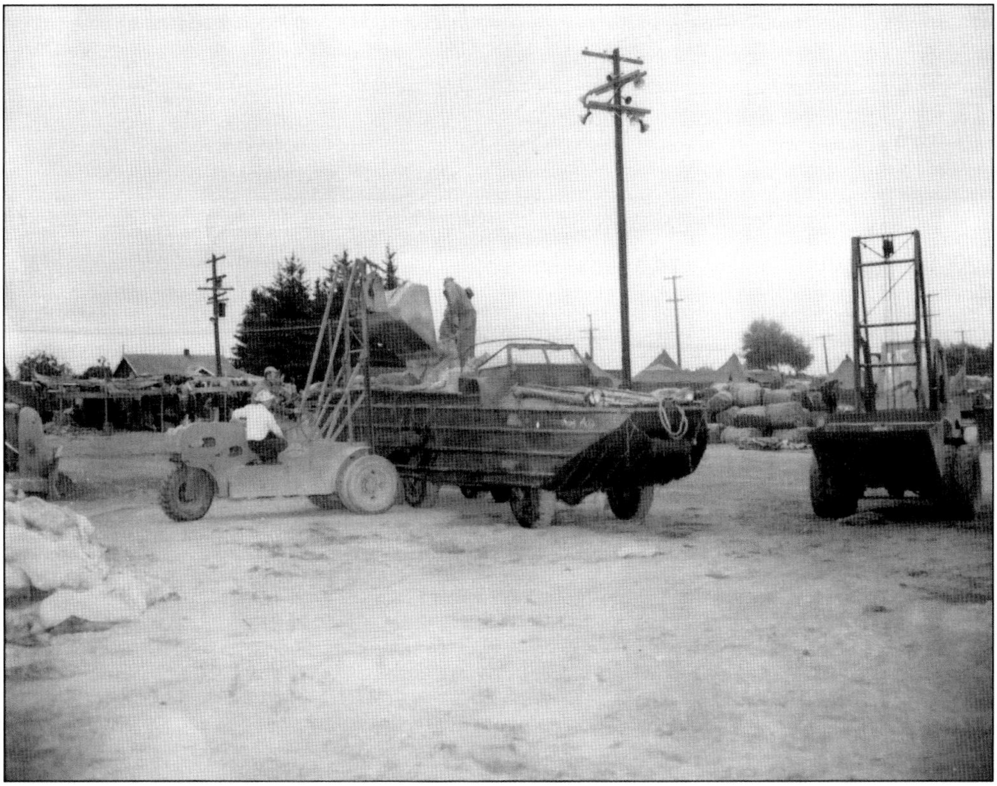

The line of defense for the Reynolds Metals Co. was an earthen barrier 18 feet high and 60 feet wide at its base. The river threatened the plant for nearly a month, and before it receded, water reached within 200 feet of the front gate.

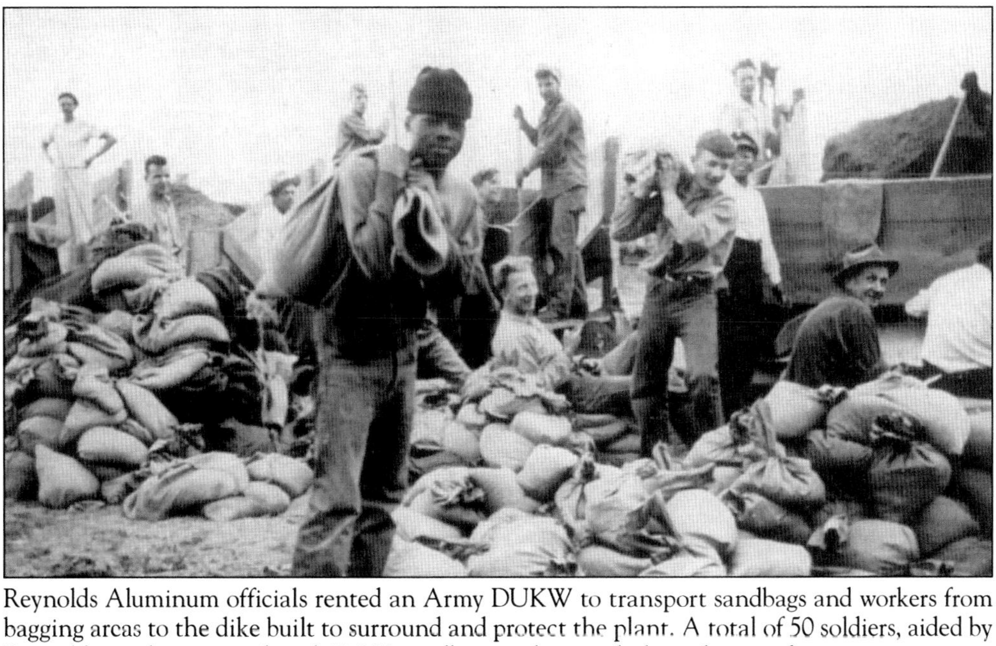

Reynolds Aluminum officials rented an Army DUKW to transport sandbags and workers from bagging areas to the dike built to surround and protect the plant. A total of 50 soldiers, aided by Reynolds employees, produced 10,000 sandbags an hour to bolster the riverfront.

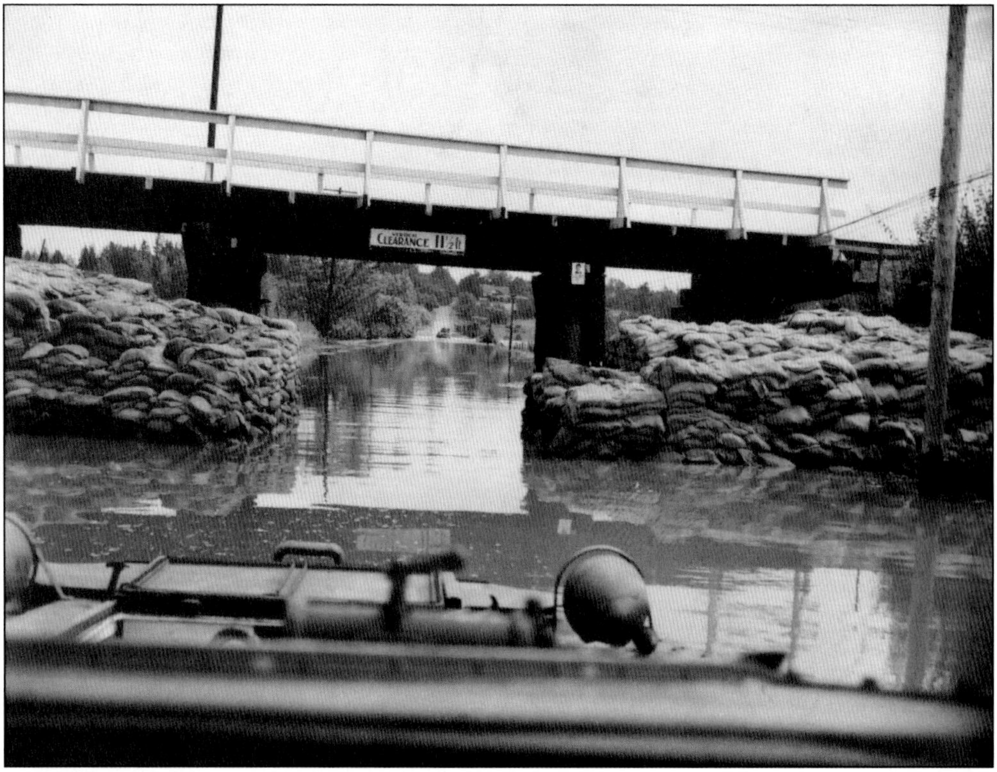

The DUKW was able to navigate in areas that were unreachable by trucks. Notice the embankment of sandbags on either side of the bridge. One worker described the dike in front of Reynolds Metals plant as being like "walking on Jell-O."

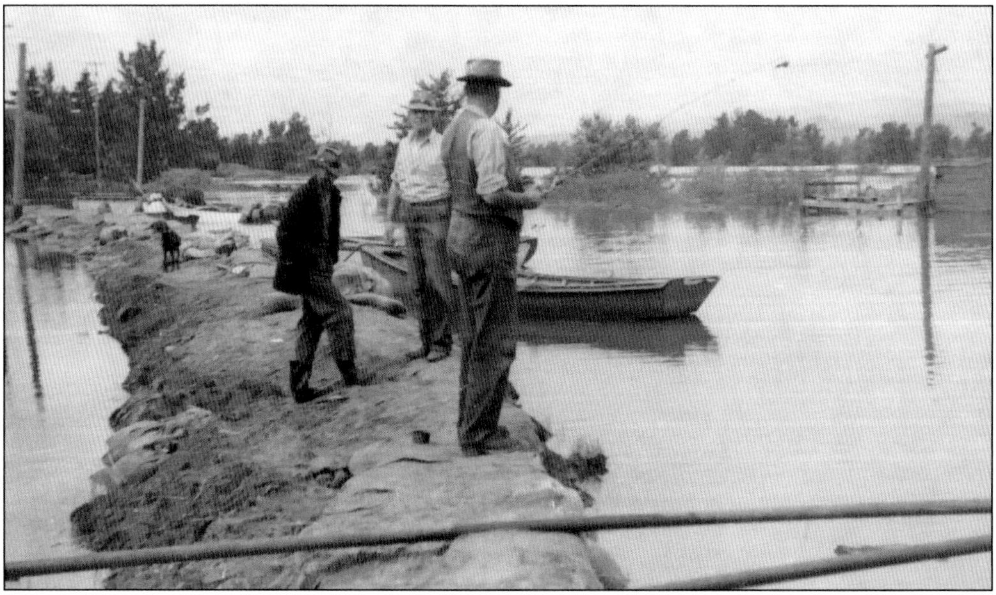

Men fish from the top of an earthen and sandbag dike erected during the May 1948 flood along the Columbia River. Although the flood swept away a community of 18,000 called Vanport in an area of north Portland, some of the dikes around Troutdale held.

Eight

Smelt Dipping on the Sandy River

Oregon fishermen salivate at the news of the "spring Chinook" run and endure the chill of standing waist-deep in an icy river to snag a steelhead. However, one Oregon tradition, smelt dipping, is an all-but-forgotten annual ritual along the Sandy River. Between the early 1900s and 1980, the stretch of the river between the Stark Street Bridge and the river's confluence with the Columbia River drew thousands of avid smelt dippers to spring runs.

Armed with dipping nets, buckets, and boxes, they stood on the banks of the river and scooped out thousands of the small, silvery fish during the short two-to-three-day spawn in early spring, when the frigid waters were coursing down from the melting mountain snow packs. A local sheriff's deputy reported that on a single day in 1945 more than 5,000 people lined the river. The event was so popular that cars lined every road, bridge, and parking area within walking distance of the site. Women in dresses and high heels symbolically lifted loaded nets to commemorate the occasion, while local restaurants and food vendors sold plates of fried smelt to eager crowds.

Whether the smelt were for home consumption, smoking for a hard winter's "survival rations," used as fertilizer, or commercial ventures, the enthusiasm for smelt was entrenched in the Troutdale community culture. In the earliest years, with no license required and no limit on catches, some dippers took home wagonloads of the fish for fertilizer.

The boom years of smelt runs on the Sandy River, from around 1900 to the early 1970s—the last record run—seemed to foreshadow the inevitable: smelt were no longer returning with the same frequency. From the largest commercial catch of fish in 1945—more than one million pounds—to several years when there was a dearth of runs, the smelt fishermen remained faithful. The Troutdale Historical Society playfully created a Smelt Court, complete with a Smelt Queen and Sir Smelt, in royal regalia, during the annual Troutdale Summerfest.

Those who experienced the thrill of smelt dipping fondly remember the annual spawns, but even the most hard-core smelt devotee can feel his zeal wane. As one local smelt fisherman confessed, "All I know is that I would give you $5 for the first smelt of the season and after that you couldn't pay me $5 to eat one!"

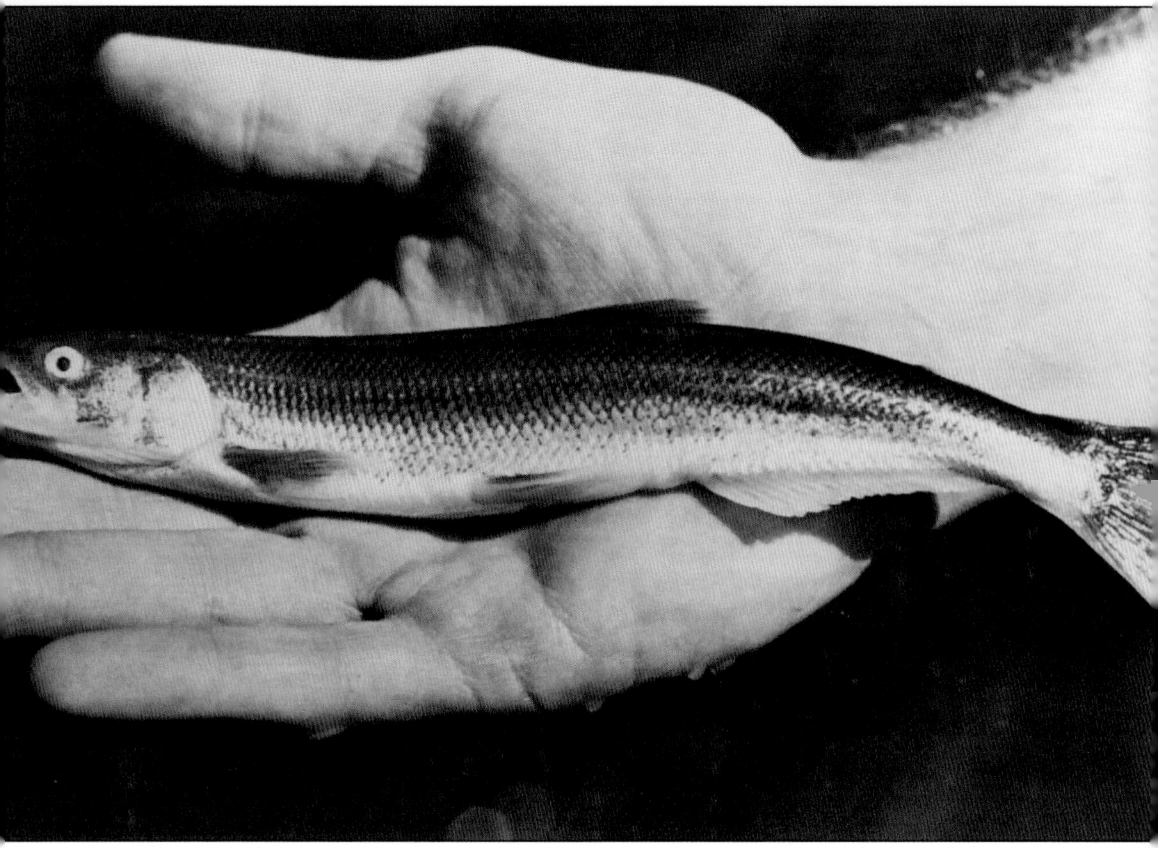

Smelt are small, silvery fish, four to eight inches long. Now protected as a threatened species, these creatures swam up the Sandy River to spawn, where they died and became food for other fish or flocks of gulls. Also called "candlefish" by Native Americans and early settlers, they were used by some people as a light source. A wick could be inserted through the fish's body, and the oil from them would produce a faint light. Smelt dippers figured about 10 smelt equaled a pound.

This swarm of smelt, caught in the eddies and current of the Sandy River, shows the prolific number of fish that used to appear nearly every spring. They could be dipped in nets from a boat by commercial fisherman or from the shore, from improvised docks or slippery rocks along the bank.

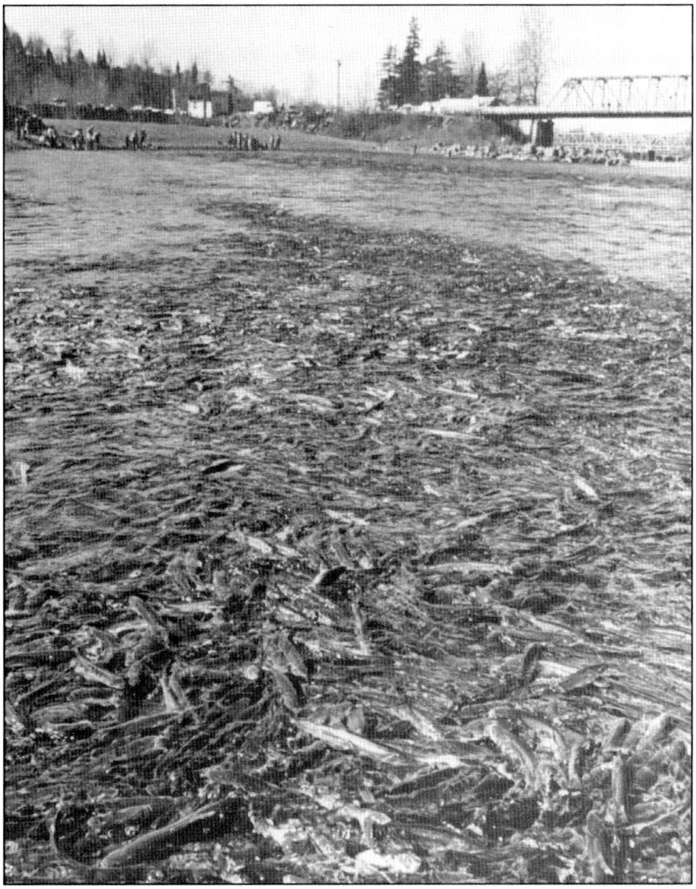

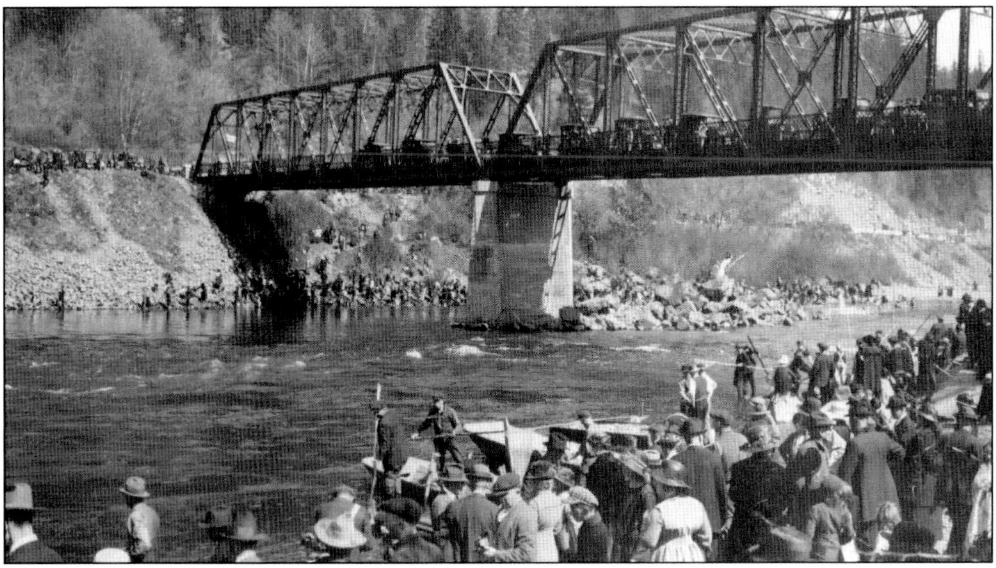

Throngs of people line both sides of the Sandy River as well as the bridge over the river in this photograph. For many years, the sheriff's office enforced a one-way traffic scheme during smelt runs to help control the chaotic traffic jams.

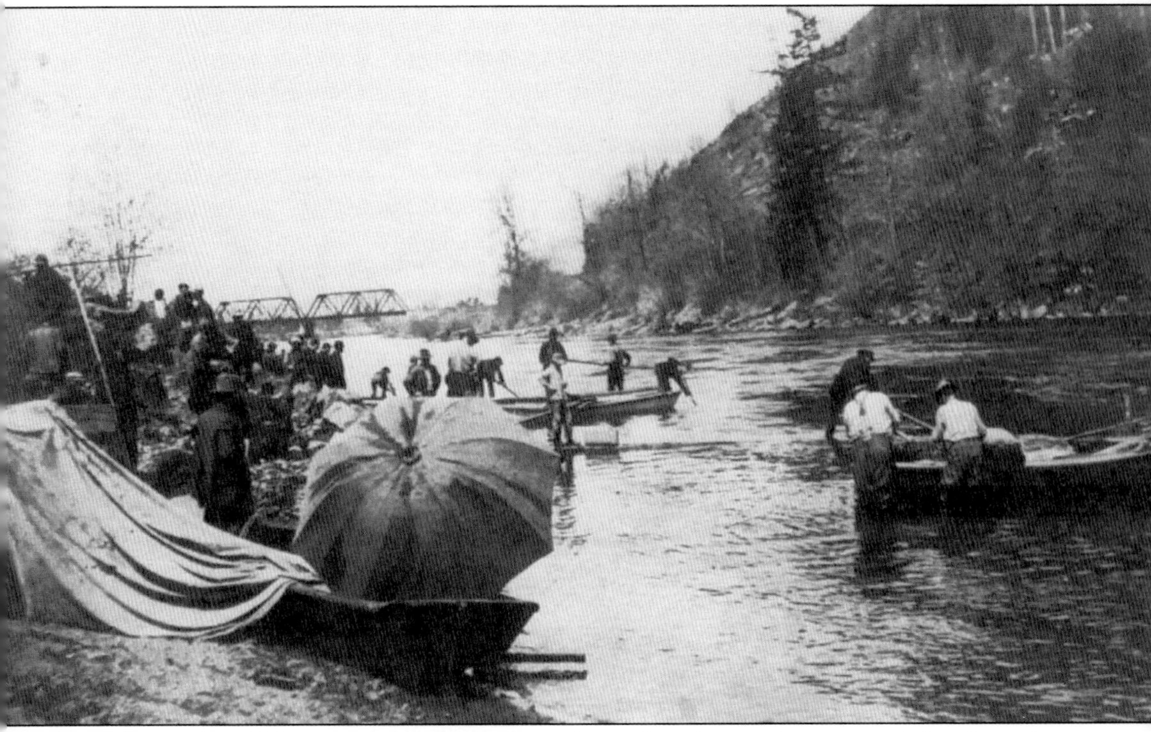

A nostalgic 1908 scene on the Sandy River shows that the activity was carried on for as long as the dippers' arms could lift the heavily laden nets from the water. The umbrella on the left might have been protection from the sun, spring rain, or wind, or a combination of all three. Smelt were known about long before these fishermen went to the river to net them. William Clark wrote of smelt on the expedition he and Meriwether Lewis made to the Pacific and back in 1805–1806, expressing a personal taste for the fish.

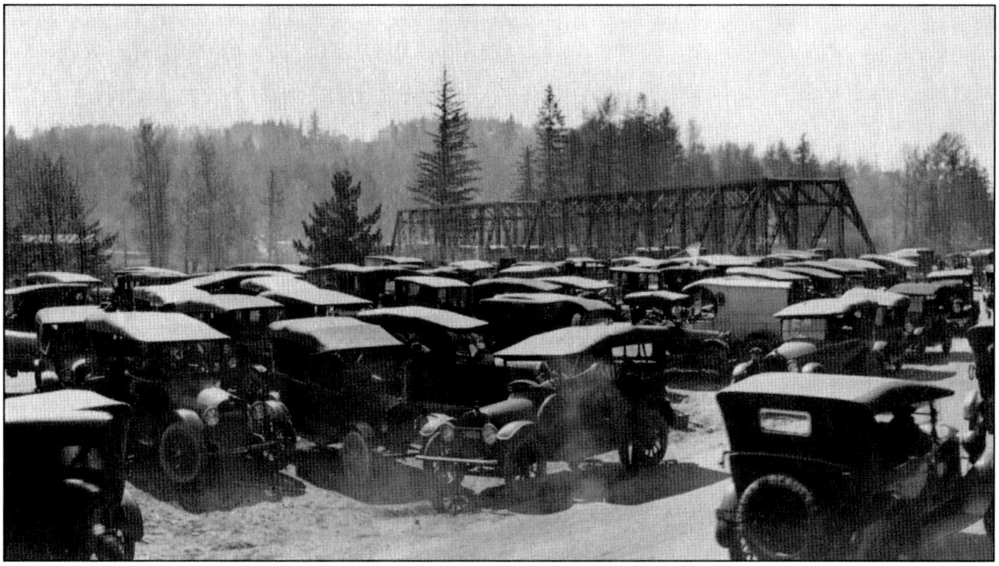

The dust from emerging and departing vehicles from a gravel parking area clouds portions of these photographs from the early 1920s. Vehicles in the photographs have been identified as a 1917 Franklin, a 1914 Ford Model T, a 1920 Ford Model T, a 1918 Hudson, and a 1918 Buick.

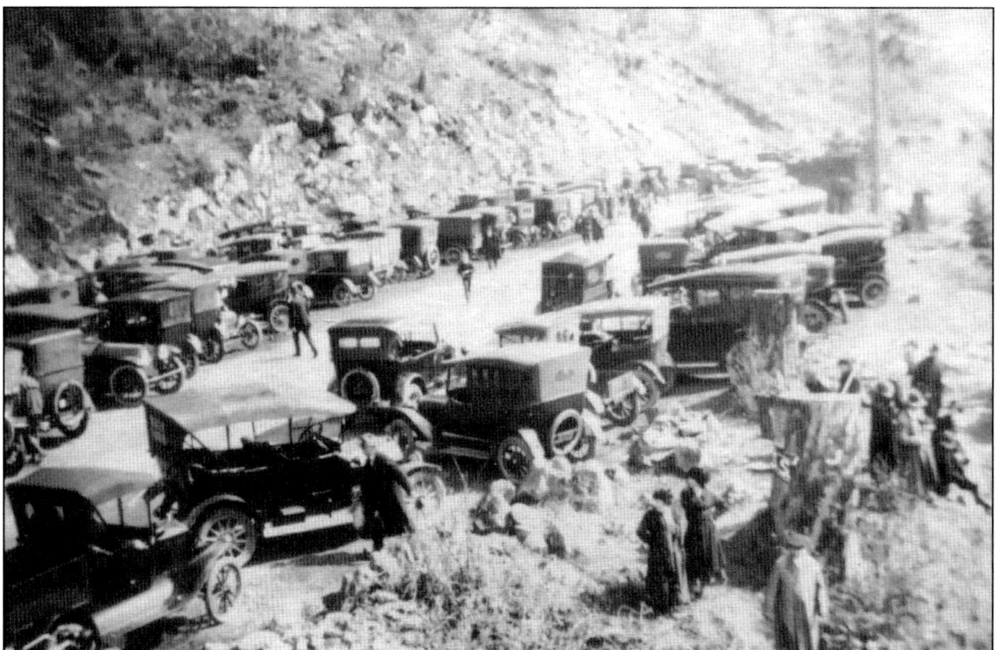

The volume of traffic increased dramatically along the Sandy River during smelt runs. Parking spaces were at a premium since it was a popular spectator sport, as well as a source of fun, food, and income for those who dipped the smelt from the river.

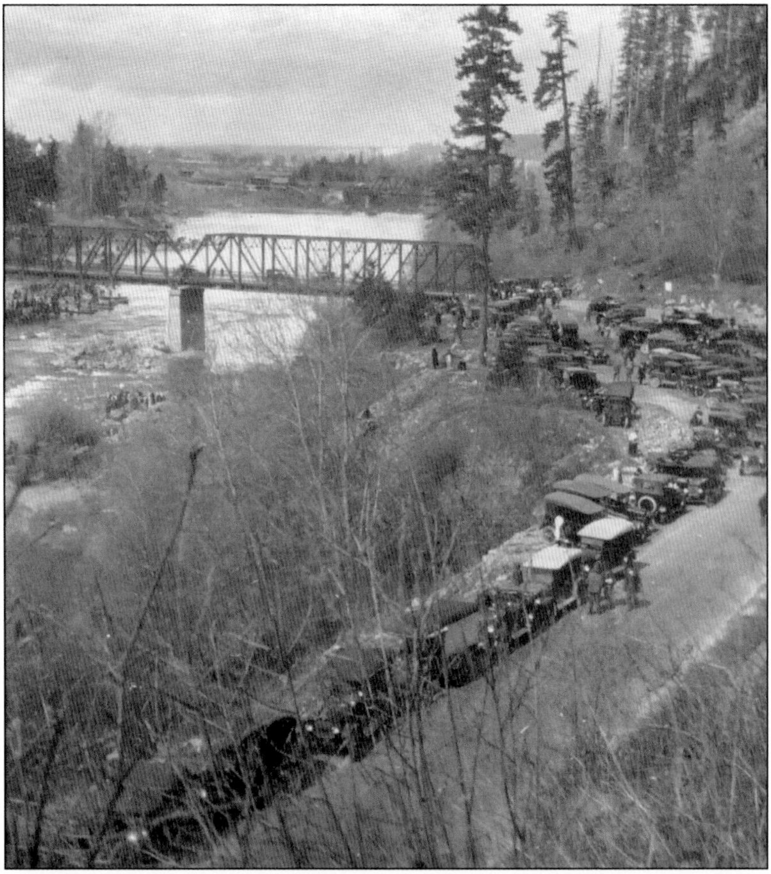

Smelt dippers and casual onlookers had a considerable hike to the river from available parking spots along the road to access the riverbanks. The term bumper-to-bumper traffic may not have been in use in the 1920s, but it describes the opening days of smelt seasons.

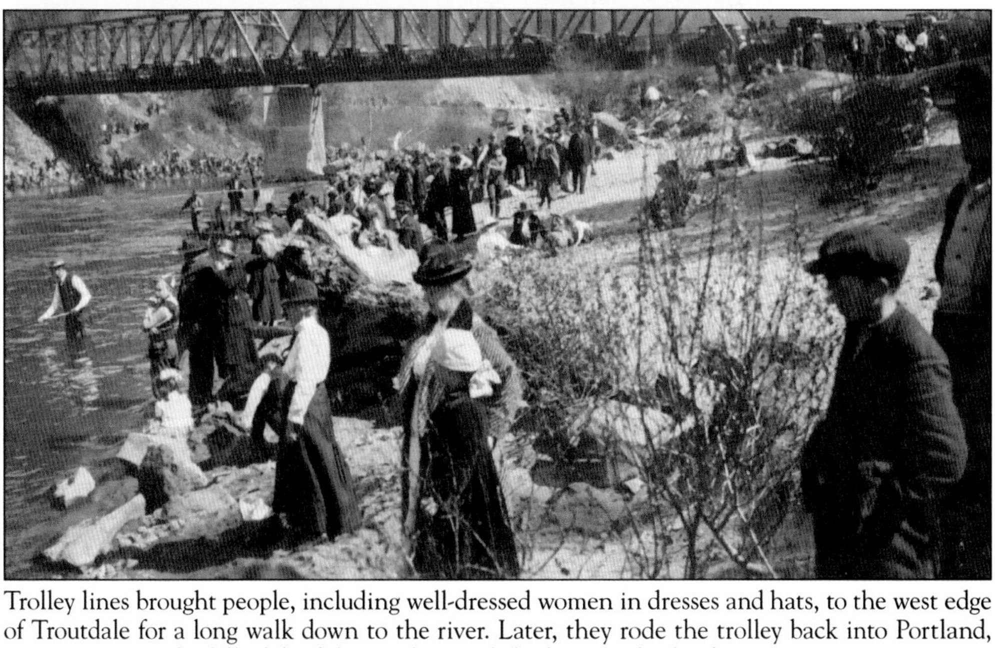

Trolley lines brought people, including well-dressed women in dresses and hats, to the west edge of Troutdale for a long walk down to the river. Later, they rode the trolley back into Portland, towing gunnysacks full of the fish to either cook fresh or smoke for the winter.

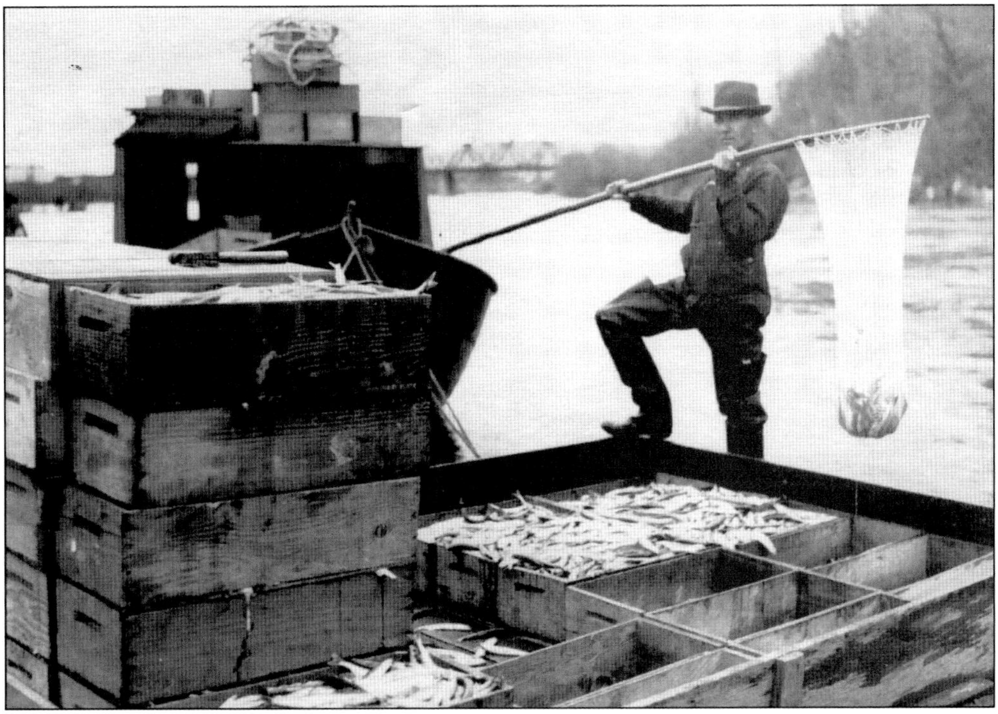

One veteran smelt dipper wrote a 12-step set of tips for the neophyte smelter, compete with appropriate hand movements, net-sweeping techniques, and net retrieval in one swift motion to avoid any "gritty" taste from the fish being dragged over the gravel that lies along the riverbanks.

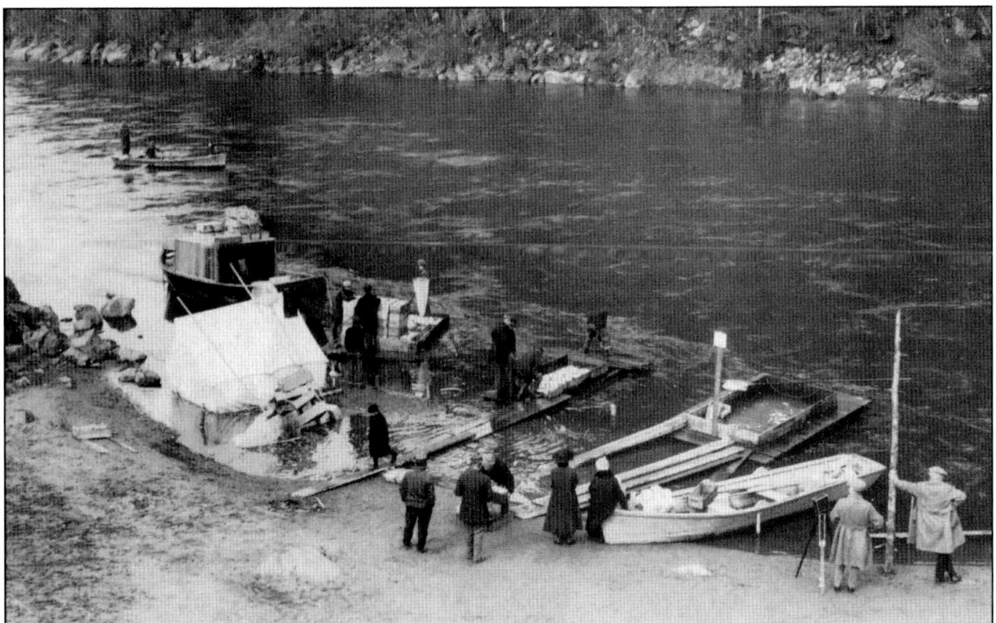

Commercial smelt dippers and their barges and boats unload their catch for the day in this early 1900s photograph. Notice the boxes loaded with smelt onboard as well as the empty live box on the barge to the right. Live boxes had an open center with a screen on the bottom.

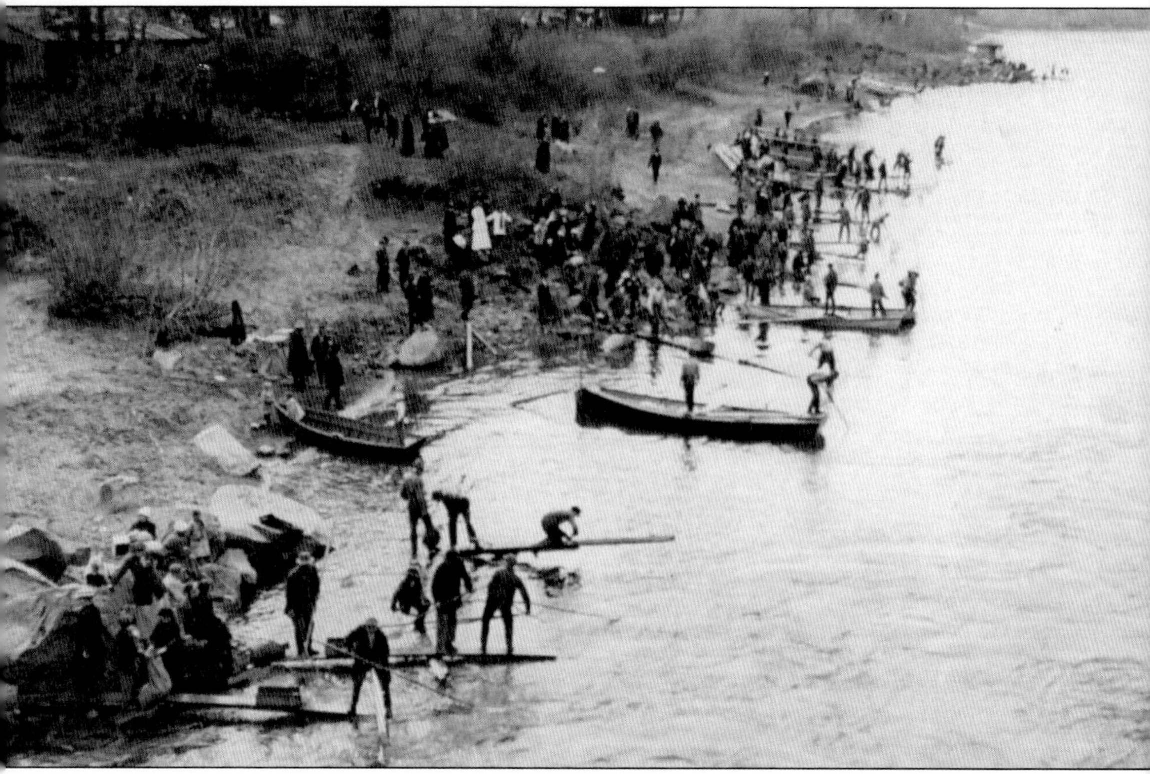

Boats were permitted for commercial fishermen, allowing them to go to the middle of the river to reach fish that tended to follow the current. One smelt dipper, Walter Nasmyth, warned, "Something to keep in mind is that if a person is dipping smelt in an area where the current is swift, a net full of smelt may cause one to go for an unscheduled swim, and the water is mighty cold that time of year." Here, smelt dippers use springboards and rocks to dip from the Sandy River.

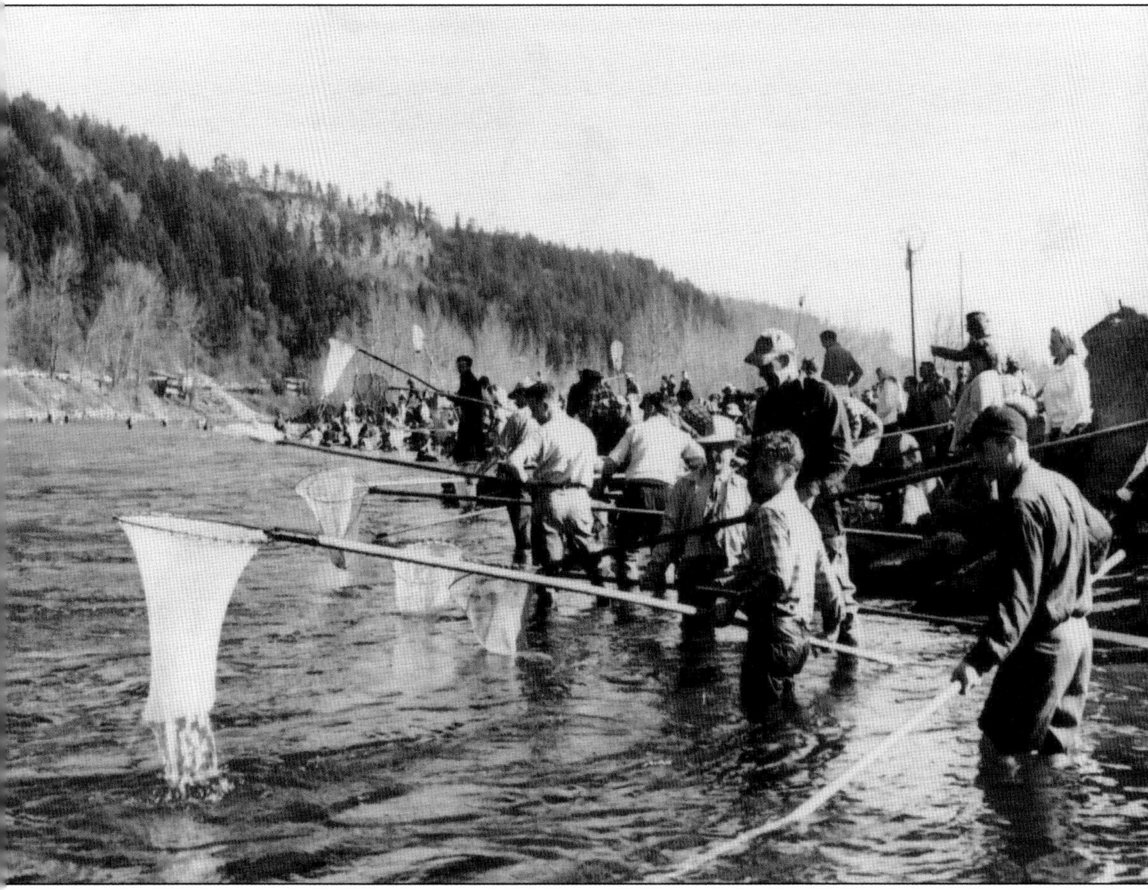

Dedicated smelt dippers line the banks and stand in the cold water of the Sandy River, dipping their nets again and again, lifting smelt into boxes, gunnysacks, and buckets. After a day of dipping, some could barely lift their arms from fatigue. Heart attacks were common. Some of the smelt were sent to Sea World and some fed soldiers during World War II. (Photograph courtesy of Len Otto.)

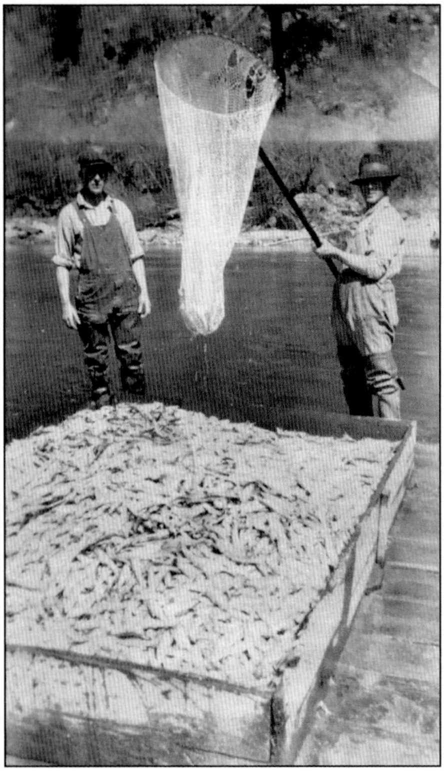

Flat-bottom boats were used by commercial smelt fishermen. Most of the large boats were built with plywood and powered by outboard motors. They could hold up to five tons of smelt. The largest commercial catch of fish occurred in 1945 when 1,393,098 pounds were taken.

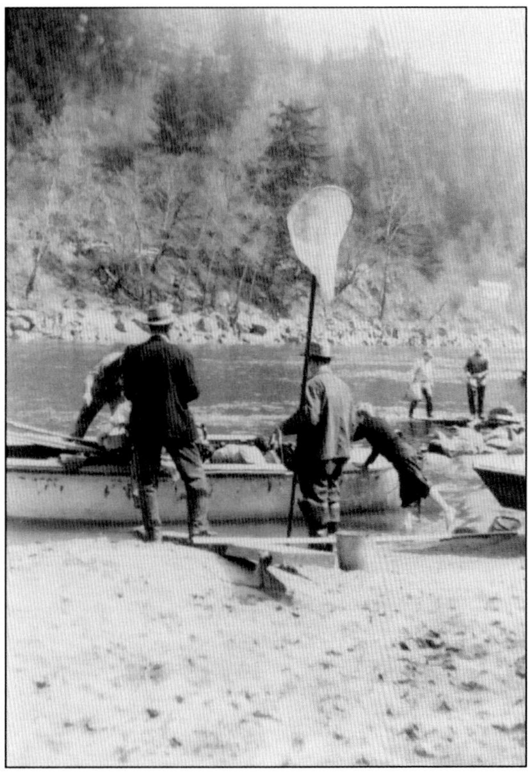

Smelt dippers were diehard fishermen, but they had a sense of humor about it. One man commented, "I'm suffering from a terrible malady. It is known as 'toomuchsmeltdippingitis'. Symptoms include sore back and arms, a lame shoulder from carrying heavy buckets of fish, and a damaged ego from friends who refuse a gift of fishy offerings."

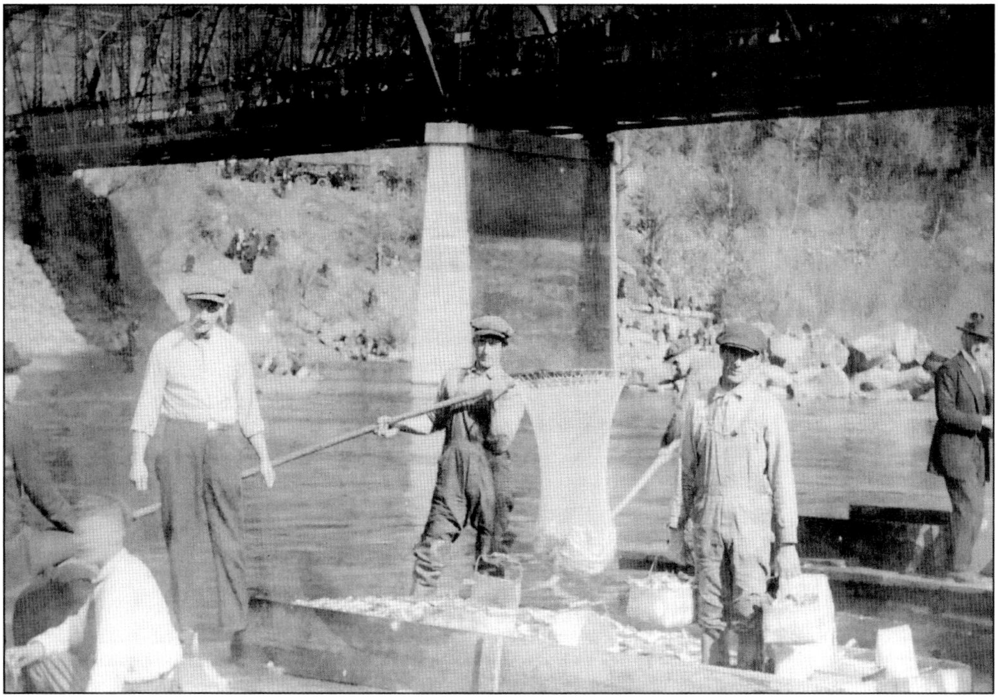

Commercial smelt fishermen stand in waders, netting smelt. The dippers worked over the stern of the moored boat, dipping upstream to downstream and then swinging the net into the boat and dumping the smelt, which were loaded into wooden boxes and hauled by horses to the railroad depot for shipment.

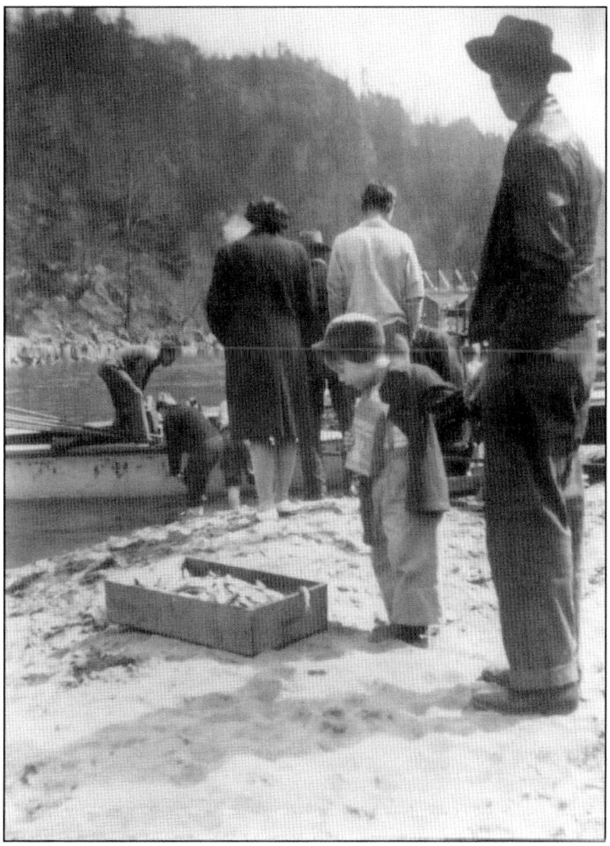

A likely future smelt dipper looks at a box of smelt lying on the bank of the river. Part of the appeal of the event was the camaraderie that developed among the dippers, often fueled by beer, good-natured rivalry, and adrenalin.

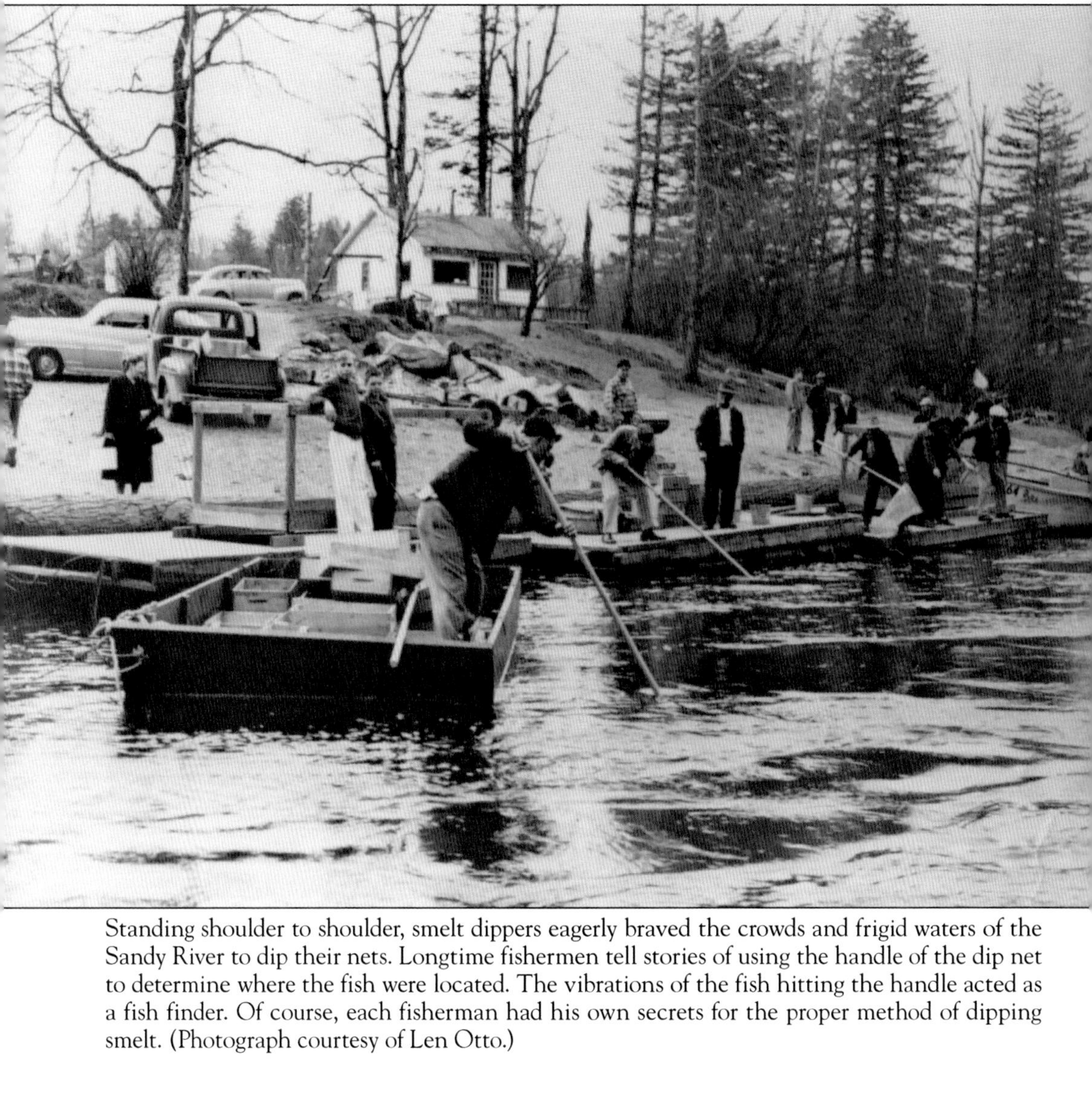

Standing shoulder to shoulder, smelt dippers eagerly braved the crowds and frigid waters of the Sandy River to dip their nets. Longtime fishermen tell stories of using the handle of the dip net to determine where the fish were located. The vibrations of the fish hitting the handle acted as a fish finder. Of course, each fisherman had his own secrets for the proper method of dipping smelt. (Photograph courtesy of Len Otto.)

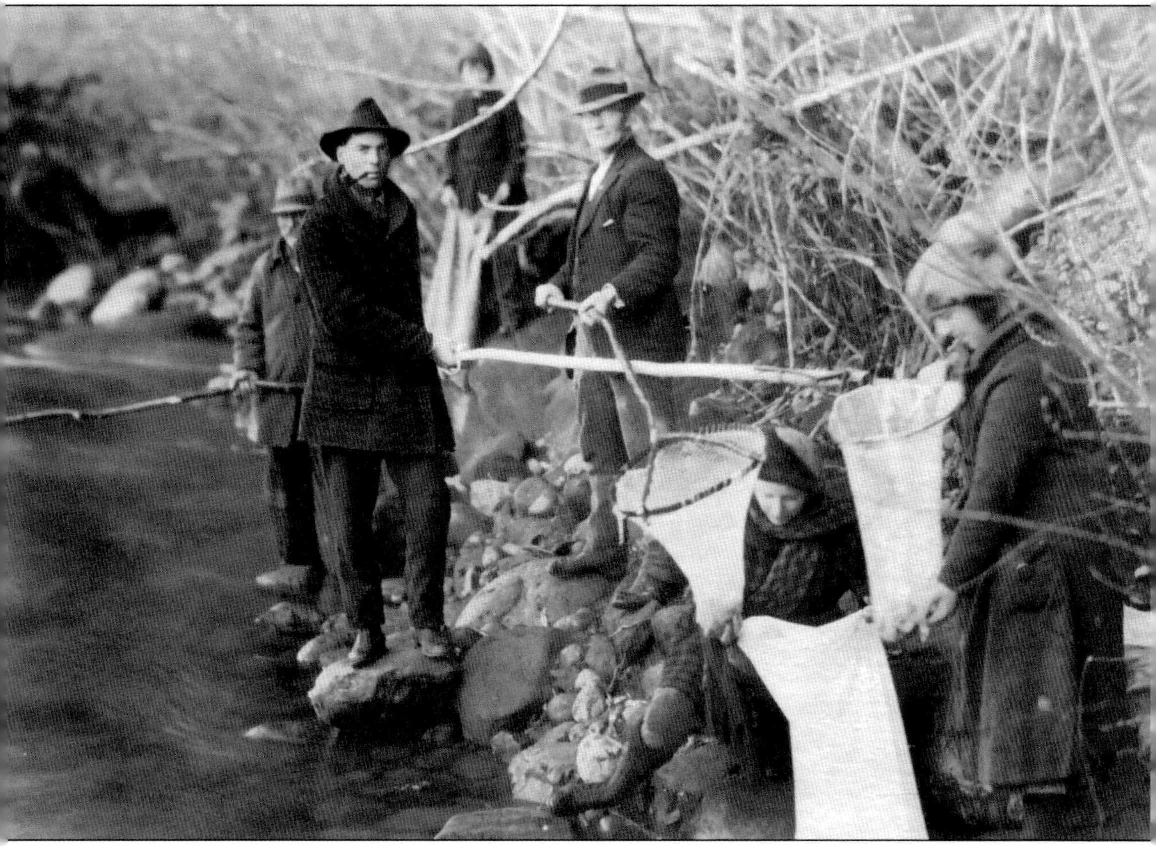

This photograph of a family of smelt dippers was taken by prominent Troutdale citizen and professional photographer Harlow Douglass. The women seem to be in charge of removing the smelt from the nets. Their heavy coats, hats, and scarves suggest that it is a cold day for the dipping, which was typical for the time of year when the smelt runs occurred.

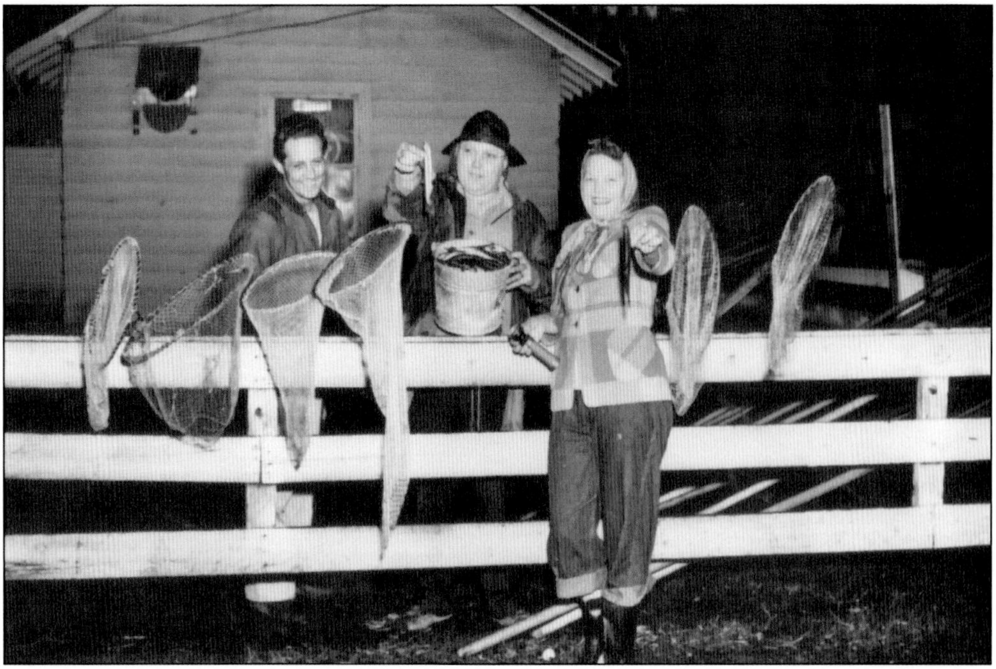

Partygoers at the Rustic Inn during the 1948 smelt run mug for the camera by holding multiple dipping nets and a bucket of the small fish. The caption on the back of the photograph reads, "Want to rent a net?" Part of the appeal of the smelt run was the festive atmosphere that accompanied it.

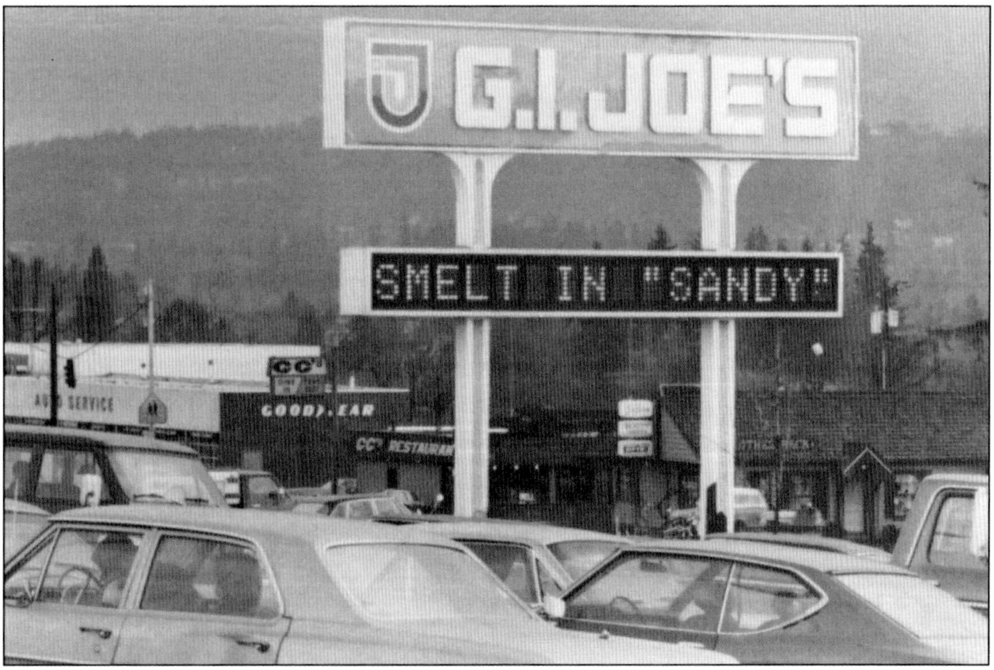

When the smelt season began, area fishing and sports stores announced the run on billboards. Avid smelt dippers scooped up nets, boots, and any other equipment they needed, making it a popular sales event for area merchants and entrepreneurs who set up concession stands along the river.

Citizens compete in a smelt-eating contest in a community-sponsored "Smelt Fest." This man eats his way through a plate of smelt while his official "counter" records each fish consumed. The all-time record for the eating contest was 150 smelt.

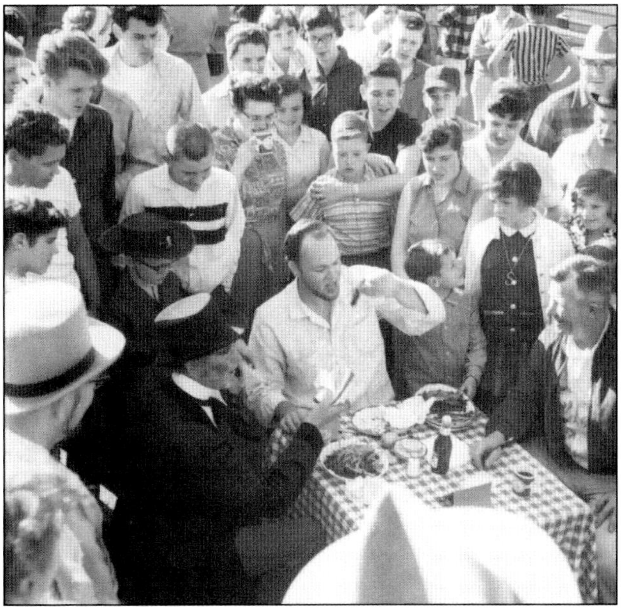

The contest results board listed the time it took the contestants to eat the smelt and the point at which each man dropped out. Notice the winner ate a total of 84 smelt for a plaque, a full stomach, and bragging rights.

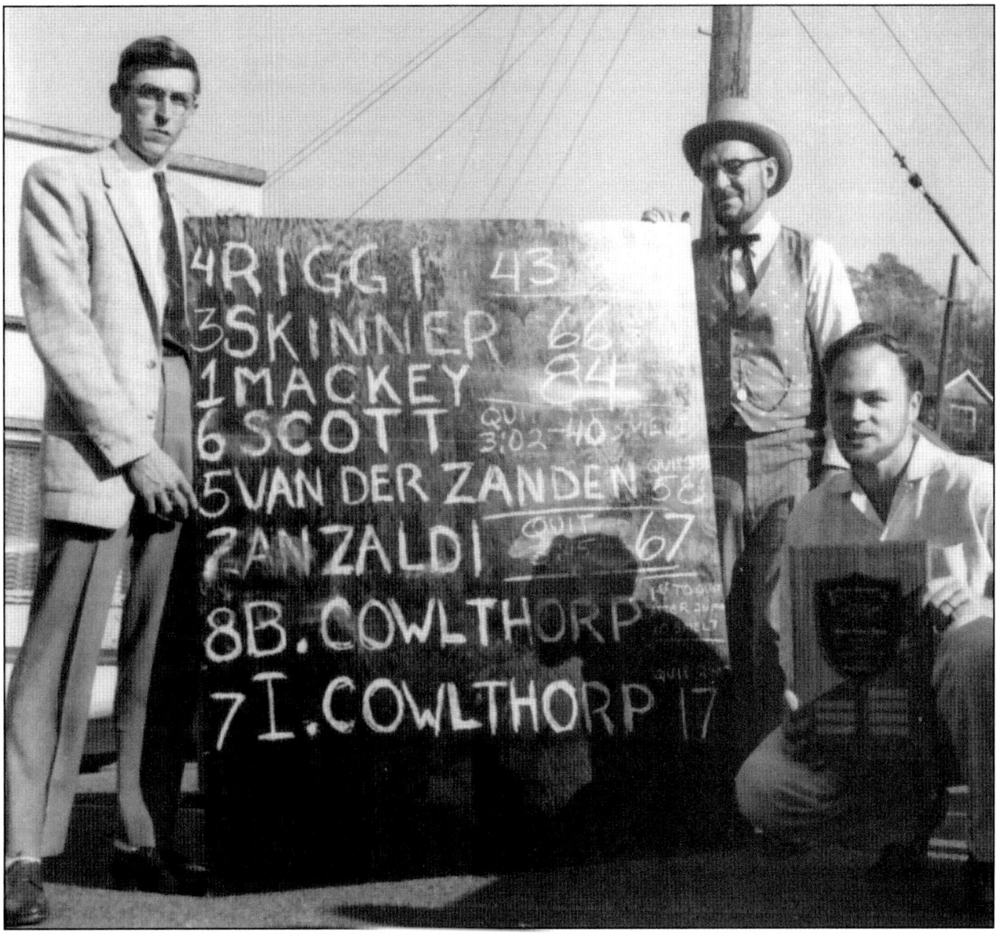

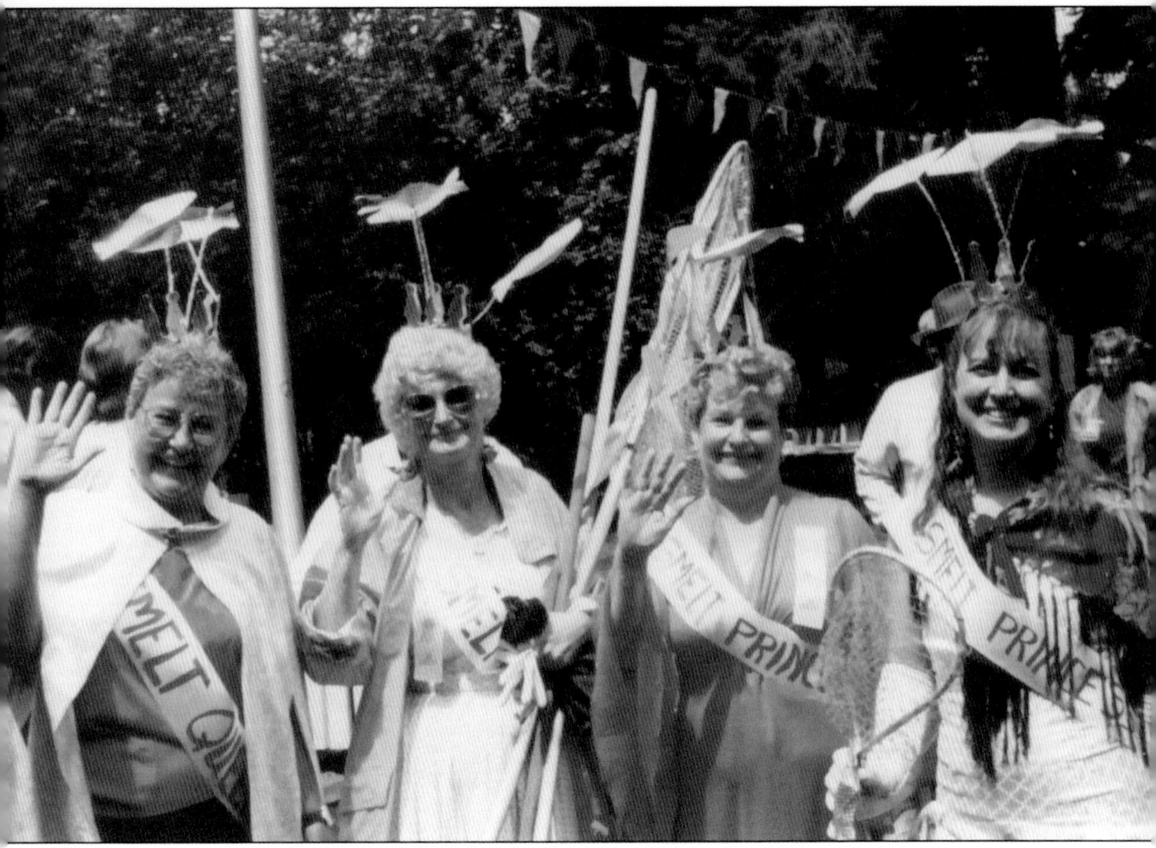

Although the last record smelt run was in 1974, in the late 1990s, the Troutdale Historical Society recreated its Smelt Queen and court for a Troutdale Summerfest parade. Smelt Queen Sharon Nesbit (left) and her court, (from left to right) Jean Holman, Dorothy Sturges, and Cathy Hamme, pose with dip nets and a cooler. Crowns with smelt "swimming" above their heads complete their royal raiment.

Nine

THE COUNTY POOR FARM, EDGEFIELD

Before social security, welfare, and Medicare, there were few options for sheltering people who had little income or means to support themselves. In the early 1900s, social advocates sought a solution for long-term care for those in need.

Oregon initially assigned local counties the task of providing care for paupers in 1858. In response, Multnomah County opened Hillside Farm on Portland's west side in 1868 to house those who had fallen on hard times. In 1910, county authorities and local charitable organizations decided to relocate the facility to an area of eastern Multnomah County near present-day Troutdale.

The 345-acre enterprise was named the Multnomah County Poor Farm and opened its doors to 211 residents in November 1911. They arrived by railroad boxcars, passenger cars, and trolleys. The cost of the facility was $100,000, barely enough to buy a modest one-family home in today's money, but the building boasted clean and cheerful wards, a dining room with wooden floors, and a separate tuberculosis hospital. To many of the residents of the farm, this offered the best housing they had ever experienced.

Residents who were able-bodied and ambitious enough to work were offered opportunities to earn a small paycheck by tending the farm's dairy herd, hog farm, and chicken flock. The meat and produce from the farm furnished food for not only the poor farm itself, but also the county jail, a hospital, and a juvenile home.

By the 1930s, the faces of poverty began to change with the Great Depression. The county facility experienced a swell of new residents who were casualties of the financial crash, but its size decreased as jobs opened up in World War II and the government introduced welfare and other programs. Over the next 15 to 20 years, the facility was renamed the Multnomah County Farm and Home and transformed into a nursing home for the aged and disabled.

By 1975, the home had begun to fall into disrepair, and the estimated $400,000 needed to bring the building up to minimal standards was more than could be raised. Over the next seven years, the residents were transferred to other nursing homes and facilities. In April 1982, the doors of the facility were closed.

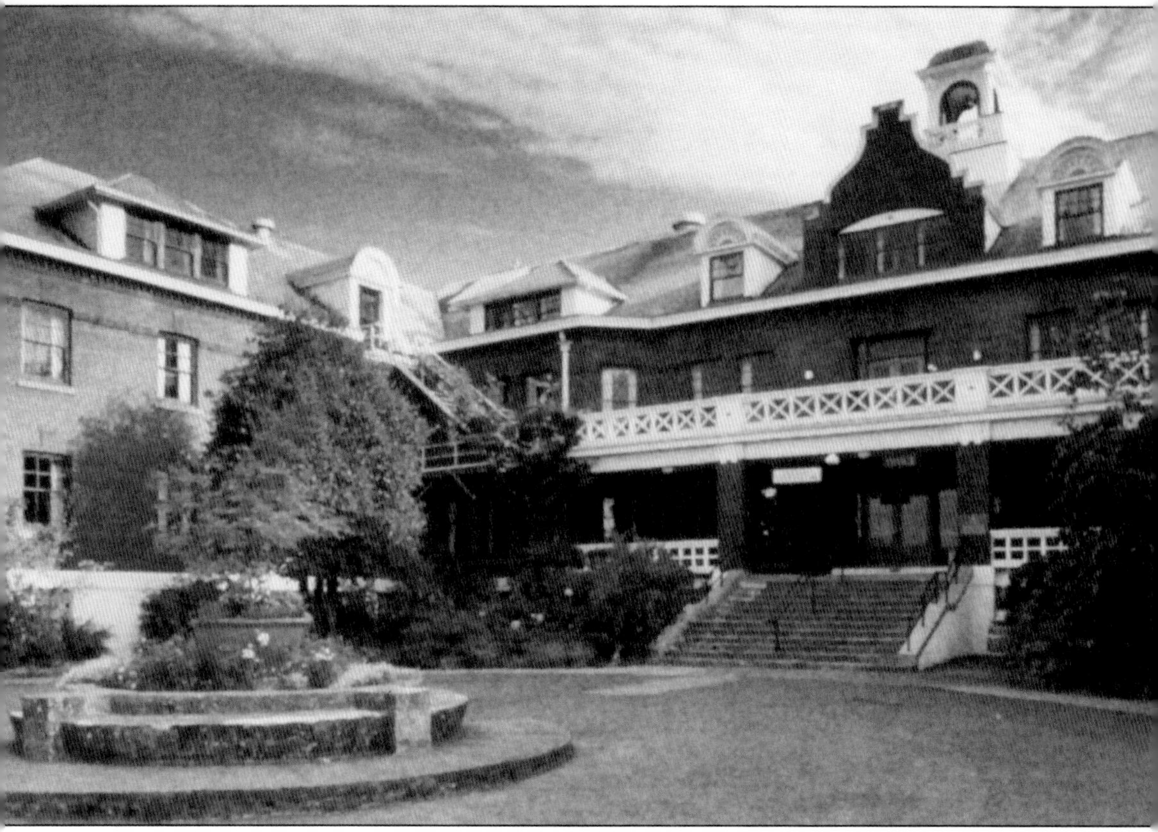

In 1911, Multnomah County commissioners decided to move the county poor farm from the West Hills area of Portland, near the zoo, to a parcel of land near Troutdale. Although the politicians at the time touted it as a "no-frills" structure, the building was far classier than any of the homes of the farmers and loggers in the Troutdale area. The main building had a cupola with a bell to summon the farm's workers from the field.

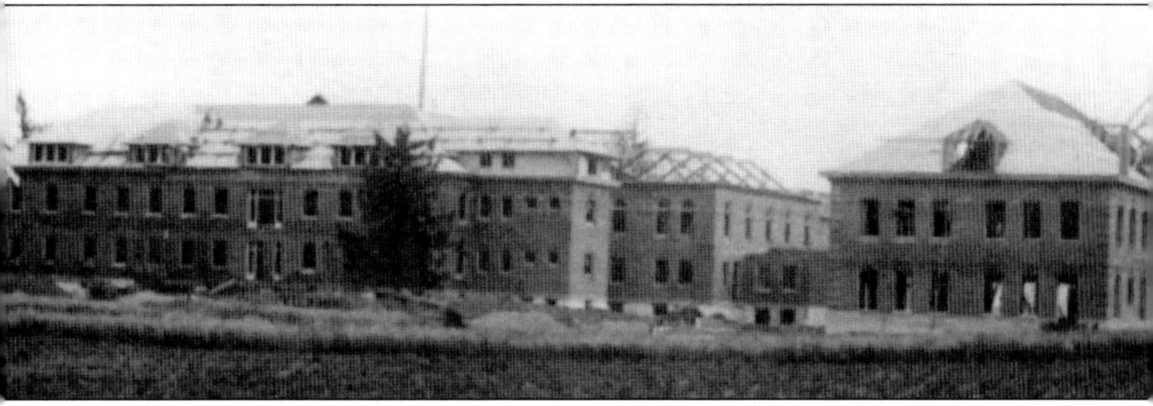

From its opening in 1911 until 1947, Edgefield was the largest county-funded relief institution in Oregon. An article in the March 12, 1912, issue of the *Oregonian* wrote, "A poor farm is asserted to be a cheerless institution at the best, but it is declared by those who have inspected the Multnomah farm that it comes nearer furnishing a real home for the unfortunate aged cripples and destitute persons than any other institution in the West." (Photograph courtesy of Steve Kenney.)

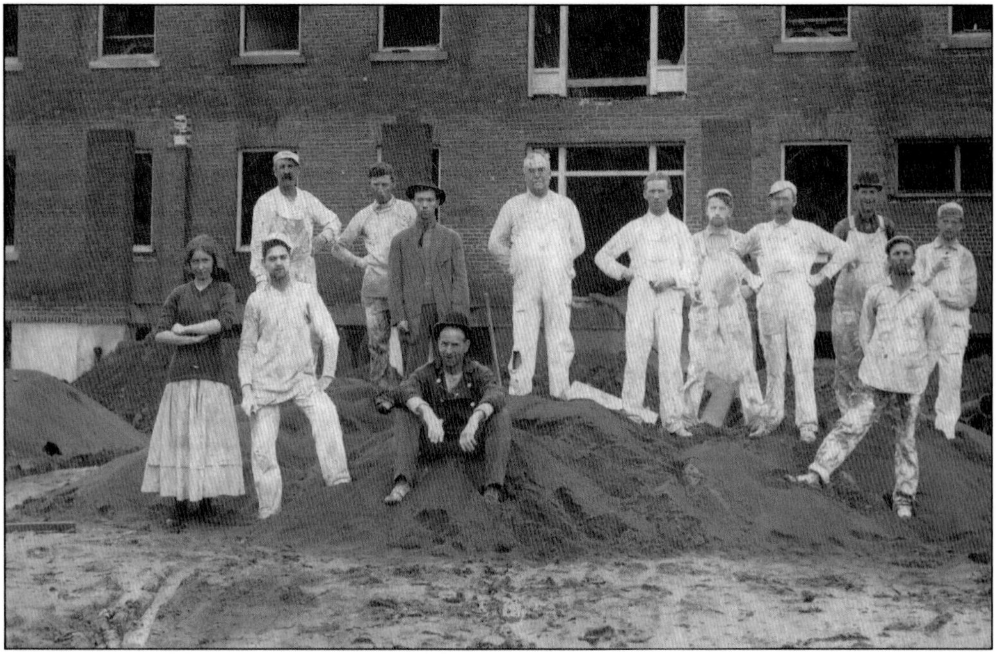

Hundreds of workers were hired, including this plastering crew, to construct the two-story Georgian-style building. Swedish carpenters and bricklayers helped construct the initial building. Once the facility opened, local residents found jobs there as service workers in the kitchen, laundry, wards, and office.

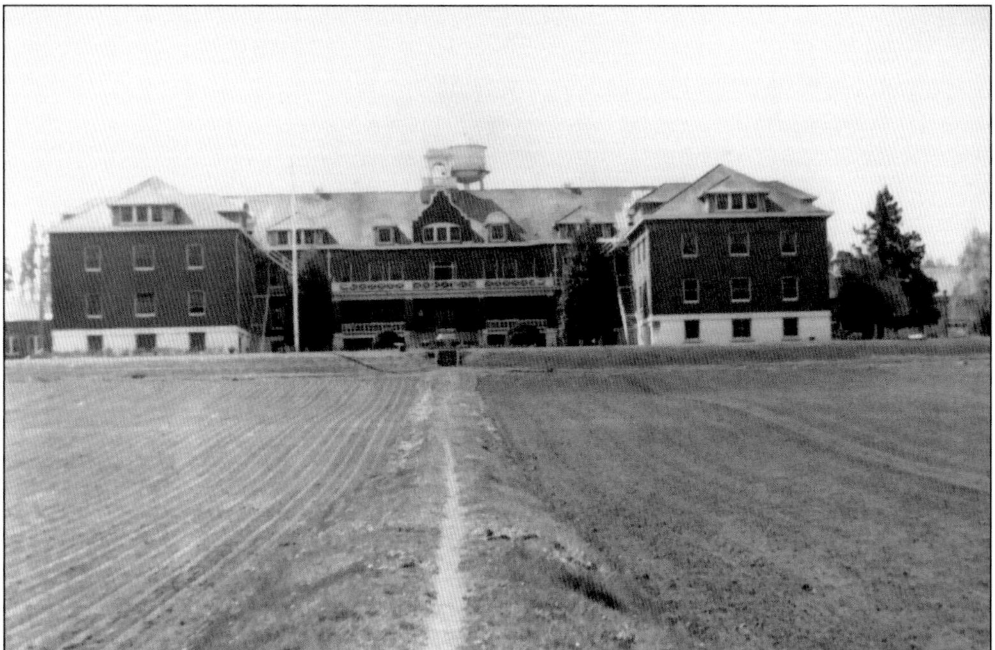

Erected in a large U-shape, Edgefield was built with bricks and roof shingles that were "guaranteed for the life of the building." Those original shingles remain in use today. Large windows allowed air and light into the facility. The *Gresham Outlook* reported that the new farm cost $100,000.

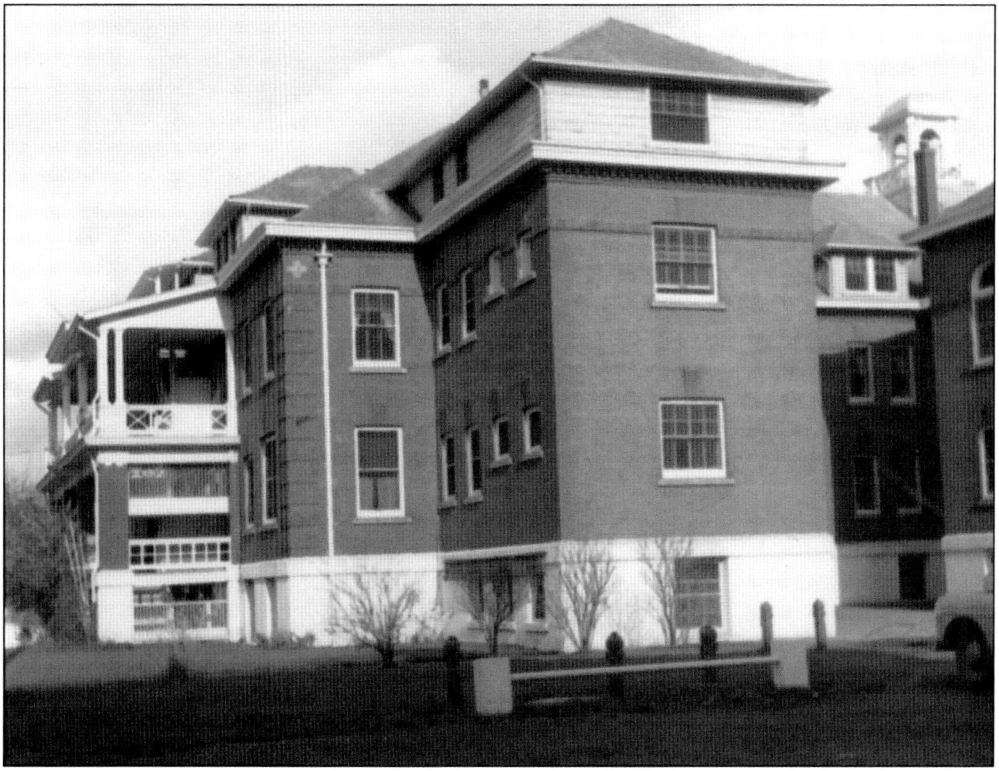

The county facility was also a working farm for able-bodied residents who wanted to earn some spending money. They helped tend the farm's Holstein cattle, Duroc hogs, and 645 hens and chicks or worked in the fields that furnished vegetables, fruit, and potatoes for the home.

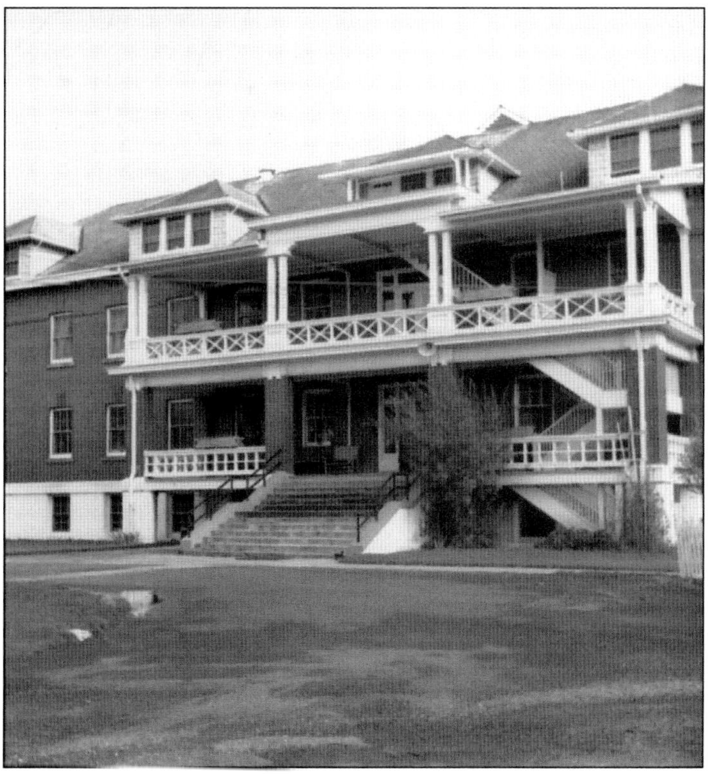

The main lodge of the county farm initially housed 211 people when it opened. Residents included loggers, domestics, hack drivers, deserted wives, a retired circus performer, and the well-known Frankie Baker of the "Frankie and Johnny Were Lovers" song.

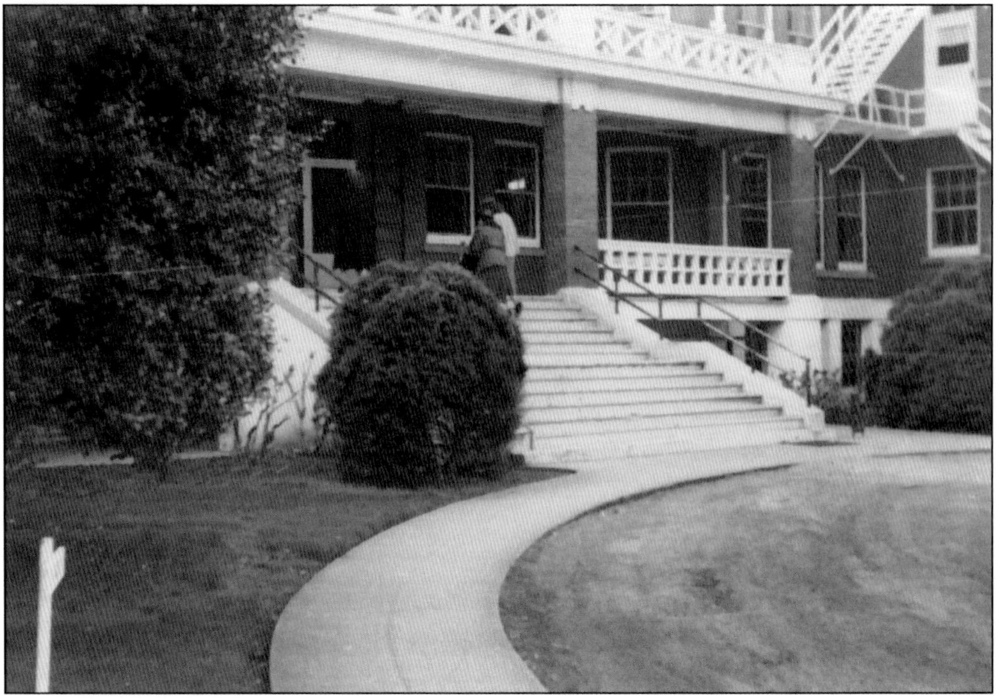

Those who lived at the poor farm were not just indigent; many residents suffered from typhoid, malaria, tuberculosis, and skin diseases or had alcohol habits. A separate building housed a tuberculosis hospital. Hospital emergency rooms in Portland frequently discharged patients with alcohol-related problems to the poor farm.

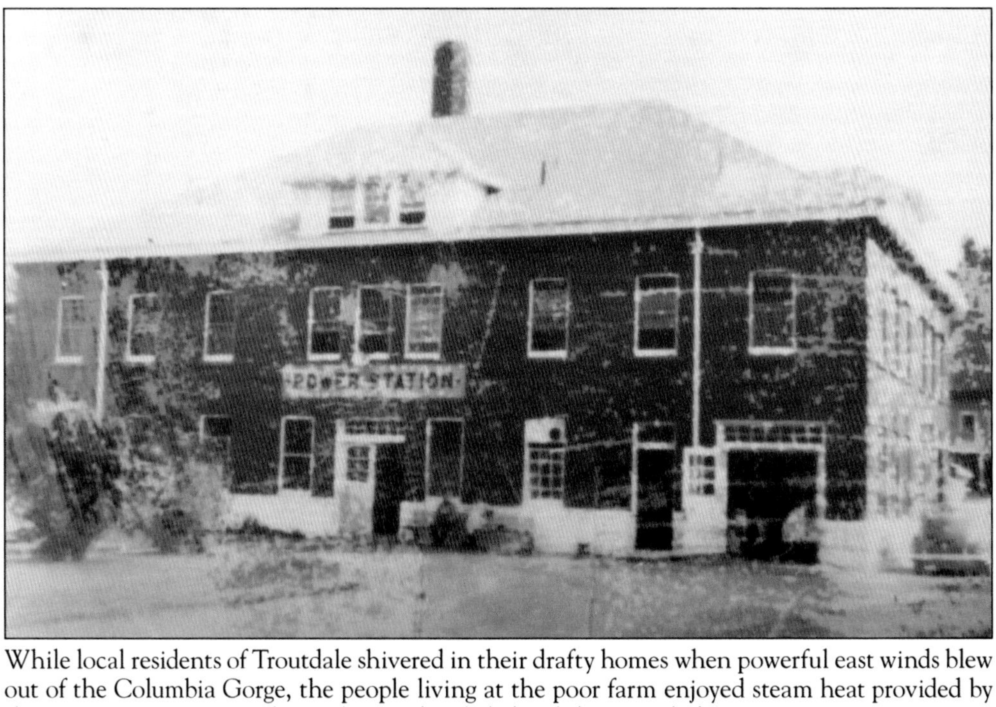

While local residents of Troutdale shivered in their drafty homes when powerful east winds blew out of the Columbia Gorge, the people living at the poor farm enjoyed steam heat provided by the on-site power station, located immediately behind the main lodge.

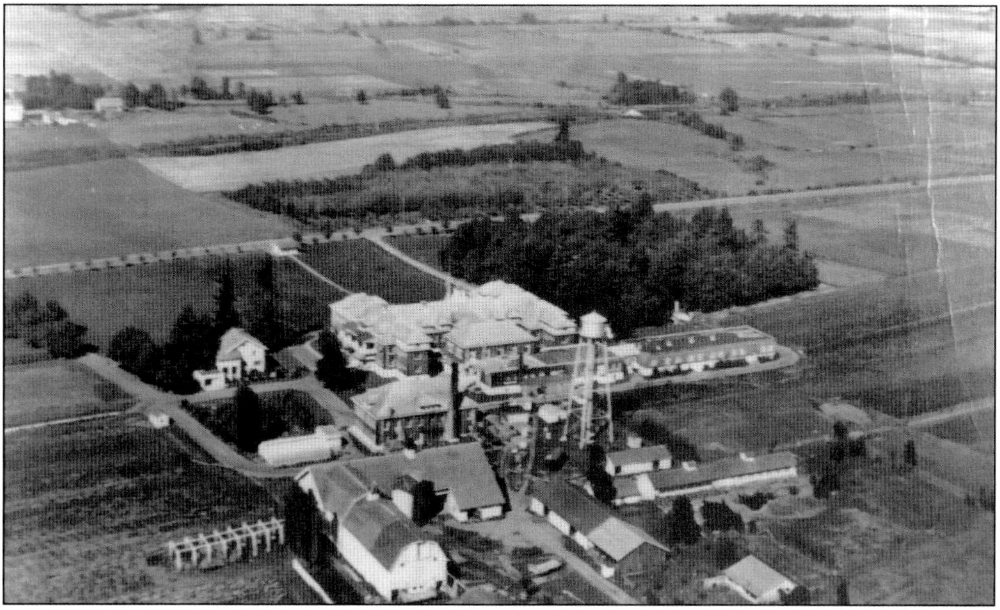

This aerial view of the Poor Farm when it was still in full operation in the early 1950s shows the 345 acres that held the main lodge, the tuberculosis hospital, the barns, the power station, the fields, gardens, and administrator's home. The farm was a self-sufficient facility.

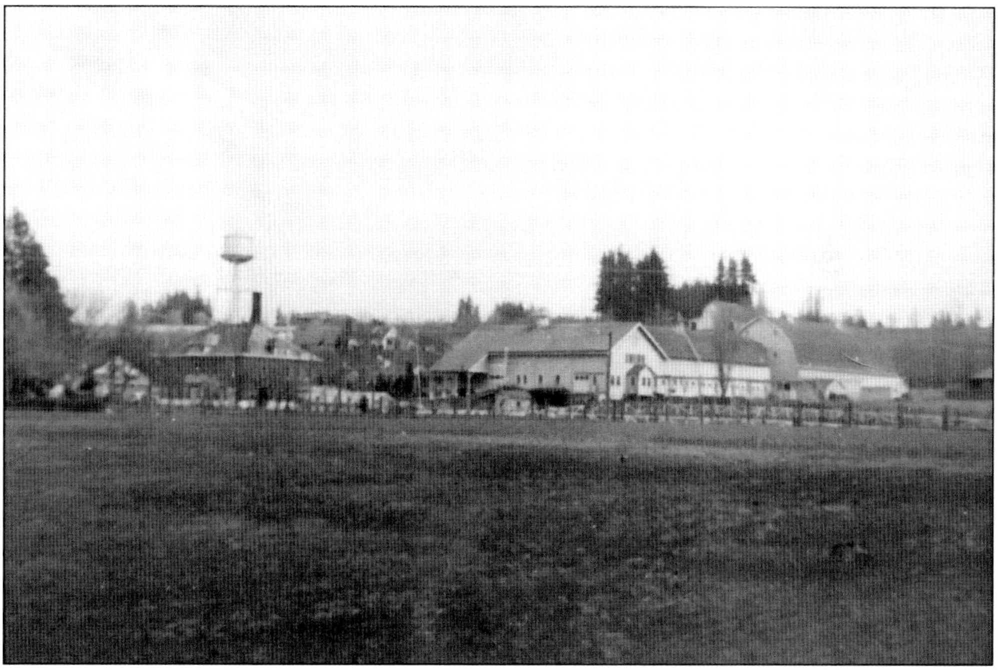

Much of the 345-acre farm was used as pasture and fields for growing hay and grain for the farm's 65 cattle that produced fresh milk. Additionally, 225 hogs were raised there, two of which were delivered each week to the kitchen to become breakfast or dinner for the residents.

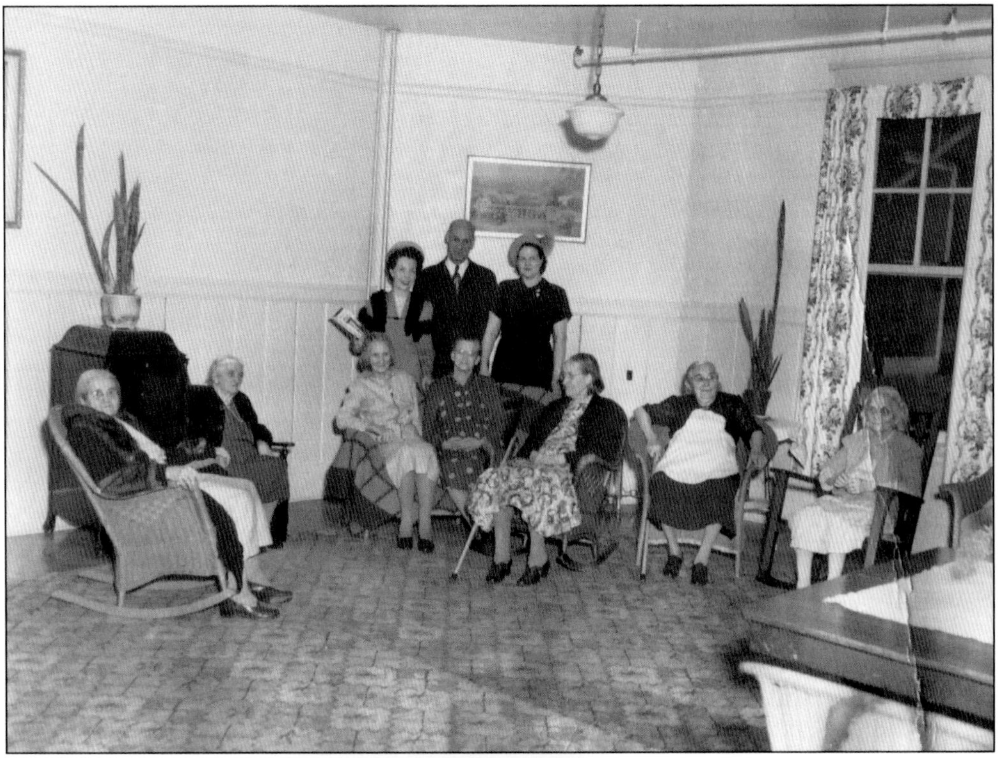

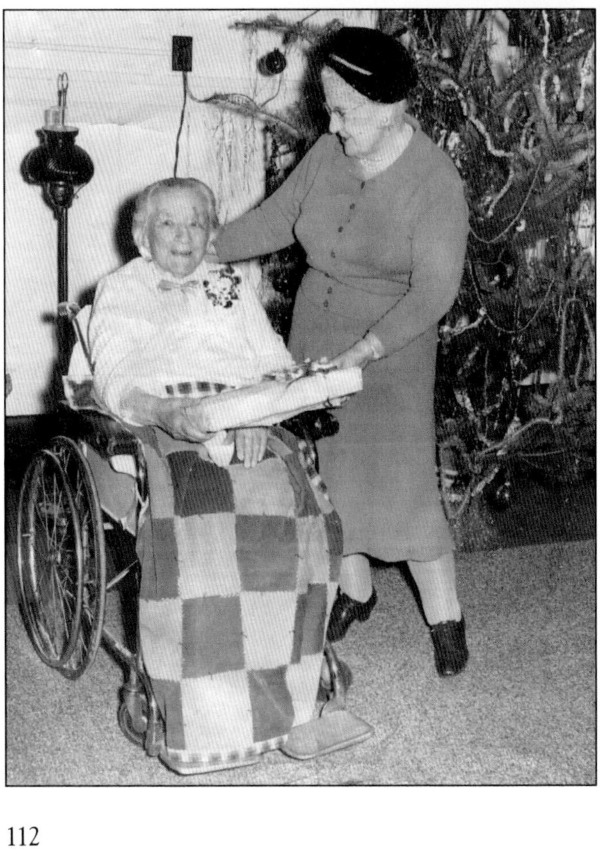

Elderly residents and some visitors sit in the women's parlor at the home. Some of the women who lived there have been immortalized by local artists in fanciful paintings that hang in various rooms and hallways of the current McMenamins' Edgefield.

Eve Meyer, the wife of local merchant Fred Meyer, visited 100-year-old Sarah Harris at Edgefield Manor at Christmas in 1959. The manor was a popular place for area philanthropic and civic-minded groups to do community service outreach work. Their participation helped sponsor some extra activities for the residents.

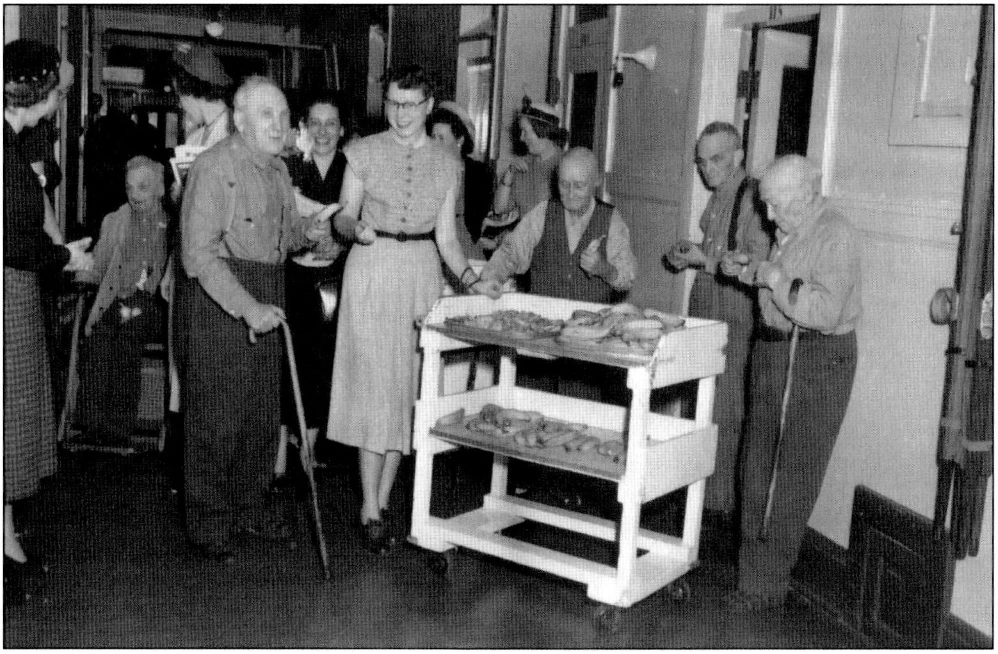

Members of the Beta Sigma Phi sorority serve fruit and rolls to some of the residents in this 1951 photograph. By this time, many of the residents were elderly, and in the 1950s, "Edgefield Manor" became a demonstration project to help stroke patients walk again in the rehabilitation center there.

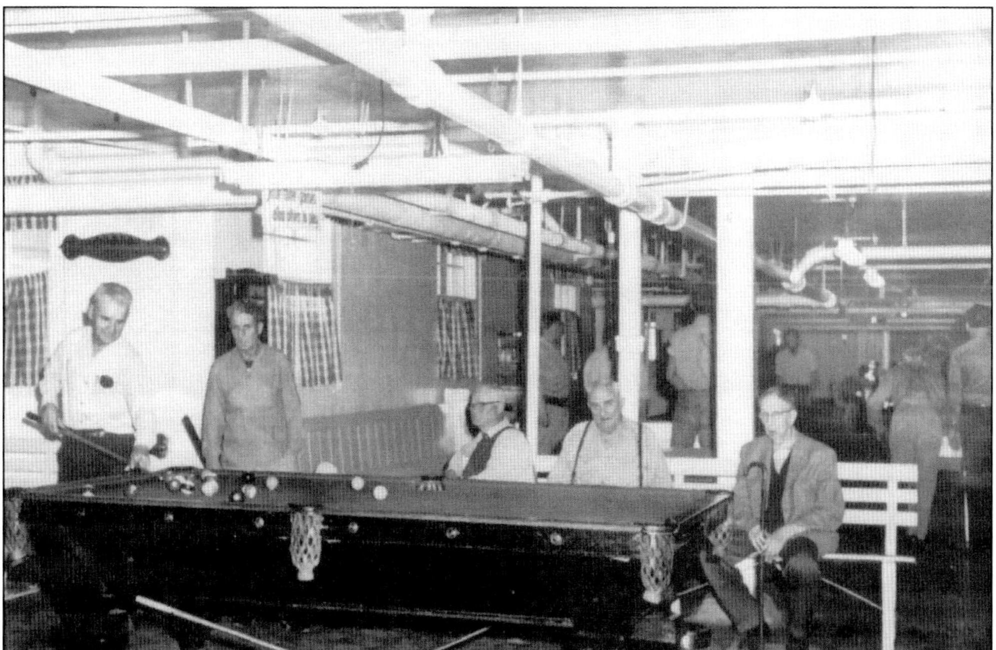

Pool sharks line the pool table in the basement of the Multnomah County poor farm. The son of the farm manager became an accomplished pool player under the tutelage of the old men who circled the green felt tables. Workers at the farm said it was "like a family" there.

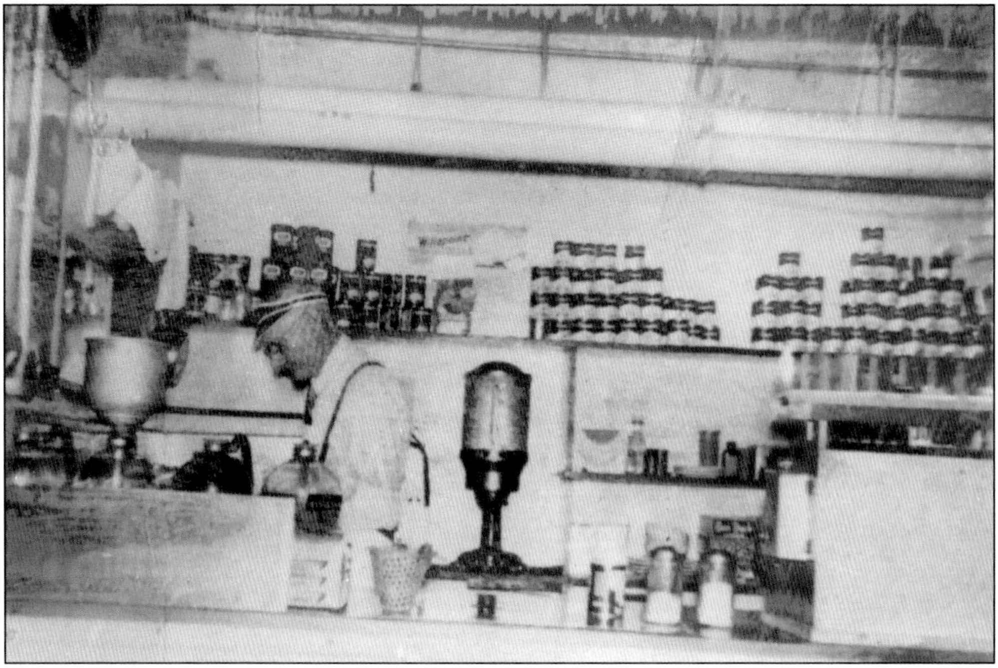

A basement canteen area for residents, staff, farm workers, and even children of the staff offered a place to buy snacks or the Campbell's soups displayed on the shelves. A can of pipe tobacco could be bought there as well, and coffee was a nickel a cup.

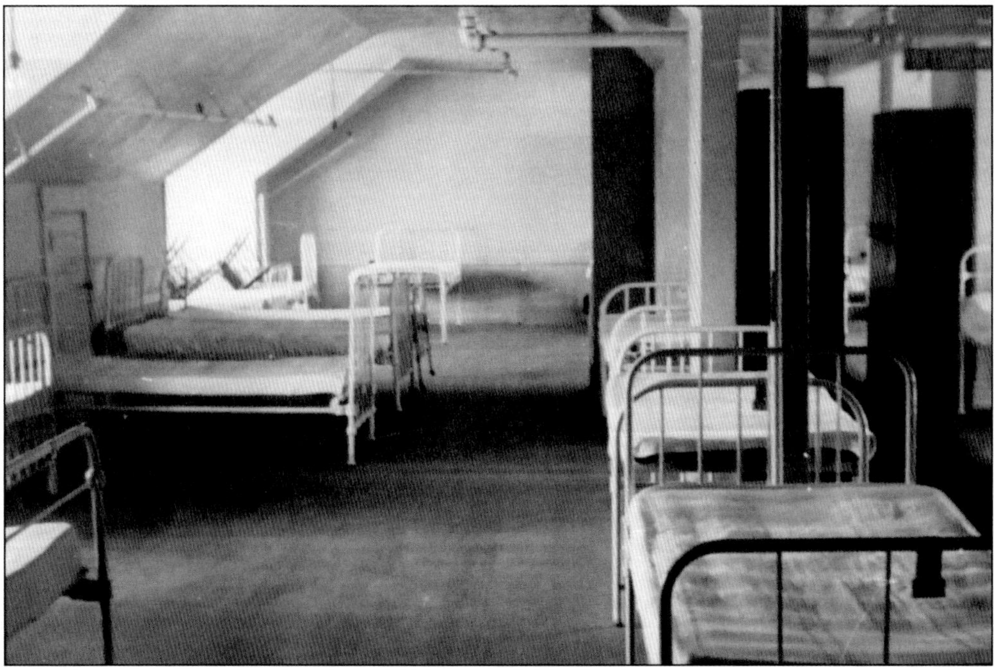

An upstairs dormitory-style room housing iron bedsteads with plain bed linens shows the sparse style of the institution. By the late 1930s, the facility began to fill with those seeking shelter from the Great Depression. The dorm rooms were pressed into service as the population soared to more than 600 people.

Ten

Having Fun in Troutdale

Every community, be it a major metropolitan area or a rural burg, creates its own enrichment and celebrations to mark its uniqueness. For a small town encamped on the convergence of two rivers and buffeted by gusty winds barreling through the Columbia River Gorge, Troutdale has figuratively put on its Wellingtons and lifted its skirts to embrace its sylvan locale and lifestyle.

Like most small towns, Troutdale's citizens help define its culture. Its early proximity to industries ranging from railroading to lumbering to meatpacking made Troutdale a sometimes lusty version of a frontier town. Saloons lined its main street prior to and after prohibition despite the objections of local wives and politicians. Regulations and ordinances in early Troutdale mirrored the rowdiness in the village: prohibitions against carrying concealed weapons, roaming the streets after midnight, rolling dice for drinks, selling liquor to minors, and throwing fireworks in the city streets were on the books as early as 1908. Women helped govern the town shortly after they were granted the right to vote.

Copies of local papers over the decade discussed Troutdale's society in the usual newsy notes about bridge clubs, church socials, county fairs, and family dinners held in honor of visiting relatives. However, on a more organized level, Troutdale boasted a garden club and a Ladies Aid Society for the women and baseball teams and a rod and gun club for the men.

Early culture included sheep-butchering contests and tent revivals down near the river as well as winding bandages or making peanut brittle for local soldiers serving overseas in one of the wars. Local band performances and dances sponsored by a neighboring community stepped up the pace of life for those who wanted something livelier than church circles and PTA meetings. Children had the Sandy River and a nearby lake to swim in during the summer and plenty of mountain slopes to ski down in the winter.

After the Ford Model T was introduced in 1908, Americans wanted to travel. By the end of World War I, the American government began to tout tourism with the slogan "See America First." Early travelers often camped in a newly invented canvas motor camper that was self-sufficient in areas that had not yet been developed to accommodate adventurous excursions to places like Oregon's Mount Hood.

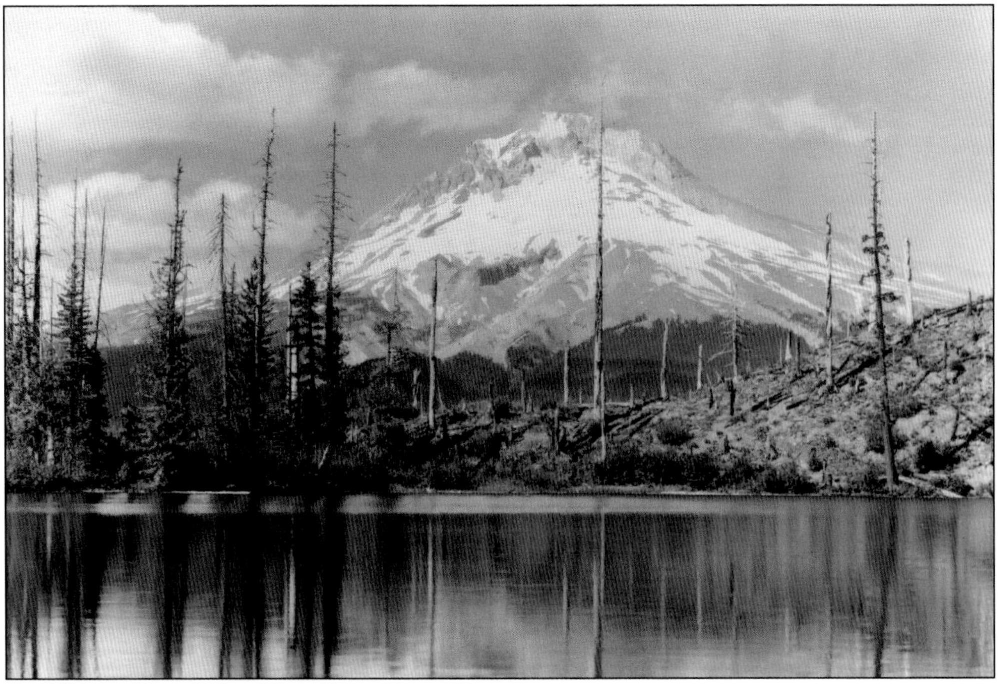

This Harlow Douglass photograph from the mid-1920s shows the beauty of Mount Hood and Mirror Lake, which drew outdoor enthusiasts during the golden age of motor touring. Although traveling by automobile was relatively new, people began to drive, hike, and camp in wilderness areas.

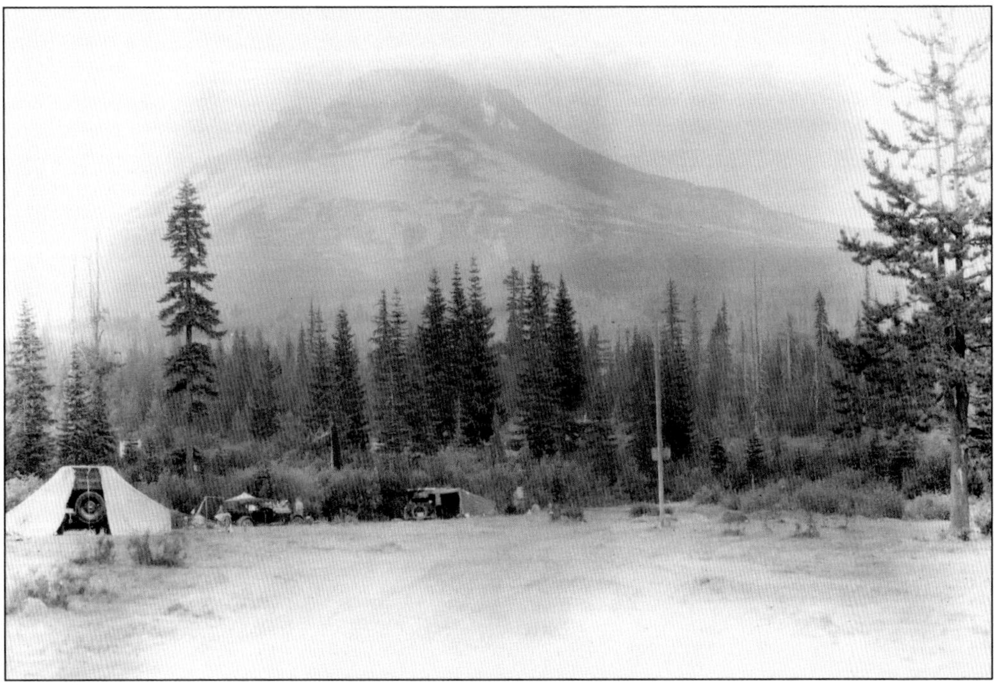

These campers have set up their tent in a relatively barren spot. Few facilities offered amenities for campers at the time; however, a unit containing all the necessary gear for roadside camping could be purchased for about $345 in 1925. The tent could be attached to the side of the car.

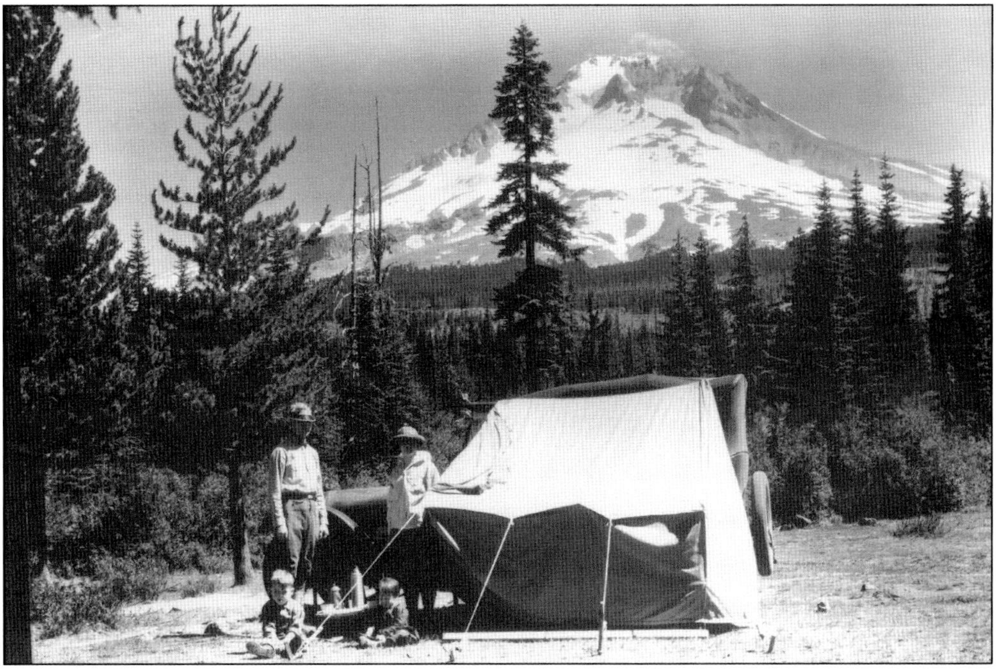

A family pitches a tent beside their automobile at Government Camp in 1925 with Mount Hood in the background. The first auto camp trailers fit into a four-foot-by-six-foot box and contained everything from folding buckets to evaporative canvas refrigerators and bathtubs.

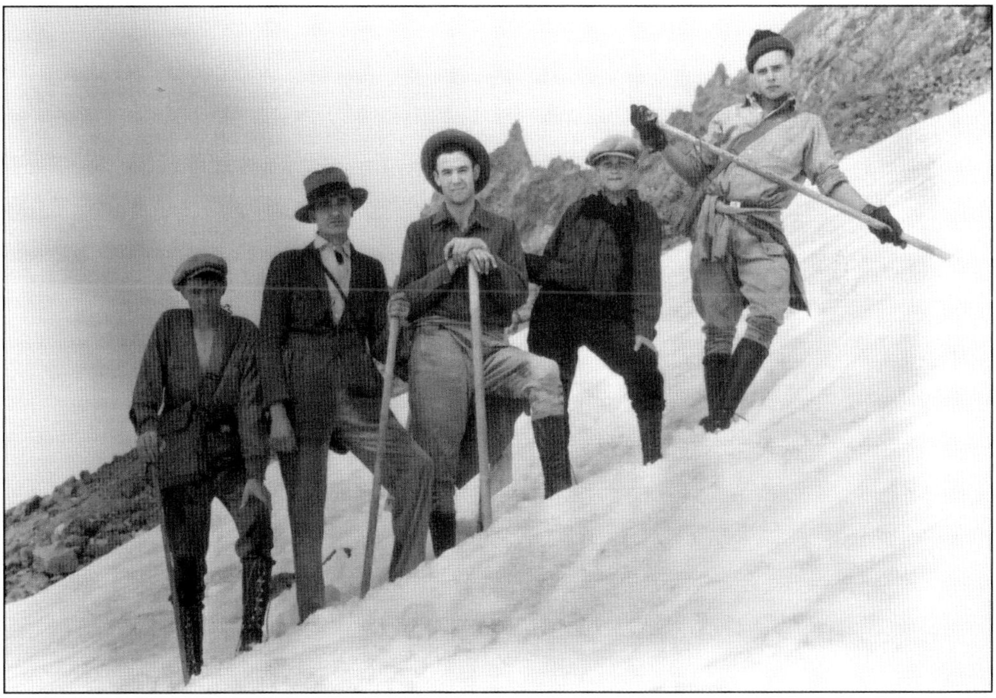

Troutdale photographer Harlow Douglass captured this shot of five mountain climbers on the slopes of Mount Hood. The advent of the automobile made day trips into the Cascade Mountains east of Troutdale possible for climbers, hikers, and campers.

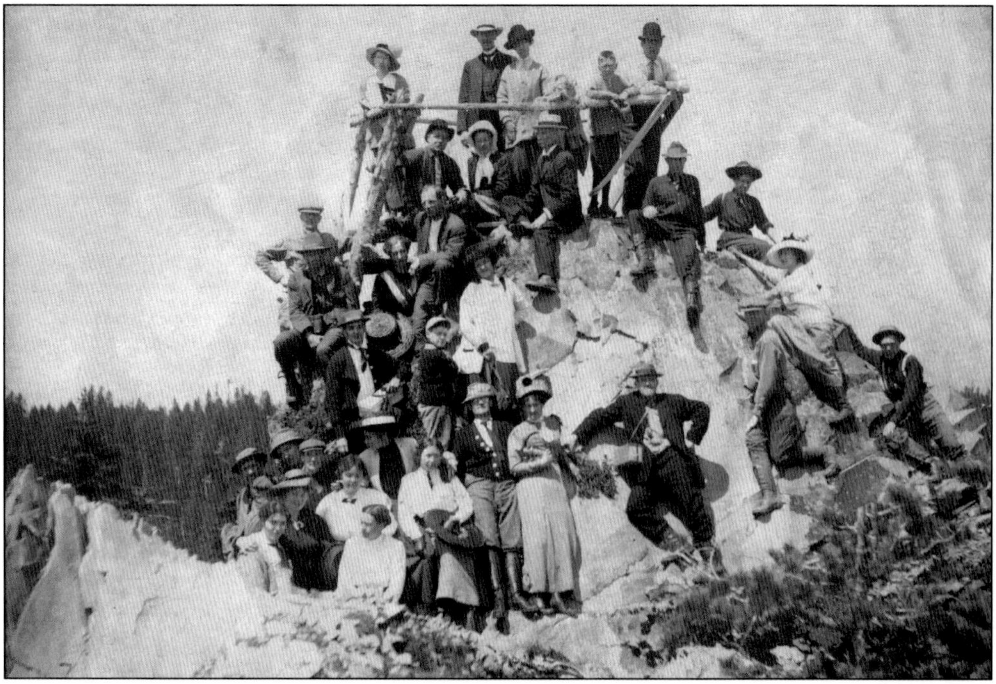

A group of the Mazamas Club, a mountain climbing group established in 1894 in Portland, poses here for a photograph on the summit of Larch Mountain, east of Troutdale, in 1912. Notice that the women were all wearing dresses and hiking boots for the climb.

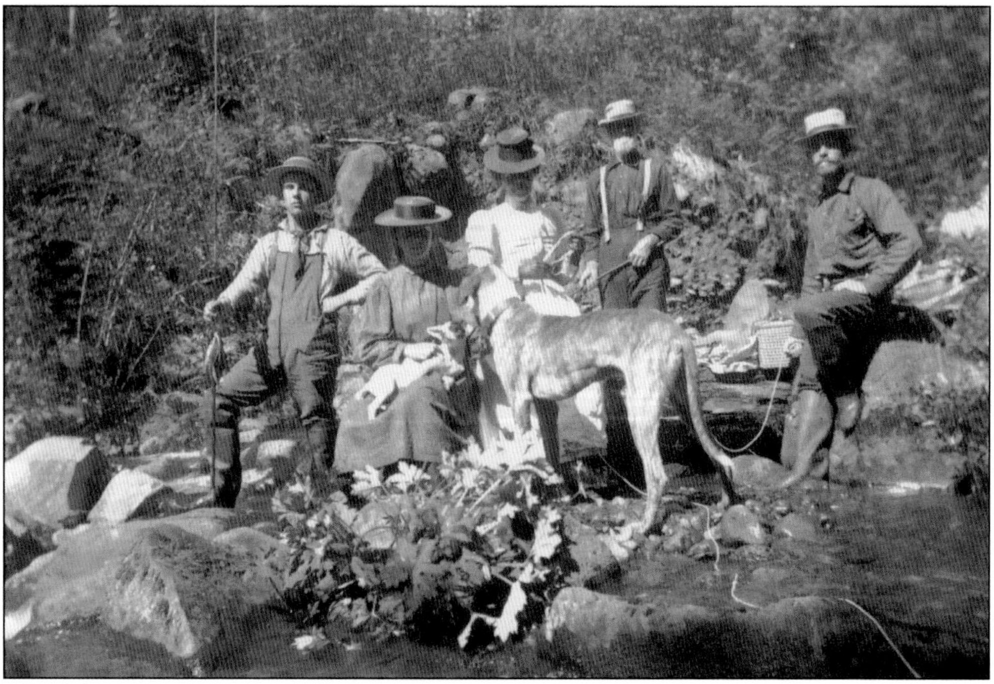

This fishing excursion at Gordon Creek, near Corbett, shows Lenore Williams and her family with her fox terrier, Gypsy, on her lap and her staghound, Major, standing. The man at the far right holds the bulb, attached to a long wire, to trip the camera.

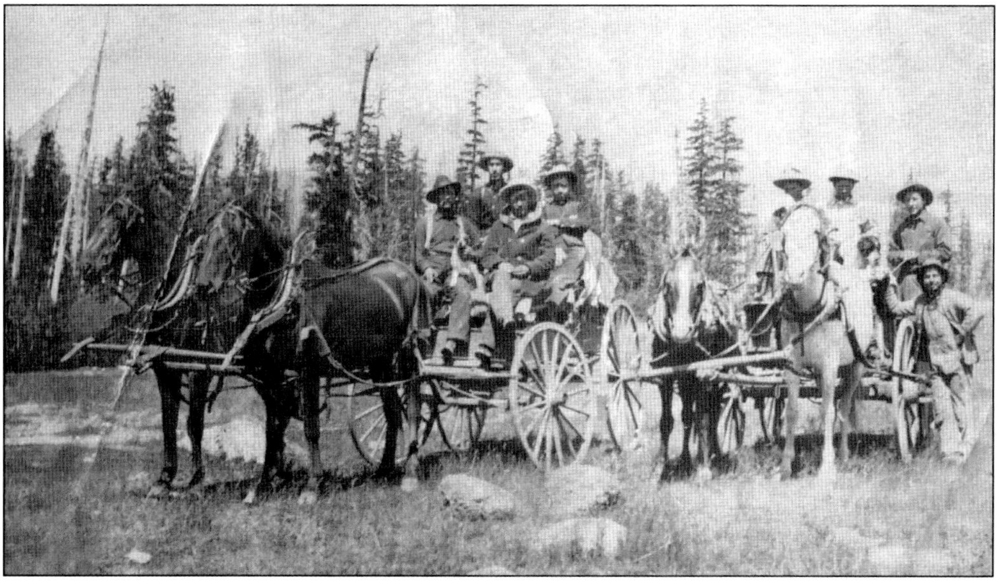

Two wagonloads of men set out on a camping trip along with their dogs in this 1920s photograph, which could have been taken straight out of a William Faulkner novel. Some of the people in the photograph are members of the Harlow family.

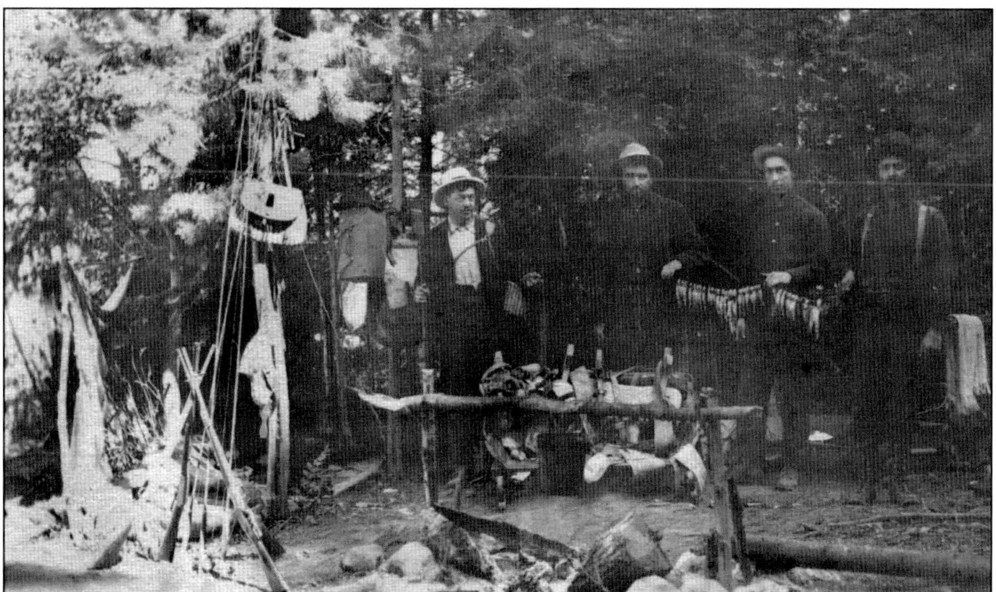

A group of men poses at their campsite on a hunting and fishing trip in about 1910. A wagon seat loaded with animal traps lies in front of the men, who are holding their stringers of fish.

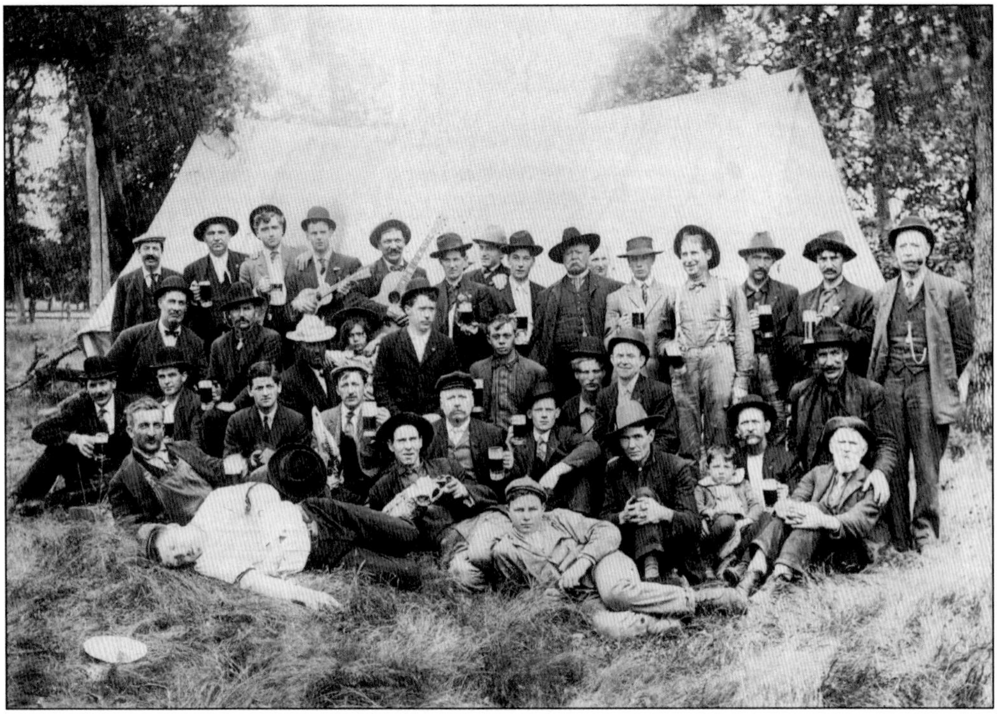

The Union Meat Company hosted barbecues with plenty of beer in the late 1880s and the early 1900s. Guitar and ukulele players and beer kept attendees happy—perhaps too happy in the case of the gentleman who appears to be passed out on the grass.

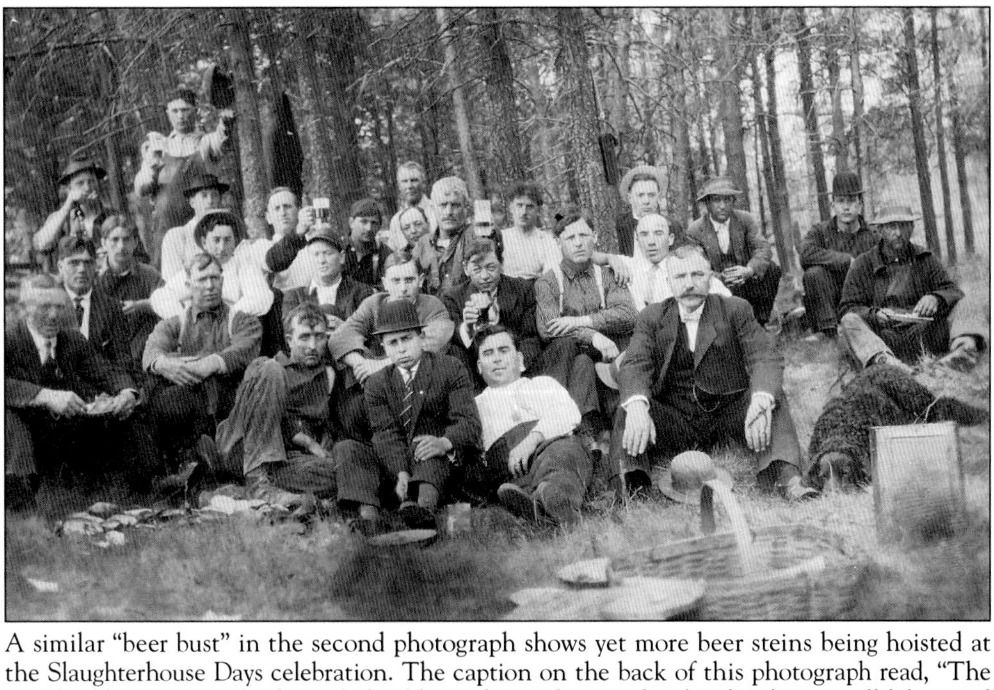

A similar "beer bust" in the second photograph shows yet more beer steins being hoisted at the Slaughterhouse Days celebration. The caption on the back of this photograph read, "The Good Old Days." Local saloons helped keep the workers at the slaughterhouse well lubricated between barbecues.

Hikers climb the trail at Eagle Creek. The extensive network of hiking trails in the Columbia River Gorge, financed by Simon Benson, was designed around the series of waterfalls in the gorge to draw hikers and tourists to the area when the Historic Columbia River Highway opened in 1916.

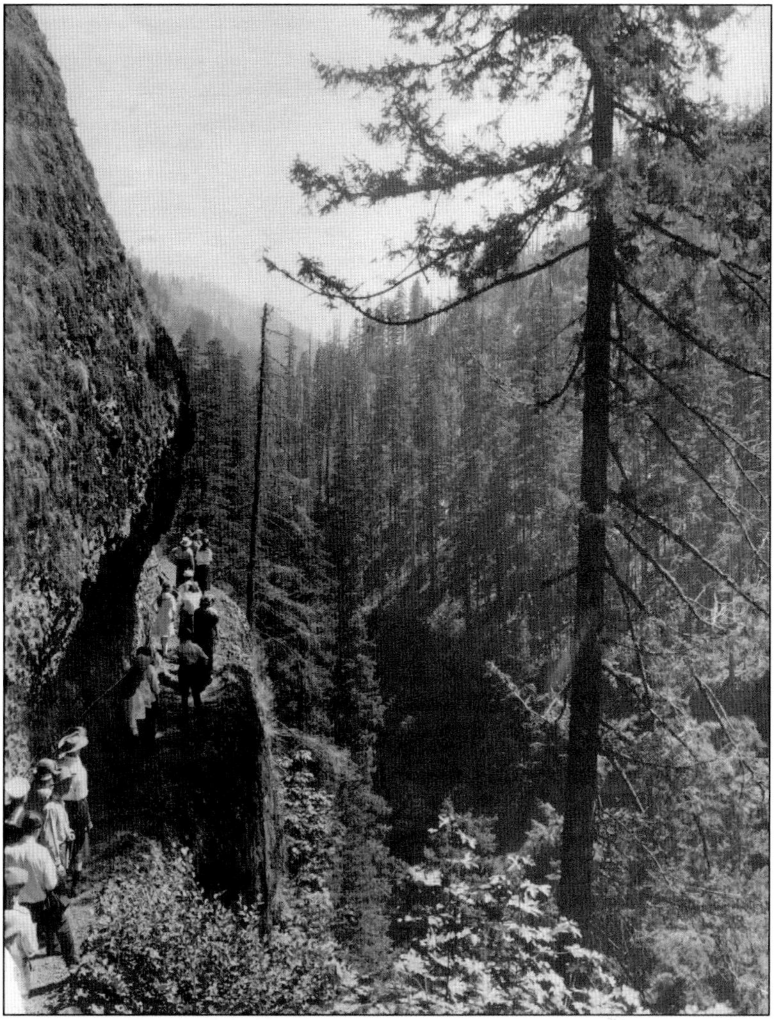

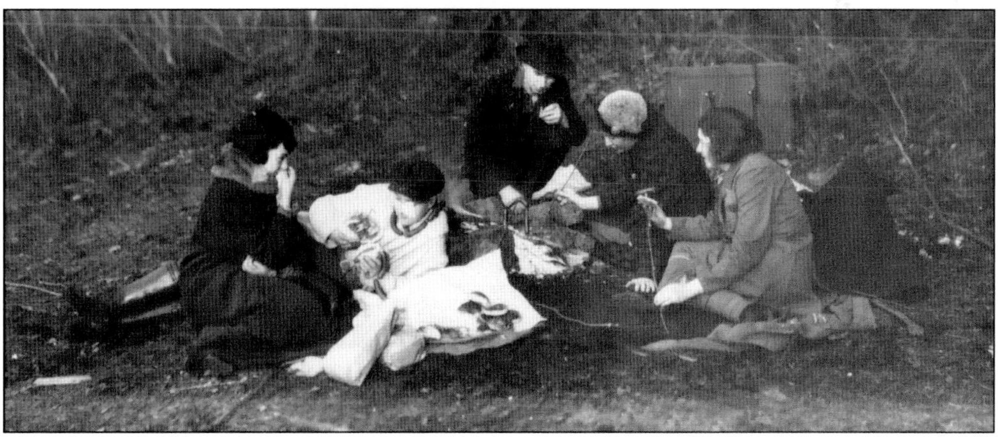

Harlow Douglass captured this intimate picnic with young people roasting hot dogs in a forested setting in the early 1900s. Chilly temperatures did not deter them, and the hefty wicker food hamper in the background indicates they came to party.

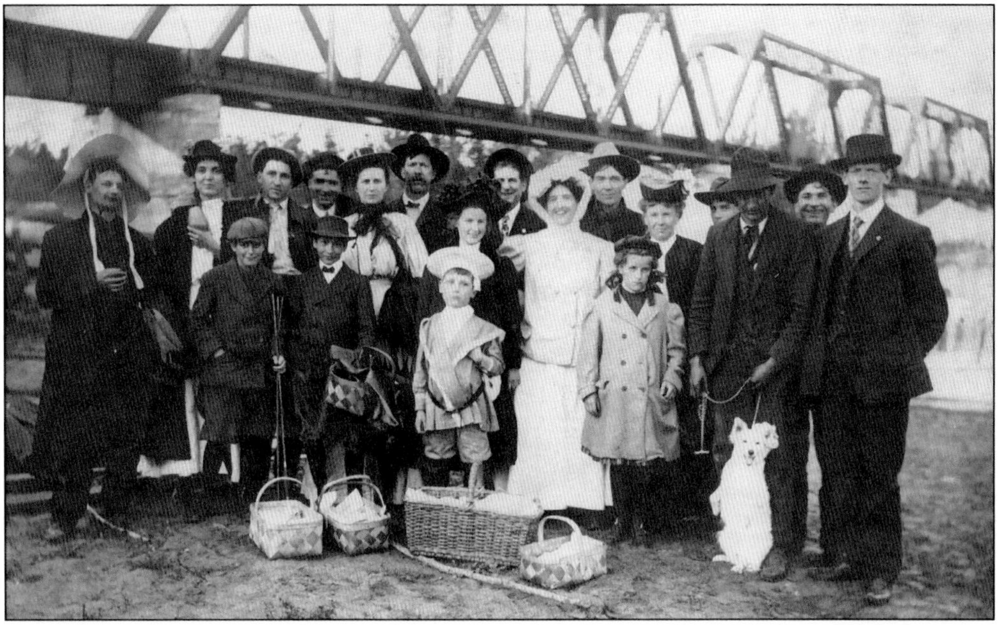

The Helming family of Troutdale enjoys a Sunday picnic down on the Sandy River. Note the rather elaborate costume on the boy in the front center and the bonnet on the man at the far left.

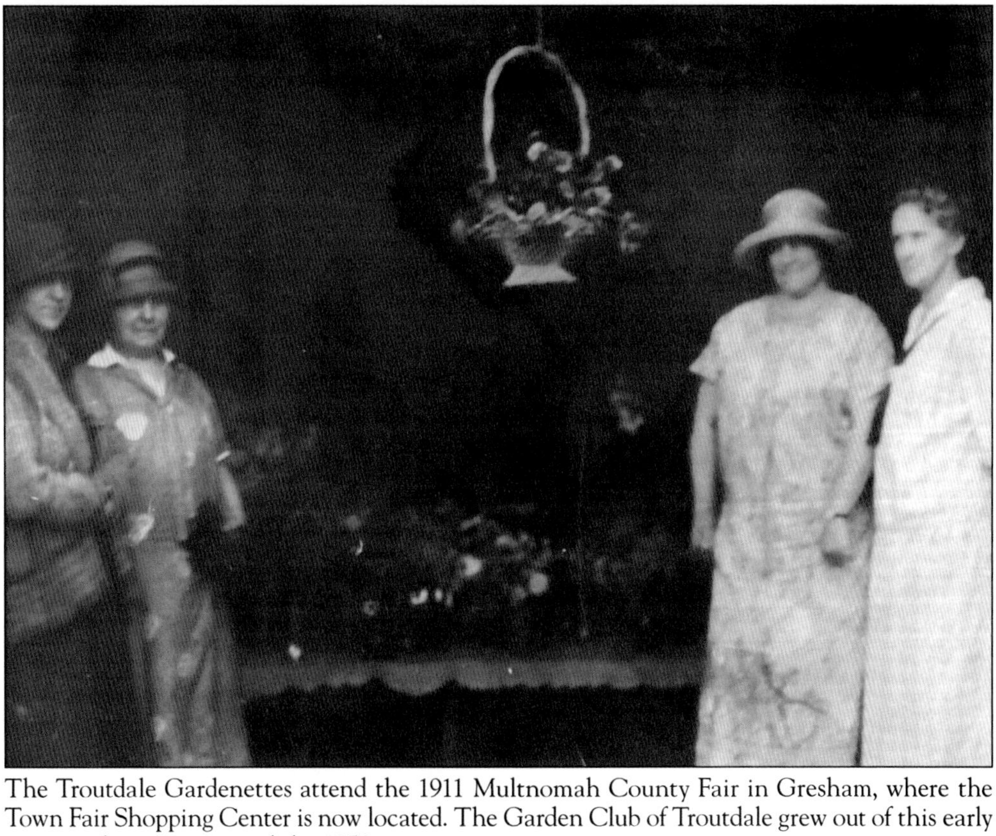

The Troutdale Gardenettes attend the 1911 Multnomah County Fair in Gresham, where the Town Fair Shopping Center is now located. The Garden Club of Troutdale grew out of this early group and was active until the 1950s.

Clarence Buxton and Olive (last name illegible) pose after a masquerade ball in 1905. Events such as this were a treat for residents in Troutdale, who created their own entertainment in the form of dancing, playing cards, and visiting friends.

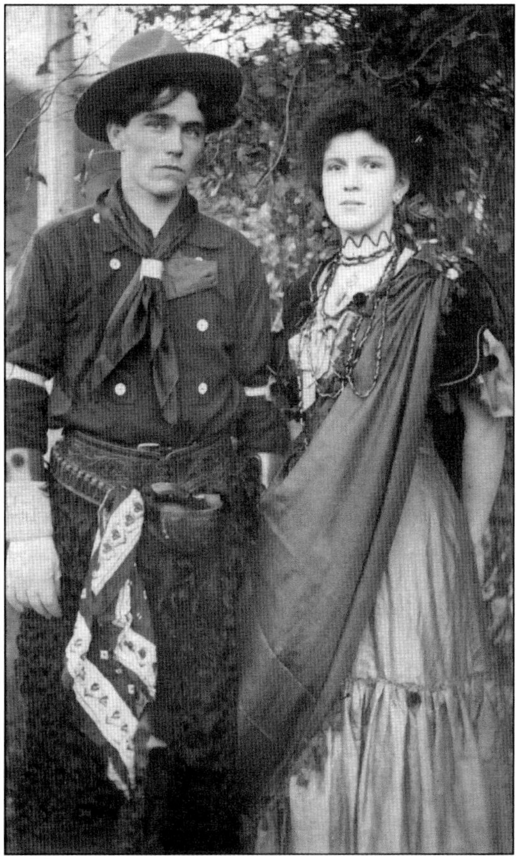

The Troutdale Rod and Gun Club, organized in 1939, led an effort to improve smelt runs in the Sandy River. Seen in this early 1940s photograph are members of the club with 20 fish they have caught in a fishing contest.

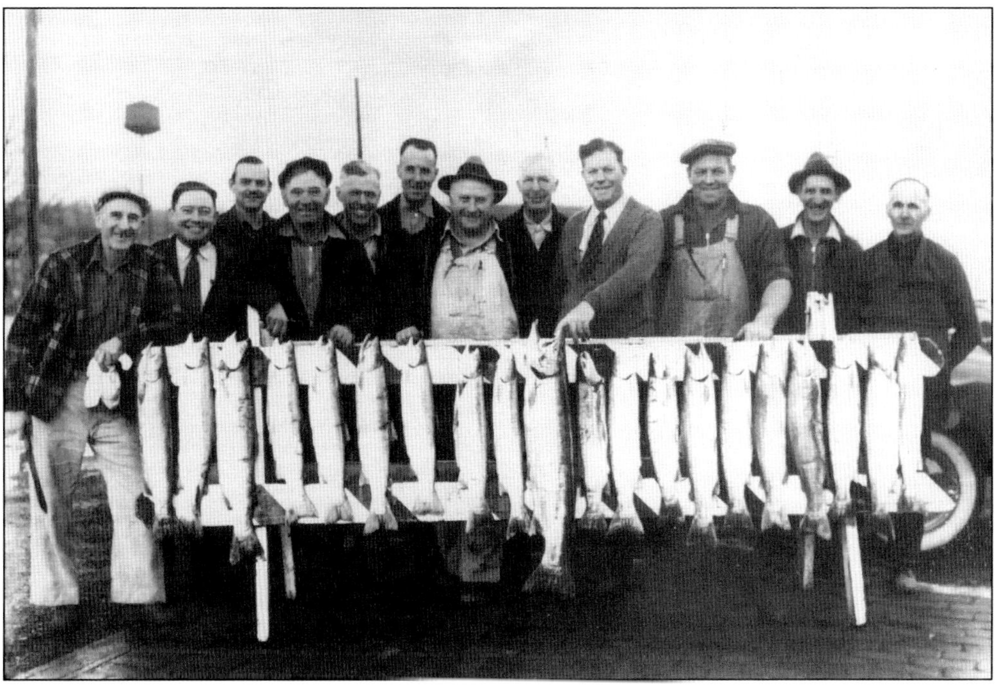

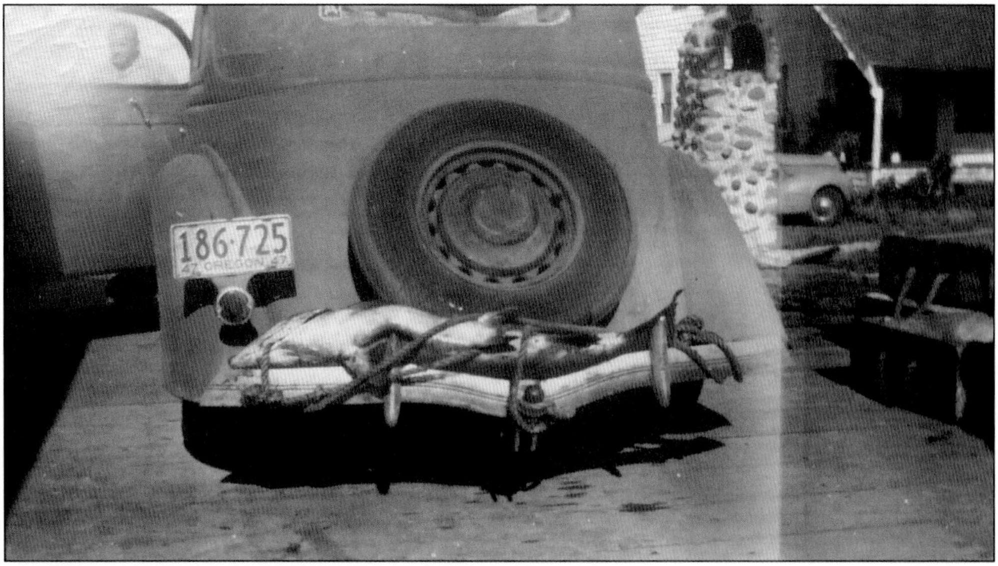

The 50-pound fish tied to the bumper of a 1935 or 1936 Chevrolet was caught in a net around 1947. Note the "A" gasoline ration sticker on the rear window. Fishermen, today, fish the Columbia and Sandy Rivers for a variety of fish, including Sturgeon, Walleye, Coho Salmon, Rainbow Trout, and Steelhead. Showing off the big catch of the day still equates to flexing muscles at the beach.

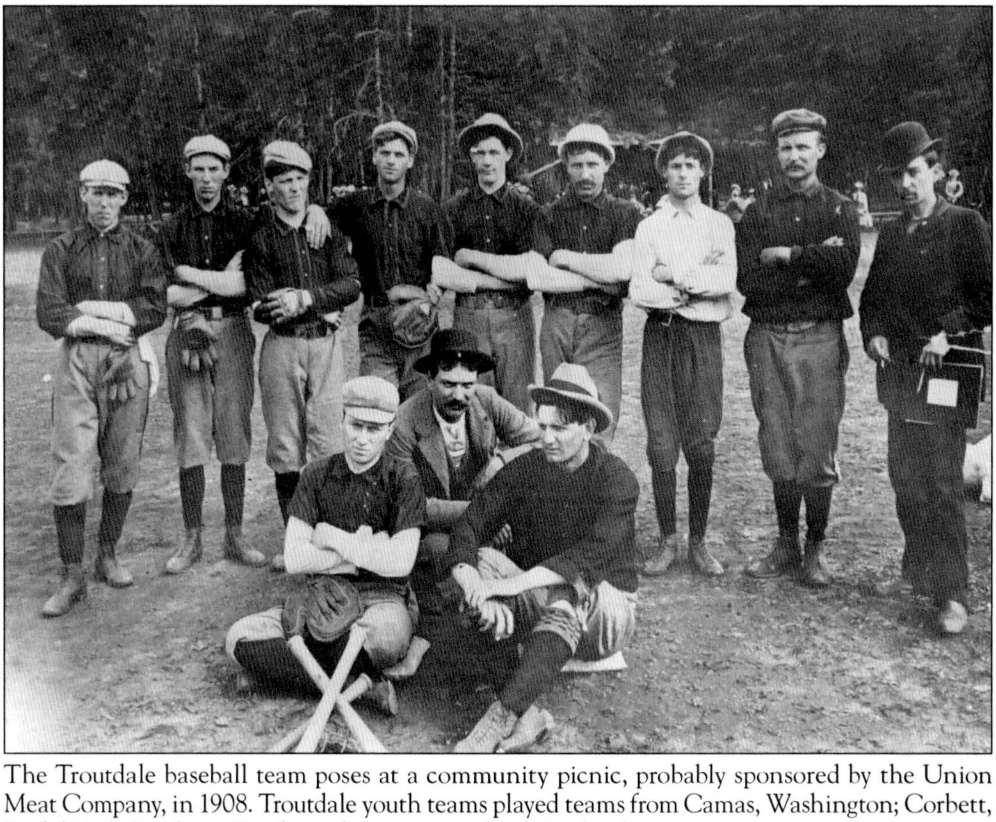

The Troutdale baseball team poses at a community picnic, probably sponsored by the Union Meat Company, in 1908. Troutdale youth teams played teams from Camas, Washington; Corbett, Bridal Veil, Gresham, Sandy, and some teams from Portland.

Living in close proximity to two rivers engenders fishermen at early ages. Here, two boys from nearby Latourell proudly display their catch, hung from a limb between them, in a photograph reminiscent of Tom Sawyer and Huckleberry Finn.

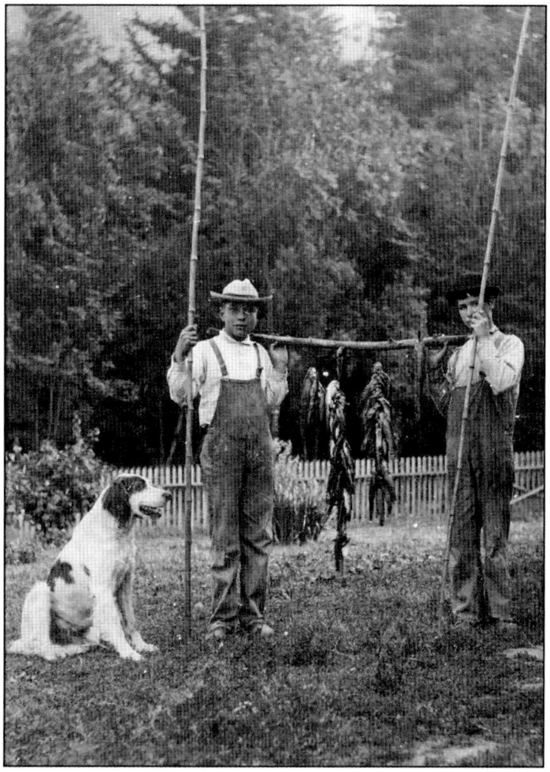

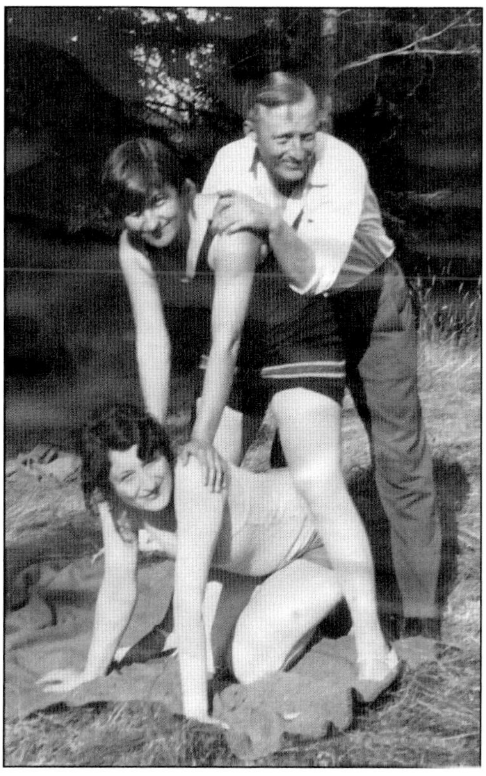

Members of the Tiller family, Bud, Helen (middle), and Laura (bottom), ham it up in this 1930 photograph, probably taken near the Sandy River. The Sandy River is still a popular spot for swimmers during hot days in the summer, when they cool off by dipping in the river.

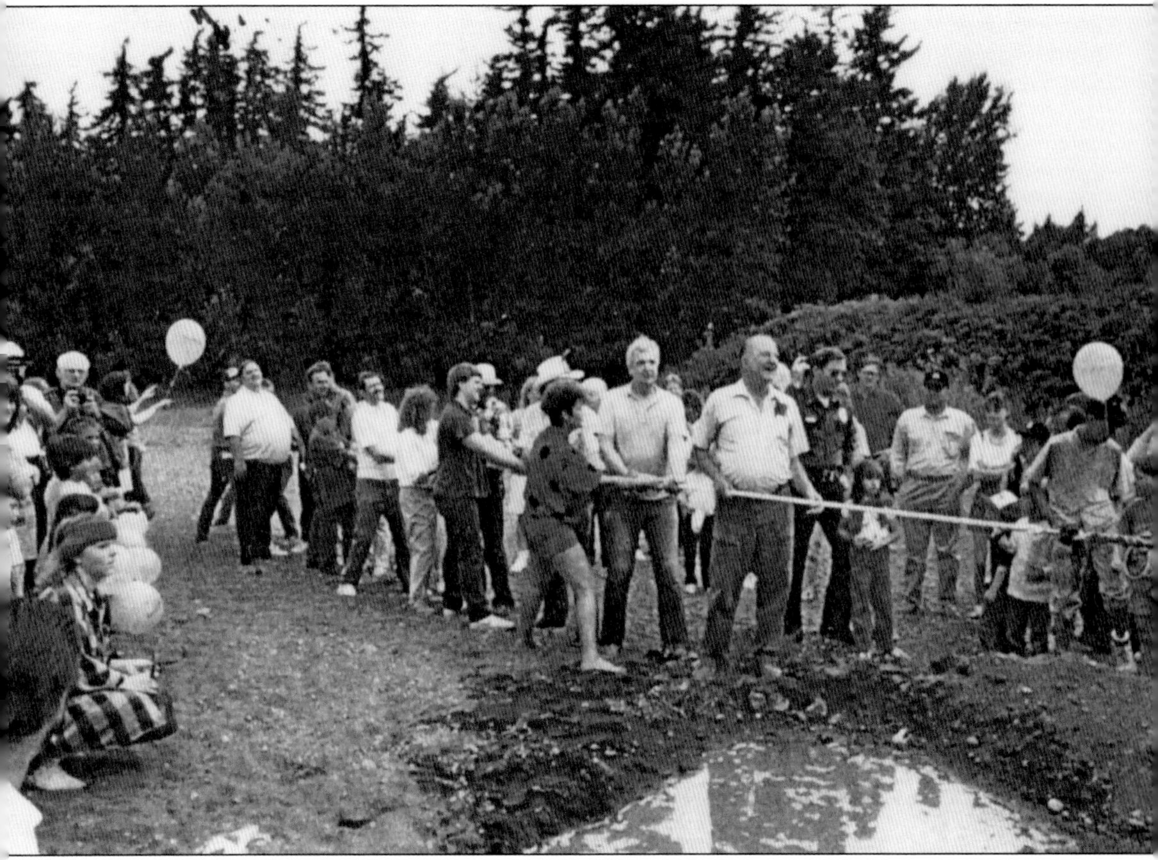

Paul Thalhofer and Troutdale mayor Sam Cox, shown at the head of the rope near the water's edge, lead the town's team in the Troutdale-Gresham tug-o-war just before the rope broke. Gresham mayor Gussie McRobert brought a busload of body-builders from a local gym as her team.

Swimmers frolic on a floating dock in the middle of the Sandy River in the 1940s with the Troutdale Bridge in the background. The numerous sandbars along the river provide good spaces for picnicking, sunbathing, and launching rafts.

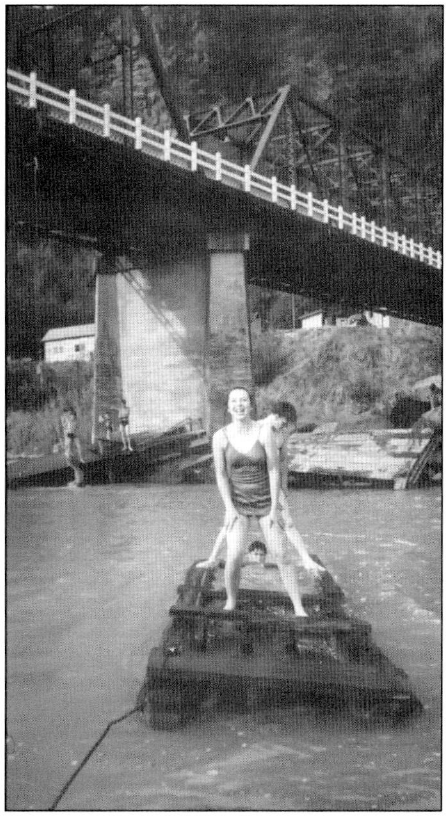

Prince Ken Owens and princess Joanne Kerslake, students at Troutdale Grade School, sit proudly in the town's floral entry in the 1946 Junior Rose Parade. Bill Elmer and Jack Quay were "a horse" that pulled the cart. The Junior Rose Parade is still part of the annual Rose Festival in Portland.

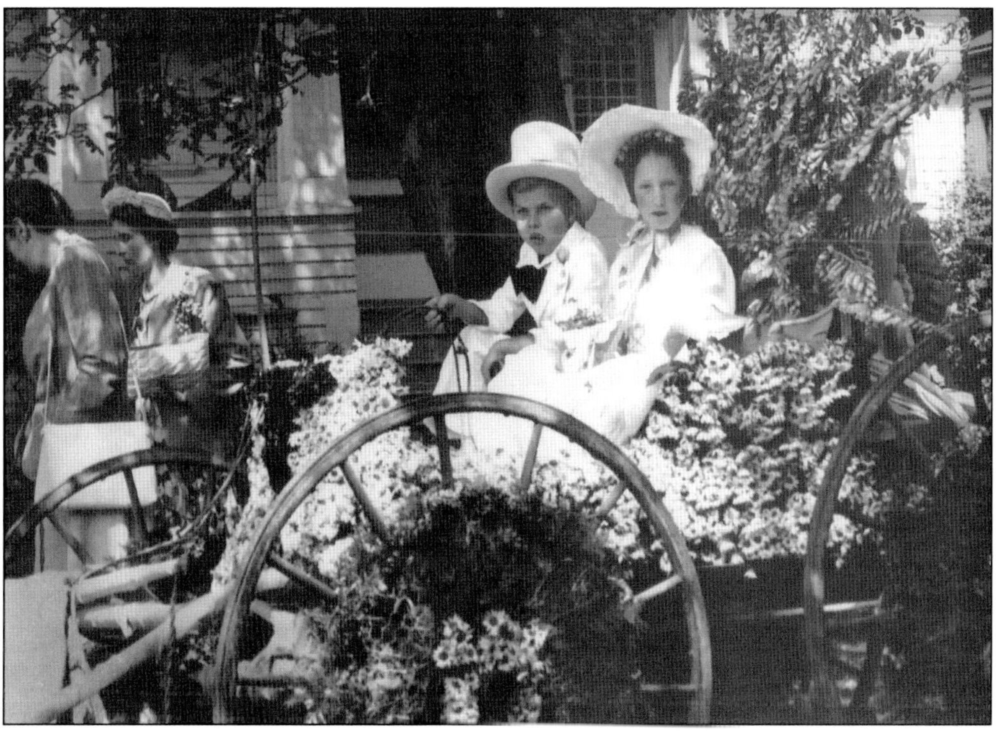